# Building a HIPAA-Compliant Cybersecurity Program

## Using NIST 800-30 and CSF to Secure Protected Health Information

Eric C. Thompson

Apress®

*Building a HIPAA-Compliant Cybersecurity Program: Using NIST 800-30 and CSF to Secure Protected Health Information*

Eric C. Thompson
Lisle, Illinois, USA

ISBN-13 (pbk): 978-1-4842-3059-6          ISBN-13 (electronic): 978-1-4842-3060-2
https://doi.org/10.1007/978-1-4842-3060-2

Library of Congress Control Number: 2017959175

Cover image by Freepik (www.freepik.com)

Managing Director: Welmoed Spahr
Editorial Director: Todd Green
Acquisitions Editor: Susan McDermott
Development Editor: Laura Berendson
Technical Reviewer: Andrew Reeder
Coordinating Editor: Rita Fernando
Copy Editor: Michael G. Laraque

Distributed to the book trade worldwide by Springer Science+Business Media New York, 233 Spring Street, 6th Floor, New York, NY 10013. Phone 1-800-SPRINGER, fax (201) 348-4505, e-mail orders-ny@springer-sbm.com, or visit www.springeronline.com. Apress Media, LLC is a California LLC and the sole member (owner) is Springer Science+Business Media Finance Inc (SSBM Finance Inc). SSBM Finance Inc is a Delaware corporation.

For information on translations, please e-mail rights@apress.com, or visit www.apress.com/rights-permissions.

Apress titles may be purchased in bulk for academic, corporate, or promotional use. eBook versions and licenses are also available for most titles. For more information, reference our Print and eBook Bulk Sales web page at www.apress.com/bulk-sales.

Any source code or other supplementary material referenced by the author in this book is available to readers on GitHub via the book's product page, located at www.apress.com/9781484230596. For more detailed information, please visit www.apress.com/source-code.

Printed on acid-free paper

*To Daina, Hannah, Daniel, and Hunter, you give me a thousand reasons to smile every day. And to my dad, thanks for teaching me to go "all in." I wish you could see this.*

# Table of Contents

# About the Author

 **Eric C. Thompson** is an accomplished governance, risk, and compliance (GRC) professional. In his GRC role as director of compliance at Blue Health Intelligence (BHI), Eric leads efforts to increase cybersecurity maturity in several domains, including governance, policy and controls, risk management, cybersecurity strategy, and business alignment. He established the risk management function, which includes assessment, analysis, and treatment of risk, threat, and vulnerability management strategy and creating due diligence assessment requirements related to third-party risk. Eric also evaluates cybersecurity technology capabilities and makes recommendations for enhancing current solutions and investing in new implementations that meet risk-reduction requirements.

Prior to joining BHI, Eric spent seven years at Ernst & Young, in the Advisory practice, where he specialized in helping healthcare organizations (providers, payers, and business associates) solve problems related to information security, risk management, and compliance. Eric led the HITRUST Common Security Framework (CSF), cybersecurity program management, and third-party risk management assessments.

Eric is also a proud member of the SANS Mentor team.

# About the Technical Reviewer

 **Andrew Reeder** serves as the HIPAA (Health Insurance Portability and Accountability Act of 1996) security officer and director of HIPAA Privacy at Rush University Medical Center, a major academic medical center in Chicago. In this role, Andy provides leadership in achieving regulatory compliance related to information-protection requirements, with major responsibilities including response and investigation into HIPAA privacy and security incidents, coordination of patient privacy rights actions, and policy development. Andy also serves as an adjunct faculty member in the College of Computing and Digital Media at DePaul University, where he teaches cybersecurity and information assurance topics at the graduate and undergraduate levels. Andy has been involved in providing privacy and information security services for many years and has previously served as director, Information Security, for a major Chicago-area regional healthcare provider and as a senior manager at a major professional services firm. He holds CISSP, CISA, CISM, CHPC, and HCISPP certifications and a master's degree in public administration.

# Acknowledgments

First, I must thank my family: Daina, Hannah, Daniel, and Hunter, for living with me during this project. Each of you picked up the slack, so that I could find time to write. To my mom, for always encouraging me to keep moving and never give up, and my dad, for teaching me to always "play hard" no matter what.

I would like to thank several of my former colleagues at Ernst & Young, who recognized my passion for this topic and for providing opportunities to learn and grow. Specifically, I want to thank Justin Greis, David Shade, Reza Chapman, and Mike Wojcik. All of you had a major impact on my professional life, and I am grateful. To my colleagues at Blue Health Intelligence, David King especially, thanks for the learning opportunities, flexibility, and support.

I also want to express my gratitude to Susan McDermott and Rita Fernando. During the last two years, I packed several Apress titles in my carry-on bags, so that I could read on airplanes and in hotel rooms while on the road. Susan encouraged me to submit a proposal for this topic, and Rita guided me through all my rookie mistakes. This project is easily one of the greatest experiences of my life.

# Introduction

Over the last several years, I had the pleasure of working with clients in the healthcare-provider sector. It is here that I learned the challenges cybersecurity and compliance teams face when it comes to protecting health information and complying with regulations such as the HIPAA Security Rule. Specifically, I saw the difficulty these entities encountered when it came to completing the risk analysis sufficiently to comply with Health Insurance Portability and Accountability Act of 1996 (HIPAA) specifications, owing to a lack of understanding about what was expected. For some, compliance and security were additional duties added to day jobs already full of expectations. For others, the perceived confusion and complexity surrounding the process and the expectations led to inaction.

The first goal of this book is to lead professionals responsible for risk analysis and risk management through the risk analysis process from beginning to end, highlighting several benefits of performing the analysis while simplifying the process. The second goal is to emphasize the importance of moving beyond thinking of this exercise in terms of just meeting compliance requirements, of going a step further in mitigating risk.

The first three chapters focus on information released by the Department of Health and Human Services (HHS) Office for Civil Rights (OCR), highlighting the difficulties entities experience with risk analysis. Examples of organizations cited by the OCR for not having a compete risk analysis at the time a breach occurred and feedback from proactive audits are illustrated. Chapters 4 through 8 lead readers through each of the necessary components of the risk analysis. Chapter 4 outlines the process of identifying instances of electronic protected health information (ePHI). Chapter 5 focuses on threats and threat actors. Chapter 6 is where documenting vulnerabilities are discussed. Chapters 7 and 8 illustrate how likelihood and impact ratings are assigned, so that risks can be documented.

Chapters 9 and 10 emphasize the need to incorporate testing into the risk analysis process, to pinpoint specific vulnerabilities through nontechnical and technical means. Nontechnical tests include assessing access management, change control and training, and awareness processes. From a technical perspective, the tests focus on vulnerability identification and management and attack and penetration testing. Chapter 11 discusses updating the risk register, based on the results of the testing performed.

The final group of chapters focuses on specific issues a risk-based cybersecurity program tackle, Chapter 12 is the chapter on how to build a cybersecurity roadmap, Chapter 13 is investing for risk reduction, and third-party risk management, in Chapter 14. Chapter 15 covers social media issues, Risk treatment through emphasizing control maturity and investments in the cybersecurity program is the topic of Chapter 16. Chapter 17 offers an example of a customized risk analysis using Monte Carlo simulations to assign likelihood and impact values to risks. Finally, Chapter 18 urges readers to become proactive and think in terms of going on the offensive.

# PART I

# Why Risk Assessment and Analysis?

# CHAPTER 1

# Not If, but When

Over the last three years, the number of breaches, lost medical records, and settlements of fines is staggering. During this span, nearly 140 million medical records were involved in a privacy breach. The Office for Civil Rights (OCR)[1] issued 22 resolution agreements, requiring monetary settlements approaching $36 million. Despite the attention and lessons learned, some very troubling themes persist. Although warnings about increasing malware attacks, the introduction of crypto-ransomware in 2016, and predictions that healthcare records will continue to be targeted, fundamental aspects of cybersecurity, privacy, and compliance are still missing. In 2015, nearly 200 privacy breaches totaling 111 million lost records were attributed to missing safeguards required by the HIPAA (Health Insurance Portability and Accountability Act of 1996) Security and Privacy Rules. This number rose to approximately 250 in 2016, and 24 were announced in the first two months of 2017. In 12 of 22 investigations, the resolution agreement issued by the OCR pointed to a "Failure to satisfactorily conduct the required risk analysis." Regulators tied this gap to incidents of lost and stolen devices, malware opening the network to attackers, or misconfigured devices not hardened properly. Essentially, shortfalls in compliance were attributed to the risk analysis gap. Table 1-1 highlights these categories and the numbers of breaches owing to weaknesses in compliance.

---

[1]U.S. Department of Health and Human Services, Office for Civil Rights, "Breach Portal: Notice to the Secretary of HHS Breach of Unsecured Protected Health Information," https://ocrportal.hhs.gov/ocr/breach/breach_report.jsf, 2017.

© Eric C. Thompson 2017
E. C. Thompson, *Building a HIPAA-Compliant Cybersecurity Program*,
https://doi.org/10.1007/978-1-4842-3060-2_1

*Table 1-1.* *Approximations of Records Lost by Category Disclosed on HHS.gov*

| Category | 2015 | 2016 | 2017 |
| --- | --- | --- | --- |
| Lost/Stolen | 674,000 | 890,000 | 16,500 |
| Access | 573,000 | 1,131,000 | 92,000 |
| Hacking | 111,814,000 | 13,428,000 | 48,800 |
| Totals | 113,000,000 | 15,400,000 | 155,000 |

The entities targeted in the Hacking/IT Incident category range from small providers to large health plans operating nationally. Any entity possessing patient information in electronic form (electronic protected health information [ePHI]) is a target.

# Evolving Regulations and Threat Landscape

The introduction of the Health Information Technology for Economic and Clinical Health (HITECH) Act of 2009 and, later, the Final Omnibus Rule created a new enforcement environment that draws attention to entities suffering a breach. The increasing number of external attacks and internal incidents affecting the healthcare sector is shining a spotlight on cybersecurity programs at these entities. HITECH, which was introduced as part of the American Reinvestment and Recovery Act (ARRA), encouraged providers to adopt the use of electronic medical records, by providing financial incentives. HITECH also required more stringent breach notification rules and made business associates liable for breaches. Incorporation of these and other requirements within the Final Omnibus Rule was one of the factors leading to this phenomenon.

As healthcare became more digitized, so did the potential for large-scale incidents. The benefits derived through digital records, such as speed, ease of use, and rapid access, meant that simple mistakes often led to devastating impacts. This created the "not if, but when," maxim that it is a matter of time before all healthcare entities experience a breach, if one has not been experienced already.

# A New Kind of Adversary

It's easy to look back and point to the breach at Target in 2013 as a turning point. There are still lessons being learned from that incident. Then Sony hit the news with a high-profile breach attributed to a state-sponsored group allegedly hacking the entertainment company in December 2014. Thus, damaging e-mails and unreleased movie footage were made public, and executives dealt with embarrassment and a public relations nightmare.

Healthcare's turn came in January 2015. Anthem announced an incident that resulted in an estimated 80 million plus lost records (the figure was later lowered to 78 million). Premera Blue Cross/Blue Shield, a health plan operating in several states, also suffered a "sophisticated" attack. In both instances, end users were victimized by phishing e-mails and directed to illegitimate web locations. These announcements sounded alarm bells for healthcare. These events were not dominos falling one after the other. Instead, the public was learning about a new adversary known as the Advanced Persistent Threat (ATP). These well-managed groups have vast resources, patience, and know how to strike without drawing attention. The time it took to steal millions of records was measured in months and sometimes years. Later, it was learned that single individuals were targeted. Intelligence was gathered from multiple social media sources to craft very specific spear-phishing e-mails. The intelligence gathered through social media made the "spoofed" e-mails difficult to detect, because of the sophistication and specificity used. The entities in Table 1-2 all suffered breaches categorized as "Hacking/IT Incidents," in 2015 and 2016, some of which were classified as "sophisticated" and similar to the attacks experienced by Anthem and Premera.

***Table 1-2.** Largest Breaches Attributed to Hacking/IT Incidents Based on Information Provided by the U.S. Department of Health and Human Services*

| 2015 | 2016 |
| --- | --- |
| Anthem: 78 million | Banner Health: 3.6 million |
| Premera Blue Cross: 11 million | NewKirk Products: 3.4 million |
| Excellus Health Plan: 10 million | 21st Century Oncology: 2.2 million |
| UCLA: 4.5 million | Valley Anesthesiology: 882,000 |
| Medical Informatics: 3.9 million | County of Los Angeles: 749,000 |
| CareFirst BC/BS: 1.1 million | Peachtree Orthopedic Clinic: 531,000 |
| Virginia Dept. of Medical Assistance: 700,000 | Community Health Washington: 381,000 |
| Georgia Dept. Community Health: 557,000 | Central Ohio Urology: 300,000 |
| Georgia Dept. Community Health: 355,000 | Southeast Eye Institute: 87,000 |
| Beacon Health System: 306,000 | East Valley Community Health: 65,000 |

Nearly two years after the breach was announced, the incident at Anthem highlights how a targeted end user initiates a chain of events leading to a breach. The kill chain presented by Mandiant (now FireEye) in Figure 1-1 highlights the series of steps attackers use to gain access to ePHI. All it takes is an attacker getting in the door.

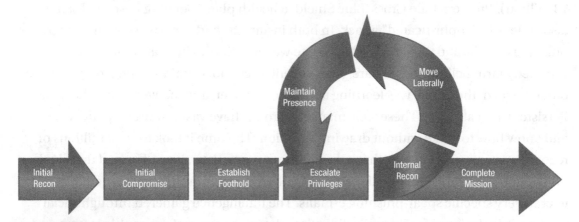

*Figure 1-1.* *The Mandiant kill chain shows the life cycle of attacks, which includes seven steps, from initial compromise to completing the mission. (Image courtesy of FireEye, Inc.)*

In January 2017, two years after the breach was announced, the findings of an investigation conducted by insurance commissioners from seven states concluded that the attack began 11 months prior to discovery. An employee at a subsidiary was compromised by a spear-phishing e-mail originating from a state-sponsored organization. The report also stated that enough intelligence was gathered from several social media sites to exploit the vulnerable end user. Speculation surfaced in 2016 that the attack at Premera, described as a sophisticated attack, used very similar attack vectors and quite possibly was conducted by the same group.[2]

Smaller healthcare providers were also targeted, including Beacon Health System, a regional provider located in South Bend, IN. Beacon confirmed that the breach experienced in 2015 also began with a phishing e-mail and ultimately allowed attackers to gain access to employee e-mails. The e-mails contained the personal health information (PHI) and personally identifiable information (PII) of 300,000 individuals, including names, birthdays, Social Security Numbers, diagnoses, and date(s) of service.

---

[2]Jeremy Kirk, "Premera, Anthem data breaches linked by similar hacking tactics," InfoWorld, `www.infoworld.com/article/2898658/security/premera-anthem-data-breaches-linked-by-similar-hacking-tactics.html`, March 18, 2017.

# Proliferation of Ransomware

It is possible that 2015 will be remembered as the year sophisticated attackers stole more than 111 million health records, and 2016 the year of crypto-ransomware, whereby attackers gain access to victim networks through sophisticated means, but rather than stealing health records, databases are encrypted and made unusable by the victim until a ransom is paid. Numerous attacks successfully encrypted key systems affecting patient care in the US and other parts of the world. One of the more recognizable cases of crypto-ransomware occurred at Hollywood Presbyterian Medical Center (HPMC) in Hollywood, CA. Initial reports stated that attackers demanded 9,000 Bitcoins, equivalent to $3.6 million, when nearly all systems required to provide patient care became unusable. HPMC refuted the initial ransom amount and reported that it paid $17,000 two weeks after the incident began, so that operations could be restored. Several more hospitals/health systems experienced ransomware attacks in 2016.

- Kansas Heart Hospital in Wichita, KS, paid the ransom demanded by its attackers; however, full restoration of the locked-down environment was not made available, and another ransom was demanded.

- Methodist Hospital in Henderson, KY, operated in a state of emergency for five days, until files and systems were restored.

- More than 30,000 records at The Rainbow Children's Clinic in Grand Prairie, TX, were affected in early August. The investigation confirmed that some records were rendered unrecoverable.

These types of attacks are considered breaches under the Privacy Rule (45 CFR 164.402).[3] Although the records were not stolen, by encrypting the records, the unauthorized acquisition of health records occurred.

In August 2016, the Department of Health and Human Services (HHS) issued a fact sheet meant to assist covered entities and business associates dealing with this new threat scenario. This guidance was very compliance-focused, emphasizing the need for analyzing risk and applying security measures to combat them, including

- Training and awareness
- Access controls

---

[3]U.S. Department of Health and Human Services, *FACT SHEET: Ransomware and HIPAA*, www.hhs.gov/sites/default/files/RansomwareFactSheet.pdf, 2017.

- Detection capabilities

- Fully tested and available backups

Since that time, various news outlets have predicted that ransomware attacks will continue to increase in frequency, the reason being it is an easier way to profit, because less experienced attack groups do not have to find a buyer on the dark web. The trade-off is that much less money is made in these scenarios. Stealing and selling health information is more complicated and requires experience. Only time can tell if the popularity of ransomware will continue.

## Malware for Sale

In January 2017, both *SecurityWeek*[4] and *SC Magazine*[5] published articles about Bankbot, malware targeting Android devices, indicating that the source code was leaked on the dark web. This piece of malicious software was hidden in benign-looking applications that, once downloaded, waited silently on the device until a financial application was opened. The malware source code contained a list of applications that, once matched, launched an attack to harvest login credentials. While this is not an attack targeted at healthcare, it sheds light on how challenging the current threat landscape has become for security professionals. Because the source code for malicious software was made available on the dark web, it gives other cybercriminals an opportunity to make improvements to the code, causing it to be harder to detect. The level of sophistication in the source code of modern malware makes it difficult to detect and analyze, once contained. Allowing others to improve upon malware code only makes the job of healthcare cyber programs more difficult. This just shows how difficult it can be for cybersecurity leaders to stay on the leading edge of threats to patient confidentiality. Speaking at the 2017 RSA Conference, Michael McCaul (R-TX), chairman of the House Committee on Homeland Security, provided a sobering outlook for private companies defending against an enemy with superior technology.

---

[4]Ionut Arghire, "Source Code for BankBot Android Trojan Leaks Online," SecurityWeek, www.securityweek.com/source-code-bankbot-android-trojan-leaks-online, January 23, 2017.

[5]Doug Olenick, "BankBot created with leaked banking trojan source code," SC Magazine, www.scmagazine.com/bankbot-created-with-leaked-banking-trojan-source-code/article/633264/, January 23, 2017.

*I'm going to be brutally honest: We are in a fight of our digital lives, and we are not winning.*

—Michael McCaul

Without a focus on risk and an understanding of what needs to be defended at all costs, developing a program to combat criminals stealing and holding patient health information hostage is nearly impossible.

## It Costs Money When Things Go Wrong

Some very eye-opening settlements have been reached with the OCR by entities that were breached in the last three years. The $36 million quoted previously includes 12 settlements greater than $1 million. Advocate Health Care in suburban Chicago agreed to the largest figure as of August 2016, totaling $5.55 million. Memorial Health System in southern Florida became the second entity to top $5 million, after agreeing in January 2017 to pay $5.50 million. These settlement amounts are public and can be found in the resolution agreements posted on the OCR's web site and go back to 2008. The five largest settlements outlined in Table 1-3 account for 63% penalties levied since 2013. What is not counted in these figures are penalties imposed at the state level or resulting from litigation of civil lawsuits. Usually, during the rigors of an OCR investigation, the state in which the breach occurred and plaintiff's lawyers tend to begin filing lawsuits as well.

***Table 1-3.*** *Five Largest Fines Posted to OCR Web Site, Representing Just over $23 million That Breached Entities Agreed to Pay at the Conclusion of Investigations*

| Entity | Settlement Amount ($) |
| --- | --- |
| Advocate Health Care | 5.55 million |
| Memorial Health System | 5.5 million |
| NY Presbyterian/Columbia University | 4.8 million |
| Cignet Health | 4.3 million |
| Triple-S | 3.5 million |

These are large amounts, but it's hard to tell if settlement agreements and civil money penalties influence covered entities and business associates to take the necessary steps and invest in cybersecurity capabilities. Several years of providing documents and being questioned by regulators culminate with reports outlining the following:

- The shortcomings in the environment that led to the breach

- A settlement of imposed fines—meaning the amounts listed in Table 1-3 were settlements of much larger penalties

- A Corrective Action Plan outlining specific remediation expected to be completed by specific dates

Breaches are public relations nightmares. When stories are reported by media outlets, healthcare organizations attempt to assure the public and its customers that confidentiality is taken seriously. However, when the OCR issues its resolution agreement, the final report outlining the findings of the breach investigation, if the conclusions state that fundamental aspects of compliance and security were not established, the brand and reputation of the entity can be damaged.

## The Approach Must Change

Historically, cybersecurity maturity in the healthcare sector has lagged, compared to other sectors, such as financial services. The gap is not as pronounced as it once was; however, investments, resources, and executive support for cybersecurity still fall short. Participation and sponsorship from a business are necessary to execute a useful risk analysis and drive the organizational changes required to tighten controls protecting ePHI. Too often, budgets increase as knee-jerk reactions to incidents or when members of the board decide cybersecurity is a hot-button issue. Then, the focus shifts to purchasing technology and other "tools" touted as the answers to solving cybersecurity challenges. This security-blanket approach misses the point. Often, there is little return on these investments, and each can wind up underutilized, if implemented at all. That's because no thought was given to what risks are being reduced with these investments. Common solutions suffering these fates over the last several years include

- Data leakage/loss protection (DLP)

- Security incident and event management (SIEM)

- Endpoint protections designed to prevent ransomware attacks

- Threat intelligence feeds

- Identity and access management (IAM) solutions

- Vulnerability scanners

Before investing in any solution, entities have to articulate the risk being mitigated. For instance, purchasing an IAM solution should be part of a remediation project targeting access management issues. This could be useful at organizations that place heavy reliance on contractors and other nonemployees. Because communication breakdowns cause deficiencies in access management, it makes sense to explore these types of solutions, if they reduce a significant risk. The risk analysis and risk management process must define use cases for new investments in technology and professional capabilities.

## Comply, but Not for the Sake of Compliance

Thinking in terms of compliance can cause defensive thinking if the goal becomes checking the box to avoid noncompliance findings. Healthcare cybersecurity leaders require a plan, one that is proactive and geared to address risks. The risk analysis forms the basis for developing the strategy and tactics necessary to fight new and advancing threats. The who, what, where, when, and how of the cybersecurity program should be based on the output of risk analysis. The language used in the HIPAA Security Rule outlines the steps required to create a cybersecurity battle plan.

---

163.308(A)—Risk analysis (Required). Conduct an accurate and thorough assessment of the potential risks and vulnerabilities to the confidentiality, integrity, and availability of electronic protected health information held by the covered entity or business associate.

---

These words might constitute a specific requirement of a federal regulation, but this requirement is documented first in the Administrative Safeguards of the HIPAA Security Rule. It makes sense, because the other safeguards cannot be implemented properly without a risk analysis.

# Going on the Offensive

This book is not about complying with HIPAA; it is about changing how healthcare entities approach risk and address it. It highlights what needs to be protected, the gaps that could lead to losses of ePHI, and where resources must be deployed. It is an iterative exercise, with each cycle providing more granular details about the environment and more useful threat and vulnerability information. There are four components to the process of developing a HIPAA-compliant cybersecurity program.

# Creating and Trusting the Process

This book is about action(s) born out of the risk analysis process, combined with the activities highlighted on the left side of Figure 1-2. Even if the healthcare sector does not have the superior tools and technology to keep ahead of threat actors, an offensive-minded strategy still adds value and improves protective measures. Three of the elements are iterative, and each cycle leads to increased maturity and improved protection. The fourth element, application, enhances the entity's ability to make decisions regarding the cybersecurity program and/or business decisions. During the risk analysis, cyber program management, and targeted testing cycle, information derived from each step feeds the next in the process.

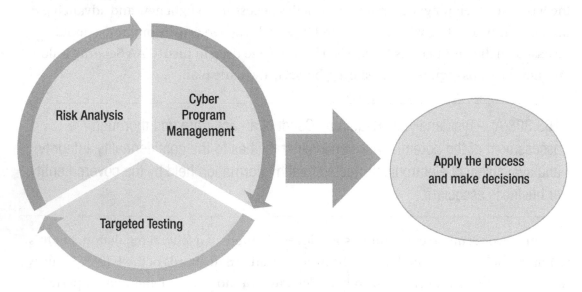

***Figure 1-2.*** *Risk analysis, implementing the cybersecurity progam and controls, and targeted testing provide data required to make adjustments to the cybersecurity program and make risk-based decisions on a daily basis*

- The risk analysis outputs highlight necessary resources and investments in the cybersecurity program.

- Based on the risk analysis and changes made to the cybersecurity program, a test plan is created, to understand if the changes worked or if adjustments are required.

- Testing results are fed back into the risk analysis. Information uncovered about assets and vulnerabilities requires the risk analysis to be updated before the process starts again.

When the initial risk analysis is completed, threats and risks are described at a higher level, but each iteration produces more specific information about threats, vulnerabilities, and risks. Table 1-4 shows how risk statements become more specific from the first year to the second.

***Table 1-4.*** *Each Cycle Through the Risk-Analysis Process Produces More Detailed Risk Information Designed to Enhance the Cybersecurity Program and Strategic Decision Making*

| Risk Year 1 | Risk Year 2 |
| --- | --- |
| Malicious outsiders can exploit end users via phishing attacks, due to a lack of training and awareness, resulting in theft, modification, or unavailability of ePHI. | State-sponsored groups could exploit data management users employing crypto-ransomware phishing attacks, rendering ePHI unavailable, owing to a lack of training and awareness in that business unit. |

# Summary

There are many reasons to have a bleak outlook about the current state of cybersecurity in the healthcare sector. There is a perception that the sophistication and advanced technology available makes it nearly impossible to protect patient data from exposure. This does not even take into account the challenge of identifying and protecting the entity against risks from insider threats. These individuals, either through ego, profit, or revenge, refuse to follow policies and cause damage to entities, based on reckless behavior.

Recently, Accenture released results of a study[6] stating that 25% of patients in America have been victimized by a breach. These consumers suffer financial issues arising from identity and medical identity theft. Some are forced to pay as much as $2,500. Trend Micro[7] also issued a report outlining how medical records are monetized. There are several ways cybercriminals can make money with healthcare records, which means that incentives exist to fuel these attacks. System- and process-level thinking are missing from many organizations, as evidenced by numerous examples of basic compliance gaps. The answer to the challenge is to establish the process to continue to improve and achieve compliance.

---

[6]Bill Swicki, "Study: One in four U.S. consumers have had their personal medical information stolen," Healthcare IT News, www.healthcareitnews.com/news/study-one-four-us-consumers-have-had-their-personal-medical-information-stolen, February 20, 2017.

[7]Trend Micro, "The Price of Health Records: Electronic Healthcare Data in the Underground," www.trendmicro.com/vinfo/us/security/news/cybercrime-and-digital-threats/electronic-healthcare-data-in-the-underground, February 21, 2017.

# CHAPTER 2

# Meeting Regulator Expectations

The Department of Health and Human Services (HHS) Office for Civil Rights (OCR) enforces HIPAA and investigates breaches, responds to patient complaints, and establishes resolution agreements, where necessary. Patients expect that safeguards designed to secure the confidentiality, integrity, and availability of healthcare records are in place. Briefly, HIPAA has been in existence since 1996. Enforcement of the HIPAA Privacy Rule took effect in April 2003, and Security Rule enforcement took effect in April 2005. Breach investigations are not new. In January 2013, the Final Omnibus Rule established several provisions of the HITECH Act and added several others. Specific to the Breach Rule were that

- Notice is provided to the media and HHS if a breach effected 500 or more individuals.

- It changed the legal test of a breach from proving significant financial or reputational harm was done to a low probability that the PHI was acquired or viewed.

- Tiered penalties based on significance of a breach were established.

- Business associates would be liable for breaches of records in their control.

Since 2009, two types of entities are subject to the OCR's enforcement actions: covered entities and business associates. Generally, healthcare providers such as doctors, clinics, psychologists, dentists, chiropractors, pharmacies, and nursing homes are considered covered entities under the Security Rule when health information is transmitted in electronic form, for example, when physicians send claims information to insurance companies for payment. Health plans that include HMOs, health insurance

© Eric C. Thompson 2017
E. C. Thompson, *Building a HIPAA-Compliant Cybersecurity Program*,
https://doi.org/10.1007/978-1-4842-3060-2_2

companies, company health plans, and government programs are also considered covered entities. Business associates are third parties that perform services for covered entities with the ability to access the ePHI of the covered entity who engaged them.

# Introduction of a Proactive Audit Program

To assess and understand compliance gaps with the Privacy, Security, and Breach Rules, the OCR conducted proactive audits of 150 covered entities, dubbed the Pilot Audit Program, during parts of 2011 and 2012. The OCR learned that two-thirds of the auditees were missing sufficient documentation to support the required comprehensive risk analysis. The breakdown of compliance gaps in the following list illustrates how pervasive missing this compliance gap was during the audit.

- One hundred one covered entities were audited against the Security Rule.

- Forty-seven of the fifty-nine providers audited had not conducted a risk analysis.

- Twenty of the thirty-five health plans audited had not conducted a risk analysis.

- Two of the seven healthcare clearinghouses had not conducted a risk analysis.

This pilot audit represented the first step in proactive enforcement of HIPAA. Shortly after the results were released, in late 2013, a report from the Office of the Inspector General (OIG), which has oversight authority over the OCR and HHS, was critical of the OCR for not doing enough to enforce HIPAA proactively.

A second phase of audits began in July 2016. Owing to the results of the pilot audits, and repeated findings during investigations, risk analysis was once again in scope. In preparation, the OCR held informational webinars and Q&A sessions for auditees. To address several questions about what documentation would satisfy the requirements for a current risk analysis, the OCR stated that it wanted to see the risk analysis that was current at the time the audit notification was sent.[1]

---

[1]Department of Health and Human Services, "OCR 2016 HIPAA Desk Audits—Audited Entity Questions and Answers," www.hhs.gov/sites/default/files/Phase2AuditOpeningMeetingWeb inarQ%26A.pdf, July 22, 2016.

# Does Language and Tone Lead to Inaction?

Why is the risk analysis so challenging and often missed? After all, it is a required administrative safeguard in the Security Rule and one the OCR has placed great emphasis on over the last several years. In an effort to educate covered entities and business associates, HHS issued guidance outlining the necessary steps required to comply with the risk analysis in July 2010.[2] The points emphasized by the guidance leave little doubt about the importance regulators place on the risk analysis.

- Risk analysis is described as foundational, and compliance with HIPAA is not possible without it.

- All PHI in electronic form must be assessed.

- The risk analysis must be thorough and comprehensive, addressing all risks to ePHI.

These expectations have remained consistent since, but the risk analysis is still one of the most common gaps related to the Security Rule. HHS recommends using guidelines issued by the National Institute for Standards and Technology (NIST) to assess risks to ePHI. Specifically, SP 800-30 outlines the activities necessary to complete the risk analysis.

HHS does not offer proscriptive guidance outlining the steps required to comply with the safeguard requiring entities to complete a thorough and comprehensive risk analysis. This document also uses a word that can create a feeling of uncertainty in individuals tasked with completing a risk analysis. The word is *all*. It means the HHS and, specifically, members of the OCR tasked with enforcement expect that *all* ePHI is assessed and *all* risks to the confidentiality, integrity, and availability of ePHI are identified. If all means all, then, technically, 99% of the protected health information can be successfully analyzed, but a breach affecting the 1% not analyzed means compliance was not met. That is a pretty tough standard to meet, but nothing short of these standards should be expected by regulators.

---

[2]Department of Health and Human Services, "Guidance on Risk Analysis Requirements under the HIPAA Security Rule," www.hhs.gov/sites/default/files/ocr/privacy/hipaa/administrative/securityrule/rafinalguidancepdf.pdf, July 14, 2010.

# Why Does This Language Exist in the Guidance?

This particular guidance, and HIPAA, for that matter, was written to be applied across entities of all sizes and types. These rules apply the same for single-physician offices and multi-state health plans, the difference being how the guidance is applied. Assessing risk at smaller entities can be simpler and more straightforward. At larger entities, the variables are greater, which adds complexity to the process.

It is also not realistic to expect any directives issued by government agencies responsible for enforcing compliance with federal regulations to state it any other way. Guidelines issued to assist entities with compliance must stay true to the requirements. It is unrealistic to think HHS or the OCR would communicate anything different. Issuing a statement that entities should just do the best they can makes it impossible to enforce regulations. To get past this issue of uncertainty regarding the need to assess all ePHI for all risks, it is important to remember that assessing, analyzing, and managing risk is not time-boxed, but, as stated in Chapter 1, it is a cyclical process. New details are learned every day about the business, IT environment, threats, and vulnerabilities. It is up to the risk-management team to periodically collect this new information and incorporate it into the analysis. Does that mean healthcare entities are 100% percent compliant one moment, then if new information comes to light, suddenly out of compliance for two days, until this new information is analyzed and risks updated? It might spark interesting debates in legal circles, but spending time and energy on perfection is unproductive.

---

**Caution**    Conducting a risk analysis, and being as thorough as possible, makes any organization required to protect patient information more effective. However, not having all instances of ePHI assessed, and missed risk documentation, does potentially create a compliance gap, and this book does not advocate noncompliance.

---

It is time to stop avoiding the problem. It will not go away, so the only choice is to act to move the cybersecurity program closer to the level expected by regulators. The result is improved protective measures that patients expect when information about them is stored electronically.

# Risk Analysis Methodology

This book focuses on the processes outlined in NIST SP 800-30, because HHS specifically references it; however, any framework or process is allowable, if the output yields all the risks, with severity, to all ePHI created and maintained. In Figure 2-1, the six steps required to conduct the analysis are displayed from left to right. The output is a list of risks, with the severity of each to the confidentially, integrity, and availability of PHI held digitally.

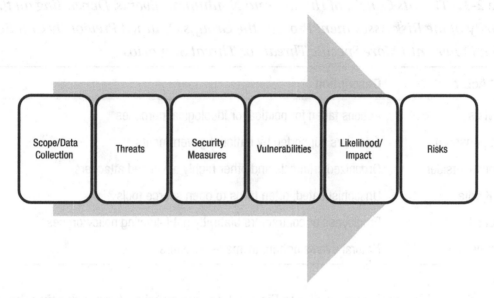

*Figure 2-1.* *Six steps in the risk analysis process outlined in NIST 800-30*

# Scope and Data Collection

The scope of the risk analysis requires documentation of all risks related to the confidentiality, integrity, and viability of *all* ePHI. This means all instances of patient information residing in applications, databases, data warehouses, share drives, thumb drives, optical media, and anywhere else data can be stored, processed, or transmitted. The entity conducting the analysis must account for each place patient data is entered, stored, maintained, or leaves the network boundaries.

# Threats

Threats are human and nonhuman sources that can have harmful effects on patient data. The human elements are made up of individuals or entities with the motive, means, and opportunity to undermine the confidentiality, integrity, or availability of ePHI.

Nonhuman elements refer to natural and environmental events. Typically, these are floods, tornados, hurricanes, and such human-made disasters as acts of terrorism. Risk analysis documentation requires entities to determine what individuals, events, or scenarios are threats to their patient data. Some threat lists are much more high-level and similar to those in Table 2-1. Others are much more detailed. These differing levels of detail make sense, based on the characteristics of the entity assessing risk.

*Table 2-1.*  *Threats Consist of Human and Nonhuman Events. Depending on the Maturity of the Risk Assessment Process, the Groups Outlined Previously Can Be Broken Down into More Specific Threats or Threat Scenarios*

| Threat Actor | Description |
| --- | --- |
| Hacktivists | Actions taken for political or ideological purposes |
| State-Sponsored | Attackers supported by national governments |
| Malicious Outsider | Organized criminals and other highly advanced attackers |
| Script Kiddie | Unsophisticated; often turns to open source tools |
| Malicious Insider | Employees or contractors blatantly not following policy/process |
| Environmental | Natural events or human-made disasters |

A high-level list of threats similar to Figure 2-1 is appropriate for conducting the analysis, but as with anything, the more detailed the analysis, the more benefits will be derived. That is why the process is conducted in cycles and operates as a program and not a project.

# Implement and Assess Security Measures

To reduce risks to an acceptable level, it is expected that covered entities and business associates implement security measures aligned to the risks. These security measures must be designed with risks in mind and placed into operation. The unique characteristics of organizations result in security measures being unique across all healthcare entities. Entities are free to choose from any cybersecurity framework available to meet requirements, multiple sources, or to design the program itself. The benefit of choosing a framework is that many are designed with information and cyber risk in mind.

# Vulnerabilities

Vulnerabilities are weaknesses in the environment that can be exploited by threat actors through different scenarios, leading to either a security event, incident, and/or breach of ePHI. Appendix C illustrates the process outlined in SP 800-30 to begin building this list, and Chapter 6 explores the process in detail. A few of the quicker ways to start compiling vulnerabilities include reviewing audits results and other assessments completed within the previous year. Referencing documents more than 12 months old may not yield relevant information.

# Risk Identification

Identifying and developing risk statements requires mapping the list of threats to the list of vulnerabilities each can exploit. This is not a one-to-one mapping but, in most cases, a mapping of one-threat to multiple vulnerabilities or multiple threats to one vulnerability. For example, state-sponsored groups and malicious insiders are examples of threat actors that may try to steal ePHI. Each could exploit noncomplex passwords and, as Figure 2-2 shows, each has multiple ways of breaking in to the entity's network. Sometimes the easiest way to complete this exercise is to list on one side of a page the vulnerabilities that exist and on the other the threats. Then it is as simple as drawing a line from the threat to each vulnerability related to it. In Figure 2-2, threats are listed on the left and vulnerabilities on the right. Each arrow represents a threat scenario, a vulnerability the actor may attempt to exploit.

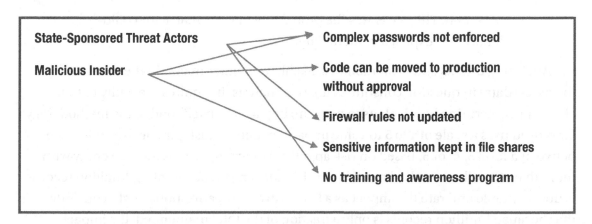

***Figure 2-2.*** *Two documented threats matched with five vulnerabilities, to create the initial list of risks*

Another benefit to this exercise is it allows individuals to visually see the relationships of threats and vulnerabilities at the time the analysis is completed. Once the mapping is complete, risk statements are written, using the following formula: state the threat actor, what vulnerability can be exploited, and what the adverse outcome is. Two examples are outlined following:

- State-sponsored groups can infiltrate the network and steal ePHI, owing to noncomplex passwords utilized to protect patient data.

- Malicious insiders can introduce code into a production environment, affecting the integrity of ePHI or rendering it unavailable, owing to a lack of monitoring and oversight of the systems development life cycle (SDLC) process.

Later, this book will illustrate how to document the analysis and create the risk register, without numerous repeated words or risks that read essentially the same, except for a word or two.

## Likelihood and Impact

A list of risks is nice, but to be useful, the severity has to be calculated. Without it, ascertaining which risks need attention is impossible. The two variables used to assess risk severity are likelihood and impact, both of which are defined following:

- *Impact*: This measures the level of adversity to the organization if a vulnerability is exploited, usually based on the types of data affected.

- *Likelihood*: This measures the probability that a threat actor could identify and exploit a vulnerability.

Analyzing threats and vulnerabilities, likelihoods, and impacts in the context of the asset (data) in question constitutes the risk analysis. It requires the entity to think about and determine how it plans to measure impact and likelihood. If the methodology employed uses a scale of 1 to 5 to value impact, an entity must quantify the difference between a level 3, 4, or 5, based on risk appetite. For example, a risk-averse entity with more than 10 million medical records may feel that any breach totaling 1 million records is unacceptable and rate the impact as a 5. Less averse organizations might conclude that because 1 million records is only a fraction of the total maintained, the impact is only a level 3. The rationale for each has to be documented in the analysis. When analyzing likelihood, it is easier to think in terms of the following two questions:

- How likely is it that the given threat actor will uncover the vulnerability?

- If uncovered, how likely is it that the given threat actor can exploit it?

In the preceding examples, both state-sponsored groups and malicious insiders can exploit sensitive data stored in unencrypted file shares. While analyzing this scenario, one might conclude that insiders could come across this weakness and exploit it more readily than the outside group. Unpatched vulnerabilities in Internet-facing servers, which are often known to the public, could be exploited more quickly by a state-sponsored group with the resources to hunt for known vulnerabilities en masse.

# Other Risk Analysis Guidance and Methodology

While the OCR specifically points to NIST 800-30 as suggested guidance for executing a risk analysis, there are other frameworks available to practitioners. The framework developed by the Health Information Trust Alliance (HITRUST) has gained traction in the healthcare provider and payer community in recent years. OCTAVE Allegro is another well-known framework and is available for download at the CERT Division of Carnegie Mellon University's Software Engineering Institute.[3]

## HITRUST

HITRUST is an organization located near Dallas, TX, that developed the Common Security Framework, now known only as the CSF, and is available on a subscription basis. The framework consists of security controls designed to guide covered entities and business associates when implementing measures to meet the safeguards of the HIPAA Security Rule. The control requirements that make up the CSF are derived from several sources, such as NIST and ISO, and are focused on security practices required to protect patient information. There is also a process for entities to achieve certification by meeting defined maturity scores.

---

[3]CERT, "OCTAVE," www.cert.org/resilience/products-services/octave/, 2017.

HITRUST also provides guidance to assist entities having to comply with risk analysis requirements. The Risk Analysis Guide[4] is available on HITRUST's web site in the publicly available downloads.

The methodology outlined by HITRUST is similar to the guidelines provided by NIST, with some nuances.

- Threats are not specifically documented in the assessment itself. The risk analysis guide considers the threat landscape within the assessment methodology.

- Each control is assessed based on a maturity rating, using a scale HITRUST created after making some modifications to NIST's PRISMA scale. The maturity score ranges from 0 to100, and the likelihood of an exploit is a function of control maturity.

- Impacts are based on control and not the asset in a non-contextual manner, which means that multiple control gaps or compensating controls are not part of the risk calculation.

- Risk ratings are calculated using a mathematical formula, with the maturity score and impact ratings driving overall risk level.

# OCTAVE

The current version of OCTAVE is the Allegro methodology. This methodology is made-up of many of the same steps outlined in NIST 800-30. The inventory of the assets is referred to as *profiles*, and to make the process easier, assets are placed into containers, allowing for grouping of common assets. Later, when asset collection is discussed, this concept can be applied to NIST, but OCTAVE begins the risk assessment process with containers, to reduce complexity. Containers can be set up based on several factors.

- Common asset owners
- Similar people, process, and technology characteristics or control operation

---

[4]HITRUST, "CSF, RMF & Related Documents," https://hitrustalliance.net/csf-rmf-related-documents/, 2017.

Threats to assets are established in the context of the containers, and risks are analyzed and mitigated in the same manner as the NIST guidelines.

- Establish the risk management criteria.

- Develop an information asset profile.

- Identify information asset containers.

- Identify areas of concern.

- Identify threat scenarios.

- Identify risks.

- Analyze risks.

- Select a mitigation approach.

OCTAVE is very business-objective focused. The initial steps in establishing the risk management criteria guide the user to focus on the organization's mission and business objectives. One benefit of this process is the effectiveness in framing risks, so that they are meaningful to members of senior management.

# Choosing a Framework Is Not Permanent

The processes described in this chapter are designed to guide organizations through the risk analysis process. Each is similar conceptually; it's the methods used to arrive at the risks to ePHI that differ.

The thing to keep in mind when getting started is whatever framework or process is chosen initially is not a permanent decision. If the first analysis is completed using OCTAVE and changing to NIST makes more sense, then NIST can be used going forward. The information already assessed can be updated into the new framework, without interrupting the process. HITRUST uses a more sophisticated means to calculate risk than the other frameworks, but it is still possible to adopt it if choosing so makes sense for the organization. NIST is an easy choice, because HHS specifically refers to SP 800-30, and it is freely available to the public. Later chapters will be devoted to walking through the NIST process.

# Summary

Risk analysis is one of the most widely misunderstood requirements within the HIPAA Security Rule. Often, it is a documented gap during proactive audits and investigations, because entities either have not taken the initiative to complete the assessment, or the assessment itself is not sufficient to meet the standards established by the HIPAA Security Rule. It does not have to stay this way. It just requires looking past the absolutes stated in press releases and guidance that create anxiety and taking actions to set up a process for assessing, analyzing, and managing risks. To effectively build a cybersecurity program designed to achieve compliance and focus on adapting to new and more sophisticated threats, developing a process to systematically assess risks is required. Risk is the starting point to identify and implement cybersecurity controls.

# CHAPTER 3

# Selecting Security Measures

The risk assessment process requires management to select security measures designed to reduce risks to an acceptable level and protect ePHI, in accordance with the HIPAA Security Rule. No specific measures are prescribed by HHS or the OCR. Rather, it is up to the entity to define the measures that meet those objectives. Successful identification and implementation of security controls requires entities to consider the following:

- Based on risk tolerance, determine the level of risk reduction required.

- Based on the risk level, identify new, or modify existing, controls.

- Conduct periodic reviews by management, to ensure that the control operation meets risk-reduction and data-protection needs.

- Recommend changes, as required, where a control operation falls short of expectations.

Risk tolerance and acceptable levels of risk are management decisions. One organization's comfort level might represent too much risk to another. These decisions are based on potential impacts to operations and objectives. Fortunately, many frameworks are available to assist entities with cybersecurity control selection. These frameworks outline control objectives that management can customize, based on current business processes, to meet risk reduction objectives.

© Eric C. Thompson 2017
E. C. Thompson, *Building a HIPAA-Compliant Cybersecurity Program*,
https://doi.org/10.1007/978-1-4842-3060-2_3

# Cybersecurity Frameworks to the Rescue

Several prominent organizations developed and published cybersecurity frameworks that healthcare entities can leverage to develop a cybersecurity program and further enhance the risk assessment process. NIST, the International Standards Organization (ISO), HITRUST, and the Center for Internet Security (CIS) have published well-known frameworks designed to aid cybersecurity leaders and practitioners. NIST, ISO, and HITRUST are built around domains or categories supplemented by control statements within each. The CIS Critical Security Controls (CSC) define 20 control activities. Table 3-1 outlines the categories or domains that make up NIST 800-53, ISO 27001, HITRUST, and CIS Critical Security Controls.

***Table 3-1.*** *Four Common Frameworks Utilized by Cybersecurity Teams*

| NIST 800-53 | ISO 27001: 27002 | HITRUST | CSC |
|---|---|---|---|
| 1 Access Control | 1 Information Security Policies | 1 Information Security Program | 1 Inventory authorized and unauthorized devices |
| 2 Audit and Accountability | 2 Organization of Information Security | 2 Endpoint Protection | 2 Inventory authorized and unauthorized software |
| 3 Awareness and Training | 3 Human Resource Security | 3 Portable Media | 3 Secure configuration |
| 4 Configuration Management | 4 Asset Management | 4 Mobile Device Security | 4 Continuous vulnerability assessment and remediation |
| 5 Contingency Planning | 5 Access Control | 5 Wireless Security | 5 Control privileged accounts |
| 6 Identification and Authentication | 6 Cryptography | 6 Configuration Management | 6 Maintenance, monitoring, and analysis of audit logs |
| 7 Incident Response | 7 Physical and Environmental Security | 7 Vulnerability Management | 7 E-mail and web browser protection |

(*continued*)

***Table 3-1.*** (*continued*)

| NIST 800-53 | ISO 27001: 27002 | HITRUST | CSC |
|---|---|---|---|
| 8 Maintenance | 8 Operation Security | 8 Network Protection | 8 Malware defenses |
| 9 Media Protection | 9 Communication Security | 9 Transmission Protection | 9 Limit and control ports, protocols, and services |
| 10 Personnel Security | 10 System Acquisition, Development, and Maintenance | 10 Password Management | 10 Data recovery capability |
| 11 Physical/ Environmental Security | 11 Supplier Relationships | 11 Access Control | 11 Secure configuration of network devices |
| 12 Planning | 12 Information Security Incident Management | 12 Audit Logging and Monitoring | 12 Boundary defense |
| 13 Program Management | 13 Information Security Aspect of Information Business Continuity Management | 13 Education, Training, and Awareness | 13 Data protection |
| 14 Risk Assessment | 14 Compliance | 14 Third-Party Assessment | 14 Controlled access based on need to know |
| 15 Security Assessment and Authorization | | 15 Incident Management | 15 Wireless access control |
| 16 System and Communication Protection | | 16 BC/DR | 16 Account monitoring and control |
| 17 System and Information Security | | 17 Risk Management | 17 Security skills assessment and appropriate training to fill gaps |

(*continued*)

**Table 3-1.** (*continued*)

| NIST 800-53 | ISO 27001: 27002 | HITRUST | CSC |
|---|---|---|---|
| 18 System and Service Acquisition | | 18 Physical/ Environmental Security | 18 Application Software Security |
| | | 19 Data Protection and Privacy | 19 Incident response and management |
| | | | 20 Penetration tests and red team exercises |

- *NIST SP 800-53: 18 families, 224 controls*: - NIST mixes controls across technical and nontechnical families.

- *ISO 27001: 114 controls in 14 domains*: ISO builds its framework around information security policies and the information security organization.

- *HITRUST CSF: 19 domains, 149 controls*: Controls making up the 19 domains of HITRUST are pulled from many authoritative sources, including ISO and NIST.

- *CIS Critical Security Controls: 20 cybersecurity control processes*

# The NIST Cybersecurity Framework

The Framework for Improving Critical Infrastructure was issued by Executive Order 13636, on February 12, 2013. This framework is commonly referred to as the NIST Cybersecurity Frameworks (CSF). The CSF is driven by business objectives and focuses primarily on cybersecurity risks as a subset of business risks. The NIST CSF consist of five functions: identify, protect, detect, respond, and recover. Each of these functions has several categories and subcategories that state targeted objectives.

One benefit of the CSF is the ability to integrate them into the risk assessment and control selection process that HHS and the OCR expect. The activities required by NIST 800-30 overlap with some CSF documentation efforts. The first function requires entities to identify assets, create governance mechanisms, and establish communication between senior management and the business, which includes cybersecurity. Identify requires entities to implement risk assessment and risk management capabilities. The

CSF flows from forming a foundation to protection, detection, response, and recover controls and capabilities. Tables 3-2, 3-3, 3-4, 3-5, and 3-6 outline the categories and subcategories of the NIST CSF by function.

# Identify

Building a cybersecurity program requires any organization, first and foremost, to understand what it needs to protect. The identify function lays the groundwork for asset management, critical business operations, proper use of asset, how behavior is enforced, and how are risks are identified and managed.

***Table 3-2.*** *Categories and Subcategories of the Identify Function*

| | |
|---|---|
| Asset Management | ID.AM-1: Physical devices and systems within the organization are inventoried. |
| | ID.AM-2: Software platforms and applications within the organization are inventoried. |
| | ID.AM-3: Organizational communication and data flows are mapped. |
| | ID.AM-4: External information systems are cataloged. |
| | ID.AM-5: Resources (e.g., hardware, devices, data, and software) are prioritized, based on their classification, criticality, and business value. |
| | ID.AM-6: Cybersecurity roles and responsibilities for the entire workforce and third-party stakeholders (e.g., suppliers, customers, partners) are established. |
| Business Environment | ID.BE-1: The organization's role in the supply chain is identified and communicated. |
| | ID.BE-2: The organization's place in critical infrastructure and its industry sector are identified and communicated. |
| | ID.BE-3: Priorities for organizational mission, objectives, and activities are established and communicated. |
| | ID.BE-4: Dependencies and critical functions for delivery of critical services are established. |
| | ID.BE-5: Resilience requirements to support delivery of critical services are established. |

*(continued)*

***Table 3-2.*** (*continued*)

| Governance | ID.GV-1: Organizational information security policy is established. |
|---|---|
| | ID.GV-2: Information security roles and responsibilities are coordinated and aligned with internal roles and external partners. |
| | ID.GV-3: Legal and regulatory requirements regarding cybersecurity, including privacy and civil liberties obligations, are understood and managed. |
| | ID.GV-4: Governance and risk management processes address cybersecurity risks. |
| Risk Assessment | ID.RA-1: Asset vulnerabilities are identified and documented. |
| | ID.RA-2: Threat and vulnerability information is received from information-sharing forums and sources. |
| | ID.RA-3: Threats, both internal and external, are identified and documented. |
| | ID.RA-4: Potential business impacts and likelihoods are identified. |
| | ID.RA-5: Threats, vulnerabilities, likelihoods, and impacts are used to determine risk. |
| | ID.RA-6: Risk responses are identified and prioritized. |
| Risk Management | ID.RM-1: Risk management processes are established, managed, and agreed to by organizational stakeholders. |
| | ID.RM-2: Organizational risk tolerance is determined and clearly expressed. |
| | ID.RM-3: The organization's determination of risk tolerance is informed by its role in critical infrastructure and sector-specific risk analysis. |

The identify function is the initial step in creating a cybersecurity program. In the five categories and subcategories, several important items are established.

- What hardware and software needs to be protected?
- How will the entity establish and enforce the protective measures?
- What business factors must be considered in the context of establishing a cybersecurity program?
- How will risk be assessed and addressed by the entity?

The elements of the identify function require management input. It is up to management to determine what to protect, how to protect it, and how to implement protections. Management also must monitor the cybersecurity and risk management program. Annually, it should review cybersecurity policies and the risk management processes, and approve or recommend changes.

# Protect

This function is the largest in the framework. It focuses on several disparate categories and capabilities of data and information protection. Examples include access control, training and awareness, configuration management, encryption, and protective technology.

***Table 3-3.*** *Categories and Subcategories of the Protect Function*

| | |
|---|---|
| Access Control | PR.AC-1: Identities and credentials are managed for authorized devices and users. |
| | PR.AC-2: Physical access to assets is managed and protected. |
| | PR.AC-3: Remote access is managed |
| | PR.AC-4: Access permissions are managed, incorporating the principles of least privilege and separation of duties. |
| | PR.AC-5: Network integrity is protected, incorporating network segregation, where appropriate. |
| Awareness and Training | PR.AT-1: All users are informed and trained. |
| | PR.AT-2: Privileged users understand roles and responsibilities. |
| | PR.AT-3: Third-party stakeholders (e.g., suppliers, customers, partners) understand roles and responsibilities. |
| | PR.AT-4: Senior executives understand roles and responsibilities. |
| | PR.AT-5: Physical and information security personnel understand roles and responsibilities. |

(*continued*)

**Table 3-3.** (*continued*)

| | |
|---|---|
| Data Security | PR.DS-1: Data at rest is protected. |
| | PR.DS-2: Data in transit is protected. |
| | PR.DS-3: Assets are formally managed throughout removal, transfers, and disposition. |
| | PR.DS-4: Adequate capacity to ensure availability is maintained. |
| | PR.DS-5: Protections against data leaks are implemented. |
| | PR.DS-6: Integrity checking mechanisms are used to verify software, firmware, and information integrity. |
| Information Protection | PR.IP-1: A baseline configuration of information technology/industrial control systems is created and maintained. |
| | PR.IP-2: A System Development Life Cycle to manage systems is implemented. |
| | PR.IP-3: Configuration change control processes are in place. |
| | PR.IP-4: Backups of information are conducted, maintained, and tested periodically. |
| | PR.IP-5: Policy and regulations regarding the physical operating environment for organizational assets are met. |
| | PR.IP-6: Data is destroyed according to policy. |
| | PR.IP-7: Protection processes are continuously improved. |
| | PR.IP-8: Effectiveness of protection technologies is shared with appropriate parties. |
| | PR.IP-9: Response plans (Incident Response and Business Continuity) and recovery plans (Incident Recovery and Disaster Recovery) are in place and managed. |
| | PR.IP-10: Response and recovery plans are tested. |
| | PR.IP-11: Cybersecurity is included in human resources practices (e.g., deprovisioning, personnel screening). |
| | PR.IP-12: A vulnerability management plan is developed and implemented. |

(*continued*)

***Table 3-3.*** (*continued*)

| Maintenance | PR.MA-1: Maintenance and repair of organizational assets are performed and logged in a timely manner, with approved and controlled tools. |
| --- | --- |
| | PR.MA-2: Remote maintenance of organizational assets is approved, logged, and performed in a manner that prevents unauthorized access. |
| Protective Technology | PR.PT-1: Audit/log records are determined, documented, implemented, and reviewed in accordance with policy. |
| | PR.PT-2: Removable media is protected, and its use restricted according to policy. |
| | PR.PT-3: Access to systems and assets is controlled, incorporating the principle of least functionality. |
| | PR.PT-4: Communications and control networks are protected. |

- Access is vital, if covered entities and business associates are not able to manage this category effectively, the value of other protective measures will be diminished.

- Awareness attempts to address a significant issue: how vulnerable end users are to exploit, and circumvention of other cybersecurity capabilities.

- Data needs to be protected throughout its life cycle. It must be secured when transferred into the environment, while in use, while in motion, and while at rest

- If data is transferred out of the entity, secure communication mechanisms are required.

- Information protection is about establishing secure configurations and ensuring that changes to those configurations are monitored.

- Technology is in place to capture logging data, access control, and protect communication networks.

This function showcases one way cybersecurity programs based on risk are designed. Once critical assets are identified and risk is measured, protective controls and capabilities are identified. The level of investment in each subcategory depends on risk.

# Detect

The numerous examples of malware and ransomware discussed earlier illustrate the need for detective controls. These controls require a mix of technical and process capabilities to be executed by the cybersecurity team.

***Table 3-4.*** *Categories and Subcategories of the Detect Function*

| | |
|---|---|
| Anomalies and Events | DE.AE-1: A baseline of network operations and expected data flows for users and systems is established and managed. |
| | DE.AE-2: Detected events are analyzed to understand attack targets and methods. |
| | DE.AE-3: Event data are aggregated and correlated from multiple sources and sensors. |
| | DE.AE-4: Impact of events is determined. |
| | DE.AE-5: Incident alert thresholds are established. |
| Security Monitoring | DE.CM-1: The network is monitored to detect potential cybersecurity events. |
| | DE.CM-2: The physical environment is monitored to detect potential cybersecurity events. |
| | DE.CM-3: Personnel activity is monitored to detect potential cybersecurity events. |
| | DE.CM-4: Malicious code is detected. |
| | DE.CM-5: Unauthorized mobile code is detected. |
| | DE.CM-6: External service provider activity is monitored to detect potential cybersecurity events. |
| | DE.CM-7: Monitoring for unauthorized personnel, connections, devices, and software is performed. |
| | DE.CM-8: Vulnerability scans are performed. |
| Detection Processes | DE.DP-1: Roles and responsibilities for detection are well defined to ensure accountability. |
| | DE.DP-2: Detection activities comply with all applicable requirements. |
| | DE.DP-3: Detection processes are tested. |
| | DE.DP-4: Event detection information is communicated to appropriate parties. |
| | DE.DP-5: Detection processes are continuously improved. |

Detection processes are exactly what the name implies, indicators detecting that a threat actor has launched an attack. Many experts in the cybersecurity field feel that prevention is not a plausible goal anymore, and they focus on detecting and responding as the functions to which organizations should direct investment. The objectives of detection are to

- Establish and monitor the baselines of user and network traffic and establish a hardening standard for all devices on the network

- Examine all events and alerts to understand what was targeted and the attack vectors

- Aggregate log data and understand the impact of a potential breach

- Establish a threshold that transitions an alert to an event and an event to an incident

Mature detect functions can understand what is normal inside the network and alert cybersecurity when anomalous behavior occurs.

# Respond

If the five functions of the NIST CSF were laid out horizontally from right to left, respond would be adjacent to detect, because one follows the other. This function lists the requirements cybersecurity leaders must implement to appropriately respond when incidents are detected.

***Table 3-5.*** *Categories and Subcategories of the Respond Function*

| | |
|---|---|
| Communications | RS.CO-1: Personnel know their roles and order of operations when a response is needed. |
| | RS.CO-2: Events are reported consistent with established criteria. |
| | RS.CO-3: Information is shared consistent with response plans. |
| | RS.CO-4: Coordination with stakeholders occurs consistent with response plans. |
| | RS.CO-5: Voluntary information sharing occurs with external stakeholders to achieve broader cybersecurity situational awareness. |
| Analysis | RS.AN-1: Notifications from detection systems are investigated. |
| | RS.AN-2: The impact of the incident is understood. |
| | RS.AN-3: Forensics are performed. |
| | RS.AN-4: Incidents are categorized consistent with response plans. |
| Mitigation | RS.MI-1: Incidents are contained. |
| | RS.MI-2: Incidents are mitigated. |
| | RS.MI-3: Newly identified vulnerabilities are mitigated or documented as accepted risks. |
| Improvement | RS.IM-1: Response plans incorporate lessons learned. |
| | RS.IM-2: Response strategies are updated. |

Intuitively, response follows detection. The response plan must be outlined and understood by the team. The response function must

- Establish communication protocols

- Analyze the situation and determine whether an event or incident has occurred

- Engage forensic specialists

- Mitigate and eradicate the intrusion

- Alert stakeholders

- Conduct a postmortem exercise to assess what went right and what could be done better next time

Conducting regular table-top exercises to test incident response is a critical activity that should be performed at least annually. When an incident occurs, a team needs to know how to react and ensure that the plan is followed. The incident response leader has to understand how to evaluate the details known, collect additional information, and determine appropriate next steps.

# Recover

Recovery focuses on getting the organization back to business as usual. When an incident occurs, even a cyber incident, the business continuity and recovery plan will also have to be executed. This function focuses on making sure the right capabilities exist to allow the origination, in the context of its place in serving healthcare needs of the population, to continue functioning throughout and after the incident.

***Table 3-6.*** *Categories and Subcategories of the Recover Function*

| | |
|---|---|
| Recovery Planning | RC.RP-1: Recovery plan is executed during or after an event. |
| Improvement | RC.IM-1: Recovery plans incorporate lessons learned. |
| | RC.IM-2: Recovery strategies are updated. |
| Communication | RC.CO-1: Public relations are managed. |
| | RC.CO-2: Reputation after an event is repaired. |
| | RC.CO-3: Recovery activities are communicated to internal stakeholders and executive and management teams. |

# Implementing Internal Controls Aligned with Subcategories

Frameworks provide guidance for implementing cybersecurity measures; however, adopting a framework is not plug-and-play. First, management must review and understand the objectives of the framework, to confirm it meets the entities requirements. If it does, cybersecurity controls that meet framework objectives are identified and documented. Simply selecting a framework is not enough. Internal controls answer the "How will this objective be implemented?" question. Figure 3-1 shows the relationship of "How" to the controls function, by identifying who needs to perform the activity, what the activity entails, and when the activity is performed.

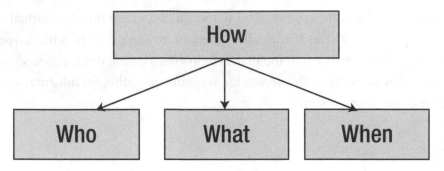

***Figure 3-1.*** *Control language addresses how objectives of any framework are implemented*

Designing effective controls incorporates current business processes while making necessary changes to instill the level of control necessary to reduce risk. Table 3-7 provides examples of applying the who, what, and where questions to the subcategory objective, to answer the question, "How do we ensure that physical devices and systems within the organization are inventoried."

***Table 3-7.*** *Internal Controls Address the "How" of Meeting Subcategory Objectives (Examples of Controls for the Remaining Subcategories Are Documented in Appendix A)*

| Category | Subcategory Example of Controls Wording |
|---|---|
| Asset Management | ID.AM-1: A complete inventory of all hardware assets is maintained by <Person> and reviewed semiannually for completeness. |
| | ID.AM-2: A complete inventory of all software is maintained by <person> and reviewed semiannually for completeness. |
| | ID.AM-3: Data flow diagrams are developed by <person> and updated annually. |
| | ID.AM-4: All external connections and systems undergo an annual risk assessment completed by <person/team>. These connections are communicated to <person> and tracked in the asset inventory. |
| | ID.AM-5: All information assets are where ePHI is created, stored, processed, and maintained are classified by the <person/team> and documented in the appropriate asset inventory. |
| | ID.AM-6: Job descriptions for all workforce classifications that have access to PHI/ePHI contain data security expectations documented by HR defined by the <committee>. |

The controls wording aligned to each subcategory throughout this framework assigns owner, place, and time elements for the required activities. Adding time elements might seem like overdoing it, such as management communicating the entity's place in the critical infrastructure or reviewing every governance document annually, but this is meant to solve some common issues in cybersecurity control environments, such as the following:

- Controls are not executed. If management is not required to communicate key business issues, a higher likelihood exits that the control will not operate effectively.

- Not forcing a review of policies, procedures, and cybersecurity strategies/roadmaps increases the risk of documents becoming obsolete and ineffective.

When designing cybersecurity controls, certain subcategories may require that more than one control be implemented to meet NIST's objective. In the following example, PR.AC-1, in the first column of Table 3-3, states the objective as limiting user access to appropriate individuals. This means that access is granted only to those individuals who need it to perform their job duties. When those individuals no longer perform those duties, access is removed. IT systems are more complex than having access granted to one environment, but a single control is too generic to properly govern access. The PR.AC-1 control requires several controls to meet the objective.

- A control for granting access at the application layer

- Each application will also require a control designed to remove access in a timely manner when users leave the entity or change roles.

- A control to govern access granted at the infrastructure level (operating system and database)

- A control to govern removal of access at the infrastructure level (operating system and database)

- Another good practice is to implement monitoring controls to periodically review access at each layer of the application stack.

The controls required to govern and secure ePHI are extensive. To comply with risk analysis requirements, it is necessary to assess the whole technology stack. These means assessing access to

- Applications

- Operating systems

- Databases

- Any other tools or components, for example, report-enhancing tools

- Directory services, such as Active Directory

- Network components transmitting data across the network

Often, ad hoc processes are in place that give off a false sense that effective processes exist. However, when assessed for the first time, gaps become more apparent.

Other considerations to keep in mind when designing the control environment include the following:

- An owner must be identified and held accountable for the operation of each control. Preferably, the accountability is built into the annual performance evaluation.

- *Segregation of duties*: No one individual should approve and execute any part of the control process. In the preceding example, individuals approving access should never grant it.

- Review controls must be executed by someone who is not reviewing his or her own activity but who possesses sufficient understanding of the process to confirm that it is operating appropriately.

Finally, the control must be monitored by management. Over time, changes to internal and external characteristics require some controls to be removed, and others adjusted, to fit the organization's needs.

# The Cybersecurity Policy

Cybersecurity and compliance policies add strength and governance to cybersecurity programs. This is where all the dos and don'ts live and where enforcement measures are identified. These policies can also ease some of the anxiety surrounding requirements to identify all instances of ePHI and document all the risks to confidentiality, integrity, and availability.

Practitioners working for larger health systems university-based medical centers, health plans, and business associates rarely have the insight into end user behavior required to document every instance of ePHI. End users engage with and send data to third parties and store it in places where ePHI is not intended to rest. This is referred to as shadow IT. Shadow IT can refer to members of a workforce using IT solutions and ePHI in a manner not approved by, or without the knowledge of, the organization. Some of the common issues heard include:

- Medical students and educators saving data to share drives, either on-premise or in the cloud, to facilitate collaborations

- Use of stand-alone servers located in offices, which store data without restricting access or applying other required security controls

- Contractors and consultants who transmit data outside the network boundary to circumvent controls perceived to be hampering speed and innovation

Information security policies should govern these issues and clearly state expectations for handling PHI and the ramifications of operating outside of policy. In later Chapter 10, specific tests to find instances of misuse are outlined. When uncovered, cybersecurity leaders, human resource leaders, and business leaders should work together to ensure proper enforcement.

In the context of the risk analysis, the scope includes instances of known to the entity based on expected compliance with policies at the time of the analysis. Instances of ePHI that exist because users acting outside of allowable policy guidelines cannot be assessed are considered out of scope.

---

**Note**    The one exception to this approach applies to any reasonably anticipated activities that violate policy. Any reason to believe a single user, group of users, or subset of the entity might act inappropriately with ePHI must be identified as a risk.

---

# Measuring the Cybersecurity Program

Assessing the program is necessary to understand how effective it is at protecting ePHI through risk reduction. Typically, cybersecurity programs are measured based on maturity. Two common methods are discussed in this section. Maturity assessments are executed for many reasons, but the two this book focuses on are

- Do gaps exist, creating in the program vulnerabilities that could affect ePHI?

- Do the cybersecurity controls operate effectively enough to reduce risks to ePHI to an acceptable level?

Later Chapters 8 through 13 provide more details regarding vulnerabilities, control adoption or enhancement, and risk reduction through improved capabilities. For now, just know that maturity assessments do uncover vulnerabilities attackers can exploit, and improvements made to the program reduce the risks cybersecurity gaps present.

# Capability Maturity Model

The Capability Maturity Model (CMM)[1] is a process-improvement model used in software development. The model consists of five levels, ranging from ad hoc to optimized. At the lowest level, processes are unorganized and lack documented policies and procedures. Entities using the model strive to optimize processes with defined metrics that are consistently measured and improved by management. This model is applicable to measuring cybersecurity program management as well.

*Level 1*: Information Security processes are unorganized and often unstructured. Success is likely to depend on individual efforts and not considered to be repeatable or scalable.

*Level 2*: Information Security efforts are repeatable. Characteristics of this level include establishing basic project management and enabling repeatable process capabilities. Control processes are documented, defined, and implemented.

*Level 3*: Information Security efforts have greater attention to documentation, standardization, and maintenance support.

---

[1]https://csrc.nist.gov/publications/detail/nistir/7358/final/

*Level 4*: At this level, an organization monitors and controls its own cybersecurity processes, through data collection and analysis.

*Level 5*: Optimizations are achieved by continual process improvement, by monitoring feedback from existing processes owners and independent monitoring. When necessary, improvements are made to existing processes, or new processes are introduced.

# PRISMA

The Program Review for Information Security Management Assistance (PRISMA)[2] was developed to support improvement of information security programs. PRISMA is used to review the maturity of information/cybersecurity programs. Users can also assess strategic elements of information security programs or strategic and technical elements. Each of these is available at NIST's computer security site.

*Policies*: These are up to date, use the words *shall* or *we*, assign IT security responsibilities, establish the implementation and monitoring of the risk assessment process, and define penalties for noncompliance.

*Procedures*: Procedures exist in a specific document and are made available in a central location and communicated to the workforce. One example are procedures for requesting and granting access. Procedures often contain the same elements as the cybersecurity control wording.

---

**Tip**    Policy documents often list the procedures required by the policy in the same document. This practice is acceptable, but clearly calling out which statements are policy statements and which are procedures is advisable.

---

[2]Pauline Bowen and Richard Kissel, "Program Review for Information Security Management Assistance(PRISMA)," NISTIR 7358, http://csrc.nist.gov/publications/nistir/ir7358/NISTIR-7358.pdf, January 2007.

*Implementation*: This focuses on the existence of cybersecurity control processes that are documented and followed throughout the organization. Ad hoc or noncompliant processes are discouraged, and reinforcement of this standard is conducted through training and initial testing of controls.

*Test*: Testing is measuring. Management must understand if the cybersecurity program and controls are operating as expected. Testing takes the form of technical tests—attack and penetration tests, for example. It also includes nontechnical testing, such as access control or change management. These tests are performed by internal resources or external firms that management engages.

*Integration*: Integration means management needs to evaluate the effectiveness of the control, by reviewing metrics and testing identified in the previous step. A complete review by management includes which metrics were reviewed and what changes to the program need to be made.

# Addressing Compliance Requirements

Quite often, organizations mistakenly focus efforts on complying with HIPAA, thinking this approach provides sufficient protection of electronic health information. Instead, the focus should be on the cybersecurity program itself. Focusing on building controls and capabilities of the NIST CSF ultimately achieves compliance with the HIPAA Security Rule. A crosswalk between the NIST CSF and the HIPAA Security Rule is available at the HHS[3] web site. Tables 3-8, 3-9, and 3-10 illustrate subcategories of the NIST CSF that meet safeguards of the Security Rule.

# HIPAA Security Rule

The mapping of NIST CSF controls to the HIPAA Security Rule in this section focuses on the administrative, physical, and technical safeguards of the regulation. These safeguards are covered across all categories and subcategories of the CSF. The job of

---

[3]DHHS Office for Civil Rights, "HIPAA Security Rule Crosswalk to NIST Cybersecurity Framework," `www.hhs.gov/sites/default/files/nist-csf-to-hipaa-security-rule-crosswalk-02-22-2016-final.pdf`, February 2016.

governance, risk, and compliance professionals is ensuring that documentation of cybersecurity program control maturity and capability is carried over to compliance assessments.

> **Note**    Not all NIST CSF subcategories are mapped to the following HIPAA Security Safeguards. Instead, focus is placed on key controls of the NIST CSF. A full mapping is available in Appendix A of this book.

## Administrative Safeguards

Administrative safeguards in Table 3-8 cover nearly two-thirds of implementation requirements under the Security Rule. The risk analysis, risk management, and program- and process-related specifications are required by the administrative safeguards.

***Table 3-8.***  *Administrative Safeguards Mapped to Controls/Subcategories of the NIST CSF*

| Standards | CFR Section | Implementation Specifications | NIST CSF Control Subcategories |
|---|---|---|---|
| Security Management Process | 164.308(a)(1) | Risk Analysis | ID.RA-1, 2, 3, 4, 5, 6 ID.AM-1, 2, 3 |
| | | Risk Management | ID.RM-1, 2, 3 ID.AM-2, 3 |
| | | Sanction Policy | ID.GV-1 |
| | | Information Activity Review | ID.RA-3 |
| Assigned Security Responsibility | 164.308(a)(2) | None | ID.GV-2, ID.AM-6 |
| Information Access Management | 164.308(a)(4) | Isolated Clearinghouse Function | ID.AM-6 |
| | | Access Authorization | PR.AC-1, 5, ID.AM-4 |
| | | Access Modification | PR.AC-1, ID.AM-4 |

*(continued)*

*Table 3-8.*  (*continued*)

| Standards | CFR Section | Implementation Specifications | NIST CSF Control Subcategories |
|---|---|---|---|
| Security Awareness and Training | 164.308(a)(5) | Security Reminders | PR.AT-1, 4, 5, ID.RA-3 |
| | | Protection from Malicious Software | DE.CM-1, 4, 5, 7 |
| | | Log-in Monitoring | PR.PT-1, DE.AE-3 |
| | | Password Management | PR.AT-2, 4, 5 |
| Security Incident Procedures | 164.308(a)(6) | Response and Reporting | |
| Contingency Plan | 164.308(a)(7) | Data Backup Plan | PR.AC-2, PR.IP-4 |
| | | Disaster Recovery Plan | PR.IP-4 |
| | | Emergency Mode Operations | ID.BE-1, 2, 3 |
| | | Testing and Revision Procedures | PR.IP-4, 7, 10 |
| | | Application Data Criticality Analysis | ID.GV-4, ID.AM-5 |
| Evaluation | 164.308(a)(8) | None | PR.IP-7, ID.AM-3 |
| Business Associates | 164.308(a)(8) | Written Contract or Other Arrangement | PR.AC-4 |

The identify and protect functions of the NIST CSF cover the administrative safeguards. Foundational controls, policies, asset management, access control, data backup, and risk management are important focal points.

# Physical Safeguards

Physical safeguards are not specific to physical security but cover contingency operations and managing removable media, which are outlined in Table 3-9.

***Table 3-9.*** *Physical Safeguards Mapped to Controls/Subcategories of the NIST CSF*

| Standard | CFR Reference | Implementation Specification | NIST CSF Control |
| --- | --- | --- | --- |
| Facility Access Controls | 164.310(a)(1) | Contingency Operations | RS.RP-1, RS.CO-1 |
| | | Facility Security Plan | PR.AC-2 |
| | | Access Control Validation Procedures | PR.AC-1 |
| | | Maintenance Records | |
| | | | PR.MA-1 |
| Work Station Use | 164.310(b) | None | DE.CM-3 |
| Work Station Security | 164.310(c) | None | DE.CM-1, 2, 3 |
| Device and Media Security | 164.310(d)(1) | Media Disposal | PR.DS-3, ID.AM-1 ID.AM-3 |
| | | Media Reuse | PR.DS-3, ID.AM-1 ID.AM-3 |
| | | Media Accountability | PR.DS-3, ID.AM-1 ID.AM-3 |
| | | Data Backup and Storage | PR.IP-4 |

The physical safeguards are primarily mapped to controls in the protect function, but detect and response functional controls are also required to meet the compliance requirements of this group of safeguards.

## Technical Safeguards

Technical safeguards (Table 3-10) are designed to allow only authorized individuals to view ePHI and determine which individuals did the viewing. That is the purpose of unique user ID controls. Generic login IDs prevent the cybersecurity and compliance officials ability to pinpoint who accessed data. Finally, auto logoff and encryption controls are also key implementations of the technical safeguards.

***Table 3-10.*** *Technical Safeguards Mapped to Controls/Subcategories of the NIST CSF*

| Standard | CFR Reference | Implementation Specification | NIST CSF Control |
| --- | --- | --- | --- |
| Access Controls | 164.312(a)(1) | Unique User Identification | PR.AC-1 |
| | | Emergency Access Procedure | PR.AC-1 |
| | | Automatic Logoff | PR.AC-2 |
| | | Encryption and Decryption | PR.DS-1 |
| Audit Controls | 164.312(b) | None | PR.PT-1 |
| Integrity | 164.312(c)(1) | Protection Against Improper Alteration or Destruction of Data | |
| Person or Enmity Authentication | 164.312(d) | None | PR.AC-1 |
| Transmission Security | 164.312(e)(1) | Integrity Controls | PR.DP-1 |
| | | Encryption | |

The organizational safeguards of the Security Rule are not mapped in the preceding sections, since these requirements are met through the security controls mapped in the administrative, physical, and technical safeguards. The implementation specifications found in the organizational safeguards include business associate, group health plan, and other policy requirements.

# Summary

Once risks are analyzed and severity levels assessed, identifying security measures designed to reduce all identified risks to ePHI is the expected next step. Security measures must be identified and assessed, to determine the level of maturity and the level of effectiveness risk reduction has achieved that can be quantified. Many organizations turn to NIST, ISO, and the CIS. This approach assists by suggesting leading practices by domain or categories and, in some cases, defined control objectives. A covered entity or business associate is free to choose any framework it is comfortable with, as long as documentation demonstrates that the organization ensures that controls exist to meet HIPAA security safeguards.

Finally, the entity must establish who owns and is accountable for the operation of the control process. As in the case of risk analysis, an iterative process of identifying, measuring, and adjusting cybersecurity controls is necessary for success.

# PART II

# Assessing and Analyzing Risk

# CHAPTER 4

# Inventory Your ePHI

Documenting all instances of ePHI, everywhere it is in use, in motion and at rest, is the one risk assessment and analysis activity that elicits the most fear and anxiety. It's been touched on before, but it is worth repeating. Cybersecurity and compliance professionals develop anxiety about attaching their names to an activity that they feel will fall short. It's a fear of being held accountable for every crazy thing end users do with patient data. If a breach occurs owing to misuse of data unknown to the entity, and that risk scenario is not documented on the risk assessment, it is quite possible that regulators may cite this as a cause of the breach. It is not possible to predict what conclusions regulators may come to when investigating a breach. What is predicable is this: when nothing is done to analyze risk, additional penalties, including steeper monetary settlements, additional corrective actions, and the appointment of independent monitors to oversee those corrective actions, often result. It's more productive to assess the risk that a malicious insider could misuse ePHI, causing another threat to steal, modify, or render the data unavailable. Next, quantify the risk and try to mitigate it as best as possible. This allows the practitioner to assess the environment, based on all known characteristics, and reasonably anticipate impermissible uses and disclosures.

## Take a Step Back and Break Down the Process

If a risk analysis does not exist, or if it is missing the qualities regulators expect, it is best to start the process from scratch. It's tempting to leverage work already completed. This is a mistake. The goal here is to free individuals from worrying about perfection and pleasing a government agency that may never see the final product. Trying to leverage internal or external artifacts will result in spending time and energy crafting the analysis to fit these artifacts, instead of creating an assessment that fits the organization. Put thought into the output and document the inventory of ePHI in a way that makes it easy to assess, analyze, and monitor risks. The risk analysis must be updated annually,

© Eric C. Thompson 2017
E. C. Thompson, *Building a HIPAA-Compliant Cybersecurity Program*,
https://doi.org/10.1007/978-1-4842-3060-2_4

so the process must be set up for success. A few tricks that might aid the process include the following:

- Make time first thing in the morning, preferably before launching Outlook, or whatever system is in use, and coworkers are buzzing around the office.

- Get back to the basics. Grab a pencil and several sheets of paper, a cup of coffee, and get started. Worry about electronic format later.

- Focus on the outcome. Analyzing risk makes the cybersecurity program more effective and helps protect patient records. Stay focused on that goal.

The Security Standards: General Rules, specifically 164.306(a)(1), expect covered entities and business associates to document where ePHI is created, maintained, stored, and processed. The goal of this exercise is to document. If a mental nudge is required, NIST has issued a "Guide to Data-Centric System Threat Modeling,"[1] which details several ways to list sensitive assets that an entity must protect. These questions are customizable to the risk analysis process that covered entities and business associates must follow.

- Where are all the locations that ePHI can be stored?

- Where are the locations where data may move through the organization and be transmitted across organizational boundaries?

- Where is data processed?

- What are the methods and locations of data input?

Notice the use of the word *may* in the NIST questions. This is another point in the process that frees risk practitioners from worry about missing the unknowns. If it can be reasonably anticipated that users are saving patient information to insecure share drives or transmitting ePHI outside organizational boundaries, those situations should be documented as risks. Later, technical tests designed to uncover improper uses of ePHI are detailed.

---

[1]Murugiah Souppaya and Karen Scarfone, "Guide to Data-Centric System Threat Modeling," NIST SP 800-154, http://csrc.nist.gov/publications/drafts/800-154/sp800_154_draft.pdf, March 2016.

The compliance requirements and security recommendations in this book apply to healthcare providers, health plans, or health payers and business associates. The healthcare providers and health plans range in size from large to small. Business associates differ not only in size but also in industry sectors. The one similarity is that all are expected to protect ePHI and follow the same guidance.

No matter which group an entity belongs to, breaking the process of documenting assets into manageable pieces moves the process along much quicker. The next several sections describe the nuances of each type of entity and ways one might organize the ePHI inventory.

## Healthcare Provider Example

Providers come in many sizes and types, which is why it is challenging to publish specific guidance for analyzing risk. No templates exist, since no two entities are the same, which creates many of the challenges and concerns about documenting all instances of ePHI. Examples highlighting the range of providers include

- Small or stand-alone hospitals

- Independent physician offices

- Regional midsize hospitals and/or physician groups

- Large metropolitan and suburban health systems made up of hospitals and physician offices, which can span entire states

- Academic medical centers and research centers

University-based hospitals and research facilities are a completely different ball game and distinct from other providers. How health information is used and who needs access is more difficult to regulate across the medical center, educational, and research areas. In some cases, disparate governing bodies exist in each area, despite the same data being used by all. It becomes difficult to direct compliance requirements when organizational politics dictate how each works in separate silos.

Providers large and small have similar IT landscapes. Most utilize an electronic medical record (EMR) system, in which much of the patient data is entered, processed, maintained, and stored. The larger, more well-known examples are modular. Specialty practices or units in a medical center might have a module, and administrative departments have specific modules. For example, based on services offered, the following modules might be needed for a healthcare provider:

- Ambulatory

- Obstetrics/gynecology

- Inpatient

- Lab

- Oncology

- Scheduling and registration

- Billing

The EMR should be a focal point early in the risk analysis process. A high percentage of the data at risk is often located in the EMR. However, it is also common, in the era of consolidation and acquisition in the healthcare provider sector, for additional EMRs and stand-alone applications to also be used, and these also require risk analysis. A simplified view of how a healthcare provider might be organized is shown in Figure 4-1. These entities centralize most IT operations and maintain the systems in one data center. An affiliated hospital or a medical center geographically separated could have IT systems managed by separate teams in separate data centers.

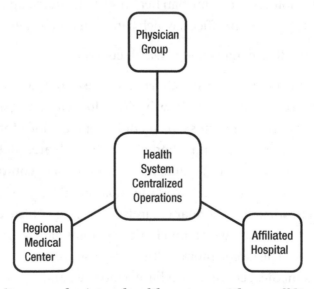

***Figure 4-1.*** *This diagram depicts a health system with an affiliated hospital and physician group geographically separated from the centralized operations*

When this occurs, sometimes several hundred instances of the same application may have to be evaluated, depending on how each is managed. In the analysis of this provider, the breakdown of assets containing ePHI during entry, processing, and storage is listed in Figure 4-2.

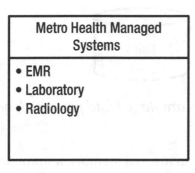

| Metro Health Managed Systems | Systems Managed Outside Corporate IT |
|---|---|
| • EMR<br>• Laboratory<br>• Radiology | • EMR2 - Affiliated Hospital<br>• Laboratory - Affiliated Hospital<br>• Radiology - Physician Group |

***Figure 4-2.*** *In this example, the central operations at the health system manage three applications with ePHI. The affiliated hospital has its own EMR and a laboratory application, while the physicians group has its own radiology system but uses the EMR at Metro Health.*

The healthcare provider analysis has six instances of ePHI that are in-scope for the risk analysis.

## Healthcare Plan/Payer Example

The primary use case for healthcare payers having access to ePHI is the claims adjudication process. Other services involve access to ePHI, but here the claims process is the primary service in-scope. The adjudication process is initiated when healthcare providers send information related to the services provided to the health plans for payment. The flow of data through the processing system displayed in Figure 4-3 shows the flow of data ingested from providers, staged, processed, and transmitted back as output to the provider. During the processing, a repository of contract parameters and another rules repository that applies information to the processing engine ensure accurate processing.

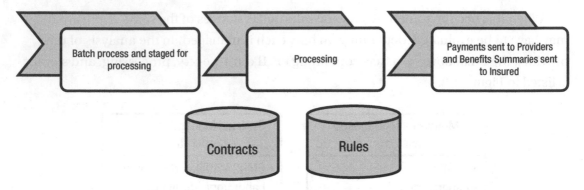

***Figure 4-3.*** *Claims arriving from providers are staged and processed, based on contractual specifications*

Thinking in terms of a single office visit by an insured member, a summary of the office visit and charges are sent to the payer entity. Summaries of services for other members are also received by the payer entity during the given period. These claims often go through a batch process that checks for errors, which interrupts processing, before moving on to the next step. The data flows to the processing engine, which pulls information from the contract and from rules repositories, which guide the processing engine. Finally, output is generated, payment is sent to the provider, and an explanation is sent to the insured member.

# Business Associate Example

Business associates are third parties that provide services to covered entities and create, store, or maintain ePHI. Business associates can view the ePHI of the covered entity with which the business relationship exists. These entities require access to health information to perform the agreed to services. Business associates are required to comply with the HIPAA Security Rule, and the HITECH Act and Final Omnibus Rule state that business associates are liable in the event of a breach. Business associates come in many forms. Fortune 500 companies, such as Microsoft, Amazon, and AT&T, operate under business associate agreements. Very common to healthcare providers are billing and collection firms. Information related to services provided, personally identifiable information (PII), and diagnosis or procedure codes are necessary to bill patients and health plans.

Business associate agreements (BAAs) outline expectations for protecting health information and complying with the HIPAA Security and Privacy Rules. Obtaining these agreements is required for covered entities, as one mechanism to address risks introduced by transmitting ePHI outside the network. Later, in Chapter 14, an in-depth look at the risks of moving data outside the organization's perimeter, I will demonstrate just how much risk third parties create with access to ePHI. Figure 4-4 uses the example of a medical billing company to give a picture of the IT landscape for the covered entities engaging this business associate. Data flows from three covered entities to the medical biller, where a single application, with logically separated instances for each covered entity, is utilized to create bills for patients and track the collections from the patient and health plan.

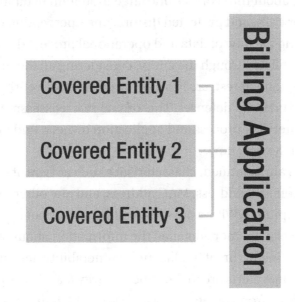

**Figure 4-4.**  *Business associates usually perform services for a number of covered entities. Data is transmitted by multiple third parties for processing by a single application; however, the expectation is that each entity's data remain logically and physically separated.*

The IT environment shown in Figure 4-3 is not uncommon. Third parties offering software as a service (SaaS) facilitate multiple clients. The risk analysis for business associates that host data in this manner is much different from other types of third parties. In fact, the application of NIST guidelines and HIPAA Safeguards across business associates varies greatly. Each entity must craft the risk analysis to encompass all the unique processes business operations, so that each unique business offering is reflected in the analysis.

Business associates require agreements with downstream third parties and subcontractors, which may also view ePHI. If the third party in Figure 4-4 engaged another vendor to provide hosting services for the billing application, the hosting entity is a business associate to the original business associate. While all downstream agreements address liability, the covered entity must be made aware of these additional agreements and account for them in its own risk analysis.

# Create the Asset List

No matter the IT landscape, the process of creating an asset ePHI inventory can be successfully completed by using the process outlined. The key is breaking it down into small pieces. Thinking about the scope as one large mountain of data needing to be identified, analyzed for risks, and protected distorts one's perception of the process and reduces clarity. Breaking the flow of data and operational process down from the highest level, and following that flow through the entity, considering all the touch points where data is in motion, in use and at rest, creates a picture risk, and security teams can use this to understand threats and build defenses. The annual risk reassessment and analysis is the opportunity to reinterview process and application owners, find others to interview, and add new details to the data flow.

When new systems are identified, characteristics such as type of system, location, version, operating systems, IP address, MAC address, and any other information deemed important should be captured. Where possible, collect data about the network hardware the ePHI traverses as well. The more detailed the information about the systems in-scope is, the more meaningful threat intelligence, vulnerability descriptions, and security event and incident alerts are to the cybersecurity team. The quicker these alerts can be tied to, or ruled out from, assets interacting with ePHI, the quicker appropriate responses are initiated. Figures 4-5, 4-6, and 4-7 illustrate sample tables created in Excel, capturing assets in-scope for the risk analysis at the healthcare provider, health plan, and business associate examples.

| Application OS or DB | Asset Name | Location | IP Address |
|---|---|---|---|
| Electronic Medical Records - EMR | MetroMedAppSrvr-1 | Corporate Data Center | 192.168.223.134 |
| Electronic Medical Records - EMR | MetroMedAppSrvr-2 | Corporate Data Center | 192.168.223.155 |
| Windows 2012 Srvr R2 | MetroMedW2012OS-1 | Corporate Data Center | 192.168.223.145 |
| Windows 2012 Srvr R2 | MetroMedW2012OS-2 | Corporate Data Center | 192.168.223.133 |
| Windows 2012 SQL | MetroMedSQL2012-1 | Corporate Data Center | 192.168.223.132 |
| Radiology - PACS System | MedCtrPACS-1 | Medical Center Data Center | 192.168.223.142 |
| Affiliated Hospital Lab System | AffHospLab-1 | Affiliated Hospital | 192.168.223.190 |
| Affiliated Hospital RedHat Linux R7 | AffHospSrvrOS-1 | Affilated Hospital | 192.168.223.182 |

***Figure 4-5.*** *This displays the initial output of the healthcare provider asset list. Each of these infrastructure components is documented in an Excel table.*

Figure 4-6 shows the locations of ePHI documented in an Excel spreadsheet. The name of the application or system, operating system, and database are documented, along with the name of the server, location, and IP address. Entities can collect more information if they feel such activity enhances the ability to assess risk and respond to incidents.

| Application OS or DB | Asset Name | Location | IP Address |
|---|---|---|---|
| Claims Processing System | HealthPayProcETLSrvr01 | Corporate Data Center | 192.168.223.168 |
| Insurance Contract Repository | HealthPayDM01 | Corporate Data Center | 192.168.223.167 |
| Insurance Payer Rule Repository | HealthPayDM02 | Corporate Data Center | 192.168.223.166 |

***Figure 4-6.*** *The healthcare payer example shows the claims processing system*

The healthcare payer processing system consists of three elements: staging, process, and output. In addition, two repositories exist that apply contract parameters and processing rules to the claims data moving through the system. Once completed, payments are remitted to providers and benefit summaries to insured members.

| Application OS or DB | Asset Name | Location | IP Address |
|---|---|---|---|
| Billing Application | Application Server | SAAS Provider | 192.168.223.148 |
| Windows 2008 Server | Operating System | SAAS Provider | 192.168.223.146 |

***Figure 4-7.*** *Business associates perform a service on behalf of covered entities and have the ability to access ePHI. This example represents an organization that provides billing services.*

The business associate example diagrammed previously, which performs billing and collection services for healthcare providers, is a single system. This scenario shows how important one system component can be to an organization. Here, the database stores all the ePHI in the biller's possession for three healthcare providers. This is a single point of risk, which is significant. As few as several hundred records may exist, or millions, depending on the size of providers and the business relationship each entered into with the billing company.

The information captured in the asset inventory is customizable and should be based on what an organization deems necessary, to understand the risks posed to ePHI. One entity may choose to name the system and document the data center the hardware is in, while another might capture more information than documented in these examples.

Once all the known items are documented, think about where outliers might exist. Check with those managing business continuity and disaster recovery operations and the project management office, if one exists. The BC/DR team may have insight into applications and data repositories identified as priorities for recovery operations. Project management offices (PMOs) have details of system implementations significant to the entity. Then consider other autonomous business units, operations separated geographically, specialized business units, and recent acquisitions. These groups are also likely to have unique IT systems, possibly in-scope for a risk analysis.

# Summary

Documenting the list of assets, either ePHI or IT assets processing ePHI, is the first step in the risk assessment process. Guidance issued by HHS and the OCR point to NIST 800-30 for key activities required to determine the risk assessment scope. Regulators require covered entities and business associates to document and assess all risks to all the ePHI each possesses. Several questions were suggested, which can be used to assist risk teams in creating the list of in-scope elements. A large percentage of the assets and ePHI are usually related to the most significant systems. That is why reviewing business continuity and disaster recovery documents is a key activity. Any systems key to business operations must be understood. Interviewing the PMO or the IT team about significant projects is another way to uncover assets that might require analysis.

The goal of this step is to document all instances of ePHI known and discoverable at the time the scope of the assessment is defined. Once all defined discovery actions listed in the risk analysis plan are exhausted, it is time to move to the next step. Understanding the next iteration of the risk analysis process provides opportunities to dig deeper and discover other unknowns.

# CHAPTER 5

# Who Wants Health Information?

Threats represent the individuals, groups, and events that create adverse situations affecting the confidentiality, integrity, and availability of patient information. The human elements include state-sponsored groups, organized cybercriminals, other malicious outsiders, including hacktivists, and malicious insiders. Nonhuman elements include natural disasters or other human-made occurrences, such as terrorist attacks. The process of documenting threats requires the risk analyst to think about the actors and scenarios that threaten ePHI. These actors and scenarios take advantage of vulnerabilities that can lead to a privacy or security incident.

This chapter focuses on risk analysis in terms of human threats. These threat actors have motive, means, and opportunity to steal, modify, or render ePHI unusable. As discussed in Chapter 1, ePHI has value on underground markets, providing plenty of motive to groups targeting the healthcare segment.

## NIST Threat Guidance

NIST 800-30 breaks down the documentation of threats, as found in Appendix D.[1] This appendix identifies threat source inputs, taxonomy, and four areas of the assessment scale.

---

[1]NIST, "Guide for Conducting Risk Assessments," http://nvlpubs.nist.gov/nistpubs/Legacy/SP/nistspecialpublication800-30r1.pdf, September 2012.

© Eric C. Thompson 2017
E. C. Thompson, *Building a HIPAA-Compliant Cybersecurity Program*,
https://doi.org/10.1007/978-1-4842-3060-2_5

# Inputs and Threat Source Identification

NIST further categorizes threat inputs into three tiers: organizational, mission/business, and information system. Table 5-1 is constructed like the tables in Appendix D, showing threat inputs and relating each to tiers two and three.

***Table 5-1.*** *Breakdown of Organizational Inputs of Threat Information Applicable to the Organization*

| Description | Provided to Tier 1 | Provided to Tier 2 | Provided to Tier 3 |
| --- | --- | --- | --- |
| Credible threat intelligence | No | Yes | Yes |
| Information and guidance | No | Yes | Yes |
| Taxonomy of threat sources | No | Yes | Yes |
| Characterization of threat sources | No | Yes | Yes |
| Previously identified threat sources | No | Yes | Yes |

When constructing the timely risk analysis, previously identified threats, credible threat intelligence provided to the entity, what or who the threat actor is, and what the tactics, techniques, and tools the threat deploys are must all be considered.

Taxonomy of threats means identifying the type of threat source, description, and characteristics of the threat. Examples of this information are shown in Table 5-2.

***Table 5-2.*** *Types of Threats Facing Entities, Based on Entities' Presence in Cyberspace, and Assessment of Vulnerabilities Available to Exploit, Based on Several Factors*

| Type | Description | Characteristics |
| --- | --- | --- |
| Adversarial: individuals, groups, organizations, and nation-states | Exploit organizations' dependencies on cyber resources | Capability, intent, and targeting |
| Accidental | Human errors by non-malicious insiders | Range of effects |
| Structural: IT equipment, environmental controls, software | Equipment, infrastructure, and facilities failures | Range of effects |
| Environmental | Natural disasters | Range of effects |

Adversarial threats come in many forms, from government-sponsored to ad hoc to individuals acting on their own. It is important to understand who these groups are and the capabilities each may use against the entity.

Last, NIST 800-30 guidance allows practitioners to assess the characteristics of threat sources, either quantitatively or qualitatively. Tables are offered to assess the capabilities, characteristics, and targeting, on a scale of very low to very high.

- Capabilities that are very low mean adversaries have very few resources and do not possess expertise to exploit vulnerabilities, while very high capabilities mean tools and expertise exist to carry out long, sustained attacks on multiple targets.

- Intent considered to be very low means that adversaries want to deface an organization or just disrupt activities, while intent rated as very high means that the attackers want to severely disrupt business operations and seek to conceal their activities, so that their goals are not impeded.

- Targeting at a very low level means the attackers may not be targeting specific organizations or classes of organizations. Threats rated as very high target specific classes of entities and put a high level of resources into reconnaissance and information-gathering.

Other guidance from NIST 800-30 to measure the effects of non-adversarial threats is provided in Appendix D of that document. Appendix E of NIST 800-30 details several pages of threat events that entities can use to think through attack patterns used by adversaries. These are loosely grouped by kill chain elements. Examples are displayed in Table 5-3.

**Table 5-3.** *Some Sample Threat Scenarios Provided by NIST*

| Attack Phase | Threat Event |
| --- | --- |
| Reconnaissance | Network sniffing, open source discovery |
| Attack tools | Phishing or spear phishing |
| Deliver payload | Malware delivery |
| Exploit and compromise | Identify additional vulnerabilities |
| Execute attack | Continue attacks against new vulnerabilities |
| Achieve results | Steal, modify, or render data unavailable |

NIST created these appendixes to assist professionals executing a risk analysis to think through threats to ePHI and consider as many adversaries as possible. Each of these specific sections in Appendixes D and E of NIST 800-30 is useful for brainstorming and improving risk analysis. They begin with high-level considerations of threat categories, adding more detail, including specific scenarios affecting ePHI.

# Types of Adversaries

Many risk assessments break threats into a list of five or six common groups. Initially, this exercise is sufficient to begin the risk analysis and can be accomplished in a short amount of time.

---

**Caution**    It is difficult to know what is sufficient in the eyes of regulatory bodies such as the OCR. Regulations require consideration of all reasonably anticipated threats. The best way to accomplish this with a short list of threats is to ensure that the entire analysis is comprehensive, covering all potential risks to ePHI.

---

This risk analysis begins with documenting the outsider and insider threats to ePHI. End users who inadvertently make a mistake, resulting in a disclosure, are considered vulnerabilities that can be exploited by adversaries. Natural disaster and other environmental items are not discussed in this analysis. The more common threats to consider initially include the following:

- State-sponsored groups

- Organized cybercriminals

- Other malicious outsiders/hacktivists

- Malicious insiders/insider threats

This chapter will dive much deeper into these threat actors and the scenarios each might use to breach healthcare entities.

## State-Sponsored Attackers

It's not surprising that Russia and China come to mind when state-sponsored threats are discussed, but other nations, including the United States, are significant players in this group. Until recently, most Russian hacking seemed to fall into the cybercriminal category: monetary gain, but the fallout from the 2016 presidential election has brought attention to the amount of espionage activities carried out in Eastern Europe via cyberattacks originating from certain states in this region of former Cold War nemeses. China and North Korea are known for government-sponsored groups targeting US corporations for financial and political reasons. President Barack Obama's administration faced several challenges emanating from these unfriendly sources in Asia, specifically, how to handle suspected Chinese efforts to steal intellectual property from American businesses. Years of diplomatic efforts achieved a drop in the number of monthly attacks from 2013 to 2016.[2] Two threat organizations working on behalf of China and Russia that are well known to cybersecurity professionals are APT 1 and APT 28.

- *APT 1*: Also known as PLA Unit 61398, identified by Mandiant (FireEye),[3] which conducts attacks on behalf of the Chinese government that focus targets that are aligned with Chinese interests. Leaders of this group have been identified as members of the Chinese military, and its computing resources are staged worldwide.

---

[2]Andy Greenberg, "Obama Curbed Chinese Hacking, but Russia Won't Be So Easy," Wired, `www.wired.com/2016/12/obama-russia-hacking-sanctions-china/`, December 16, 2016.

[3]Mandiant, "APT 1: Exposing One of China's Cyber Espionage Units," `www.fireeye.com/content/dam/fireeye-www/services/pdfs/mandiant-apt1-report.pdf`, October 25, 2004.

- *APT 28*: This group is suspected of conducting espionage attacks against Georgia and Ukraine to further Russia's interests.[4] This group is known for its skill at developing and updating malware.

The difference between state-sponsored and organized cybercriminals is primarily the attack objectives. These groups identify targets based on government interests, not financial gain.

# Organized Cybercriminals

Organized cybercriminals, also considered advanced persistent threats (APTs), operate for financial gain or to disrupt key operations of their targets. Organized cybercriminals are also well-funded and structured like any other entity, with strategic plans and objectives, and employ structured processes, such as change control. Examples of well-known organized cybercriminal groups are Black Vine and Dragonfly.

- *Black Vine*: One of the more astounding characteristics of Black Vine, as reported by Symantec in August 2015, is its ability to develop a zero-day exploit, targeting vulnerabilities not known publicly.[5]

- *Dragonfly*: Since 2013, this group has used two remote access tools to conduct attacks against energy firms in the United States and Europe.

## What Makes These Groups Sophisticated?

The attack vectors, the processes and steps used by attackers to penetrate and locate the objectives inside their targets, set the state-sponsored and organized cybercriminal groups apart from other attack groups. The Mandiant kill chain, Figure 5-1, shows the process many adversaries use to infiltrate a target, quietly moving through the entity and finding ePHI.

---

[4]FireEye, "APT 28: A Window into Russia's Cyber Espionage Operations?" www2.fireeye.com/rs/fireye/images/rpt-apt28.pdf, 2014.

[5]Jon DiMaggio, "The Black Vine cyberespionage group," Symantec, www.symantec.com/content/dam/symantec/docs/security-center/white-papers/black-vine-cyberespionage-group-15-en.pdf, August 6, 2015.

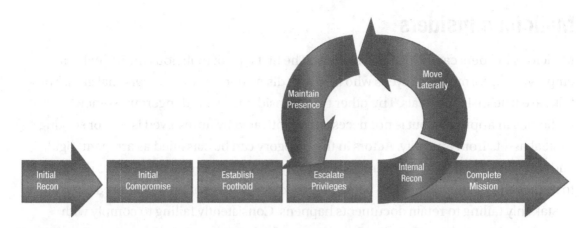

**Figure 5-1.**  *The kill chain published by Mandiant (now FireEye) outlines the chain of events, from compromise to reaching the target. (Image courtesy of FireEye, Inc.)*

According to the Verizon Breach Report[6] published in 2016, several well-known breaches began via phishing attacks. Intelligence-gathering targeted specific individuals, known as spear phishing, increasing the odds of success after initiating an attack. Highly advanced adversaries place as much importance, if not more, on reconnaissance and information-gathering. Sophisticated code wrapped by encrypted packers does not do much good if the payload does not have a path to a target's end point. Sophisticated groups utilize very common and unsophisticated means to reach objectives. The reconnaissance phase uses tools and techniques available to most Internet users. A few minutes on Shodan, a cybersecurity search engine, can yield information on devices connected to the Internet. Healthcare providers may not realize that medical devices can be discovered this way. Payers might have servers facing the Internet that the security team thinks are hidden behind firewalls. APTs also collect intelligence from many social media sites—LinkedIn, Twitter, and more—to uncover key information about employees. In minutes, e-mail addresses, patterns of behavior, and personal information can be found. Social media also reveals a lot about the technology stacks at targets.

Symantec's report on Black Vine concluded that the group directed its attack against Anthem by targeting a specific individual, directing that person to a compromised server, and gaining control over the targeted computer to infiltrate Anthem's network.

Once inside, the attacker acquires the ability to map the network, move through the system's escalating privileges, and repeat the process until the target is reached.

---

[6]Verizon, "2016 Data Breach Investigations Report," www.verizonenterprise.com/verizon-insights-lab/dbir/2016/, 2016.

# Malicious Insiders

Malicious insiders can be one of two types. The first type of malicious individuals are employees or former employees who might be disgruntled or out for personal gain. These folks are true insider threats. The other type of insider threat is dangerous, somewhat malicious in approach, but is not necessarily motivated by unresolved issues or seeking to steal assets from an entity. Actors in this category can be classified as arrogant, rigid, and unwilling to change, as required, to comply with controls and procedures designed to reduce the likelihood of ePHI being breached. A process not being followed once or mistakenly failing to retain documents happens. Consistently failing to comply with policies and procedures over time is a pattern, which creates more risk.

# Hacktivists

Individuals and groups in this category conduct activities for political or principle-based reasons. The Ashley Madison breach, although not executed completely from the outside, is an example. WikiLeaks is another. The motivation of these entities is not for pure financial gain. These attackers possess varied levels of sophistication similar to those of state-sponsored and APT groups or script kiddies.

# Summary

The attackers stealing patient information are formidable. Sophisticated groups have access to resources that put the average healthcare-based cybersecurity team behind in the fight to protect patient data. These groups can exploit vulnerabilities not yet known to the public that require significant amounts of time and money to identify. The real problem, however, is not the sophisticated tools and resources available but the success attackers have in launching unsophisticated attacks. It may not be fair to say that phishing attacks are unsophisticated, because the e-mails used are very hard to detect and are laced with attachments and links allowing attackers to gain a foothold in a network. It just feels like using e-mail, or finding vulnerabilities not patched in years, does not require the highest level of sophistication. To successfully complete a thorough risk analysis, it is important to understand and follow the process of documenting specific threats, based on groups, taxonomy, and other characteristics.

# CHAPTER 6

# Weaknesses Waiting to Be Exploited

Vulnerabilities represent weaknesses in technology, controls, processes, capabilities, and human activities that can be exploited by a threat actor and lead to a breach. Owing to limitations in resources, the need to conduct business, and the human element, most entities have dozens of vulnerabilities to document and evaluate. The key to a comprehensive and successful risk analysis lies in analyzing the environment thoroughly enough to collect a comprehensive list of vulnerabilities from across the organization. Several methods can be used to uncover these weaknesses. One way to start is by reviewing recent assessments for issues found, including any of the following:

- Cyber program assessments

- Vulnerability scans

- Penetration tests

- IT general control audits related to year-end financial statements

- Compliance examinations

Also, interview members of the organization. Often, managers and frontline employees provide insights not always gained through documentation review. Set the stage for interviews by making sure the interviewee knows that the goal of the process is to find improvement opportunities. Often, once individuals feel comfortable and develop trust, useful information previously unknown is discovered. Include associates from diverse business units and geographies, to get a comprehensive look at operations.

© Eric C. Thompson 2017
E. C. Thompson, *Building a HIPAA-Compliant Cybersecurity Program*,
https://doi.org/10.1007/978-1-4842-3060-2_6

# Predisposing Conditions

NIST (SP)800-30 guides covered entities and business associates to consider predisposing conditions when thinking through vulnerabilities that could exist inside the organization. These are inherent risks present by doing business in the healthcare sector and based on how the organization conducts business. The most significant predisposing condition in the healthcare industry is how sought after ePHI is by attackers. Because a market for selling this information exists, attackers are motivated to probe entities in possession of health information. The risk analysis must account for the types of attacks being waged specifically against healthcare organizations and consider this when analyzing threats and vulnerabilities. Also, the expectation is that security measures specific to these circumstances are selected and placed into operation. Healthcare entities might have to consider whether best-in-class detection and protection is required on end points, based on the number of phishing and malware attacks launched against them. Other types of entities may not require this level of protection.

# Documenting Vulnerabilities

Historically, regulators do not approve of approaches to risk analysis that are in a checklist form. They expect the analysis to be unique to the risks faced by the entity performing the exercise. So, on the surface, this section appears like a big "no" to the OCR, because creating a list of vulnerabilities inside each functional area of the NIST CSF appears like the entity simply went through the NIST CSF and created a list. This is not a good way to approach risk analysis. The list of vulnerabilities must be aggregated from across the entire organization and consider all the potential weaknesses in the environment. Now, once the list is created, and if it is comprehensive and includes all facets of the environment, grouping them into categories to make analyzing, mitigating, and monitoring risk easier is a sound approach.

---

**Tip**   It is important to develop the habit of documenting the thought process and rationale behind any conclusions drawn. At some point, a regulator may review the risk analysis and have questions on scope and why it was performed a certain way. Because personnel change roles, or details are forgotten, documenting these factors helps avoid some uncomfortable experiences with auditors at a later time.

---

# Vulnerability Buckets Based on the NIST CSF

Because the NIST CSF is the cybersecurity framework adopted in this analysis, weaknesses identified through the methods described earlier—interviews, reviewing audit and security assessment reports—can be mapped to the functions of the NIST CSF, to ease the organization of vulnerabilities and understand what improvements are necessary to reduce risks. Gaps in the NIST CSF alone should not be the source of vulnerabilities, because the exercise is reduced to a gap assessment vs. a comprehensive risk assessment. Grouping vulnerabilities is one way to organize vulnerabilities. The documentation of vulnerabilities begins in Table 6-1, the identify function, which highlights a failure to inventory hardware and software assets, fund cybersecurity sufficiently, and integrate compliance requirements into business operations.

***Table 6-1.*** *Vulnerabilities Identified During the Analysis and Aligned with the Identify Function*

| Identify |
| --- |
| ID.1: An up-to-date inventory of physical assets does not exist, and IT ownership and accountability for information assets is not clearly defined and documented. |
| ID.2: Data is not managed based on its classification requirements. |
| ID.3: Cybersecurity is not appropriately funded to effectively maintain and support business objectives. |
| ID.4: Compliance gaps are not monitored or resolved in a timely manner. |
| ID.5: Legal and regulatory compliance requirements are not adequately integrated into policies and procedures. |

Table 6-2 outlines the vulnerabilities identified during the analysis, which are weaknesses related to protection. This is the largest group of vulnerabilities in the analysis and represents issues with access control, change control, and data protection controls and capabilities.

***Table 6-2.*** *Vulnerabilities Aligned with the Protection Function*

**Protect**

PV.1: Infrastructure and applications (including web applications and interfaces) are inappropriately configured.

PV.2: Code changes are not tested for quality assurance.

PV.3: Access to source code is not effectively controlled.

PV.4: Standards time lines to remediate vulnerabilities are not established.

PV.5: Application access management is ineffectively managed.

PV.6: Database access management is ineffectively managed.

PV.7: Information is not adequately protected from malicious code.

PV.8: Network access management is ineffectively managed.

PV.9: The organization does not have an effective network security infrastructure.

PV.10: Responsibilities are not segregated within the organization.

PV.11: Security education and awareness training is not adequate for workforce members to understand threats posed to ePHI.

PV.12: Data at rest is not encrypted.

PV.13: Protected health information is used in development and testing environments.

PV.14: Secure disposal of media is not adequately performed.

Because phishing and spear phishing are the easiest ways to bypass network perimeter controls, detection becomes the key to limiting the damage when end users are exploited. During this analysis, it is concluded that logging and monitoring weaknesses exist. Table 6-3 displays vulnerabilities mapped to the detct function.

***Table 6-3.*** *Vulnerabilties Mapped to the Detect Function*

**Detect**

DE.1: Security monitoring is not adequately performed to detect unauthorized or suspicious activities.

DE.2: A defined logging process is not documented.

DE.3: Security incidents are not adequately logged for investigations.

DE.4: A process to collect logs in a centralized location does not exist.

The issues outlined in Table 6-4 highlight vulnerabilities related to planning for responding to incidents and events.

***Table 6-4.*** *Vulnerabilities Related to the Response Function*

**Respond**

RE.1: Security incidents do not incorporate challenges and lessons learned.

RE.2: Availability requirements to support the business are not defined.

RE.3: An incident response plan has not been documented or tested.

The analysis also uncovers two issues related to recovery capabilities (see Table 6-5). Management has not emphasized the need to review the recovery plans annually or the need to conduct post-mortem exercises to identify and incorporate lessons learned after a test of the incident response plan or when an event occurred and the response plan was invoked.

***Table 6-5.*** *Vulnerabilities in the Recovery Function*

**Recover**

RC.1: Recovery strategies are not updated annually.

RC.2: Recovery plans do not incorporate lessons learned.

# Summary

The process of documenting vulnerabilities would be cumbersome and hard to work without a structure to streamline management and monitoring. The OCR is very much against any process that is a "checklist" exercise, so risk analysis must be reflective of the organization. Assessing security measures from any framework and taking note of gaps is a start, but the process should include reviewing all assessment completed in the recent past and interviewing members of the workforce, to understand what processes and daily activities might introduce weaknesses into the environment.

# CHAPTER 7

# Is It Really This Bad?

Now comes the step in the process in which all the risks (there's that word again) have to be measured in terms of how each could impact all the ePHI identified earlier in the analysis. This is a thoughtful process that can, and should, take some time. It is also not a task that should be completed entirely by one person but, rather, should have input from others in the organization. This input can come when documenting and analyzing the risks or when reviewing the list, once complete. The desired outcome of this phase is knowledge of all the risks to ePHI and how severe each is to the confidentiality, integrity, and availability to ePHI, so that management can implement risk mitigations that reduce risk severity to acceptable levels.

## Risk Statements

Risks are comprised of three parts: the threat actor or scenario that targets the network in a malicious effort to gain access to ePHI; the weaknesses in the environment that can be exploited by the attack; and the assets that are the targets of exploits. In this case, the targeted asset is ePHI. Once all the risk statements are composed, each must be measured, based on the likelihood of occurrence and impact of a successful attack.

---

**Note**    Threat scenarios include the natural, environmental, and physical threats that cause outages leading to availability risks. For example, entities must assess risks due to floods that impact data center operations hosting infrastructure that processes ePHI.

---

Sometimes, bringing all the details together into an analysis that makes sense to users is challenging. The analysis process resembles Figure 7-1, in which threat, vulnerability, and asset information is combined into a funnel and, once mixed together and combined with likelihood and impact ingredients, produce risks.

© Eric C. Thompson 2017
E. C. Thompson, *Building a HIPAA-Compliant Cybersecurity Program*,
https://doi.org/10.1007/978-1-4842-3060-2_7

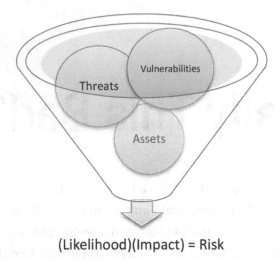

(Likelihood)(Impact) = Risk

***Figure 7-1.*** *Identifying risks takes sorting through all the lists and informaton collected, to create meaningful risk data that management can act upon*

# Likelihood

Likelihood measures the odds a vulnerability will be exploited by an adversary. NIST SP 800-30 guidance assists users through the process of measuring likelihood by thorough consideration of the following:

- What is the capability of this threat actor?

- How likely is it the threat will target the entity?

- How easy is it to uncover this vulnerability?

- What else needs to be accomplished to exploit the vulnerability?

Questions such as these allow organizations to distinguish between adversaries, based on how likely each is to successfully exploit a weakness. If two threat actors are motivated enough to attack an entity, it makes sense to focus the analysis on the threat that is more likely to be successful. That is the benefit of questions such as the ones posed previously. For example, in the initial threat list created in Chapter 5, state-sponsored and organized cybercriminals are two identified highly sophisticated threat actors that target ePHI. Each is a concern when it comes to protecting ePHI and is considered a formidable adversary. As a reminder, Table 7-1, outlines the initial list of threats included in this analysis and a brief description of each.

***Table 7-1.*** *List of Threats and Descriptions Identified As Part of the Risk Analysis Being Conducted*

| Threat Actor | Description |
|---|---|
| State-Sponsored | Groups conducting attacks to benefit government intelligence operations vs. making a profit. |
| Organized Cybercriminals | Sophisticated threats in which profit is the primary motive for launching attacks |
| Other Malicious Outsiders | Less sophisticated groups and individuals; examples in this group include hacktivists |
| Malicious Insiders | Employees and former employees who steal information, render systems unavailable, or refuse to adhere to policy and process, which could lead to a breach |

Table 7-2 displays the degree of likelihood based on information found in NIST SP 800-30, Appendix I

***Table 7-2.*** *Likelihood Determination Is Based on How Certain It Is That a Threat Actor or Scenario Will Successfully Find and Exploit a Vulnerability*

| Likelihood | Determinant |
|---|---|
| Very High | Almost certain to initiate the event |
| High | Highly likely to initiate the event |
| Moderate | Somewhat likely to initiate the event |
| Low | Unlikely to initiate the event |
| Very Low | Highly unlikely to initiate the event |

The desired outcome of this exercise is to measure the odds of success for threat actors exploiting a given vulnerability. This measurement of likelihood is one of the ingredients that aids management in understanding the significance of each weakness and the urgency required to mitigate the issue. The other ingredient, impact, is discussed next.

# Impact

Impact is exactly what it seems. It represents the damage done by the successful exploit of a weakness. Not all exploits are created equal; therefore, a successful exploit does not always lead to a breach. Evaluating where in the network the exploit occurs, and correlating it to the guidance, such as the Mandiant kill chain, discussed in Chapters 1 and 5, establishes where in the process the exploit would occur, and the downstream events required for a breach to occur. To successfully place values on this, NIST provides guidance in SP 800-30, as outlined in Table 7-3.[1] These values are used to measure the magnitude of potential damage and exposure of sensitive information to adversaries through exploitation of specific vulnerabilities.

***Table 7-3.***  *Summarized Impact Characteristics, Based on Level of Impact Identified for a Specific Risk*

| Level of Impact | Characteristics |
| --- | --- |
| Very High | Multiple severe catastrophic effects |
| High | Severe or catastrophic effect |
| Moderate | Serious adverse effect |
| Low | Limited adverse effect |
| Very Low | Negligible adverse effect |

# Measuring Risk

The risk measurement, or level of risk severity, is the intersection of impact and likelihood on the "heat map" used to track identified risks. For each risk, the likelihood measurement on the horizontal axis and the impact measurement on the vertical axis intersect at a point at which the severity of the risk is highlighted by the color-coded grid in Figure 7-2. When heat maps are developed, the audience is frequently executives. The best way to tell each the risk story without expecting him or her to dive into too many

---

[1]NIST, "Guide for Conducting Risk Assessments," NIST Special Publication 800-30, Revision 1, http://nvlpubs.nist.gov/nistpubs/Legacy/SP/nistspecialpublication800-30r1.pdf, September 2012.

details is to color-code the grid, so that it is easy to see where the risks lie. The grid in Figure 7-2 was constructed using the following color scheme:

- Very High is dark pink.

- High is pink.

- Moderate is yellow.

- Low is green.

- Very Low is light green.

| Risk Matrix | | | | | |
|---|---|---|---|---|---|
| **Very High** 5 | Very Low | Low | Moderate | High | Very High |
| **High** 4 | Very Low | Low | Moderate | High | Very High |
| **Moderate** 3 | Very Low | Low | Moderate | Moderate | High |
| **Low** 2 | Very Low | Low | Low | Low | Moderate |
| **Very Low** 1 | Very Low | Very Low | Very Low | Low | Low |
| | Very Low 1 | Low 2 | Moderate 3 | High 4 | Very High 5 |
| | | | Likelihood | | |

(Impact is labeled on the vertical axis; Likelihood on the horizontal axis.)

**Figure 7-2.** *Risk matrix used to identify severity of inherent and residual risks, based on guidance provided in NIST SP 800-30*

This makes the heat map easy to view, and executives get a snapshot of the risk profile quickly when reviewing.

Once the process for measuring risks is understood and accepted within the organization, the risk register can be developed to track these issues.

# Creating the Risk Register

The importance of analyzing, assessing, and managing risk is documented throughout this book. Risk management objectives lay the groundwork for the cybersecurity and compliance function and set the tone for protecting patient health information.

The goal of this risk analysis process is to simplify the elements and make action the key result of the process. One area that often becomes confusing and cumbersome is sorting through the numerous threat actors that can target a specific weakness. In the preceding text, in the discussion of likelihood, it was noted that differentiating between state-sponsored and cybercriminal adversaries and each's capabilities is difficult, as both use sophisticated means to achieve, steal, modify, and render ePHI unavailable. Therefore, these two threats are combined as sophisticated attackers in this analysis. This filters quite a bit of noise from the analysis process. Rather than documenting four different risks, each with different threat actors exploiting the same vulnerability, this analysis focuses on the most dangerous and significant threat. This has a trickle-down effect on any risks posed by less capable adversaries, because implementing mitigating and/or compensating controls against a much worthier adversary also mitigates and compensates for any lesser threat actor's capabilities. Assuming that each adversary would utilize the same attack vectors when exploiting vulnerabilities, each iteration of the analysis re-confirms these conclusions, so that the proper protections and risk mitigation activities are executed.

Now, the analysis consists of sophisticated threat actors, other malicious outsiders, and malicious insiders as key threats.

---

**Note**    According to some definitions, the difference between information security and cybersecurity is that cybersecurity refers to security issues related to digital assets connected to the Internet, whereas information security also includes physical and environmental issues. Based on this definition, risks and security measures related to physical and environmental concerns are not included in this risk analysis. These items would have to be covered in the comprehensive risk analysis.

---

The executive summary introducing the analysis identifies and describes how each threat actor could approach the environment.

- Sophisticated attackers could view, modify, steal, or render ePHI unavailable because...

- Other malicious outsiders could view, modify, steal, or render ePHI unavailable because...

- Malicious insiders could view, modify, steal, or render ePHI unavailable because...

The desired outcome for the analysis is to combine the verbiage about the threat actor the vulnerability generates in the first risk statement.

- Malicious insiders could view, modify, steal, or render ePHI unavailable because an up-to-date inventory of physical assets does not exist; IT ownership and accountability for information assets is not clearly defined and documented.

# Risks Identified to ePHI

Table 7-4 lists the risk number, threat actor, vulnerability, likelihood, and impact for risks identified to ePHI. For each vulnerability identified in the environment, the threat actor most likely to exploit it were matched to create the risk. Then, using the preceding criteria, likelihood and impact measures were assigned.

***Table 7-4.*** *Risks Identified by Matching Threats and Vulnerabilities Are Measured, Based on the Criteria Discussed Earlier, to Assign Likelihood and Impact Values*

| No. | Threat Actor | Vulnerability | Likelihood | Impact |
|-----|--------------|---------------|------------|--------|
| R1 | Malicious Insider | ID.1: An up-to-date inventory of physical assets does not exist; IT ownership and accountability for information assets is not clearly defined and documented. | 3 | 3 |
| R2 | Sophisticated Attackers | ID.2: Data is not managed based on its classification requirements. | 3 | 4 |
| R3 | Sophisticated Attackers | ID.3: Cybersecurity is not appropriately funded to effectively maintain and support business objectives. Compliance gaps are not monitored or resolved in a timely manner. | 4 | 4 |
| R4 | Malicious Insider | ID.4: Legal and regulatory compliance requirements are not adequately integrated into policies and procedures. | 4 | 3 |
| R5 | Sophisticated Attackers | PV.1: Infrastructure and applications are inappropriately configured. | 4 | 4 |

*(continued)*

*Table 7-4* (*continued*)

| No. | Threat Actor | Vulnerability | Likelihood | Impact |
|-----|-------------|---------------|:----------:|:------:|
| R6 | Malicious Insider | PV.2: Code changes are not tested for vulnerabilities and other bugs. | 3 | 3 |
| R7 | Malicious Insider | PV.3: Access to source code is not effectively controlled. | 3 | 3 |
| R8 | Malicious Insider | PV.4: Standard time lines to remediate vulnerabilities are not established. | 3 | 4 |
| R9 | Sophisticated Attackers | PV.5: Application access management is ineffectively managed. | 4 | 5 |
| R10 | Sophisticated Attackers | PV.6: Database access management is ineffectively managed. | 4 | 5 |
| R11 | Sophisticated Attackers | PV.7: Information is not adequately protected from malicious code. | 3 | 3 |
| R12 | Sophisticated Attackers | PV.8: Network access management is ineffectively managed. | 4 | 5 |
| R13 | Sophisticated Attackers | PV.9: The organization does not have an up-to-date network security infrastructure. | 4 | 5 |
| R14 | Malicious Insider | PV.10: Responsibilities are not segregated within the organization. | 3 | 3 |
| R15 | Sophisticated Attacker | PV.11: Security education and awareness training is not adequate for workforce members to understand threats posed to ePHI. | 4 | 4 |
| R16 | Sophisticated Attacker | PV.12: Data at rest is not encrypted. | 3 | 4 |
| R17 | Sophisticated Attacker | PV.13: Protected health information is used in development and testing environments. | 3 | 5 |
| R18 | Malicious Insider | PV.14: Secure disposal of media is not adequately performed. | 4 | 5 |

(*continued*)

*Table 7-4* (*continued*)

| No. | Threat Actor | Vulnerability | Likelihood | Impact |
|-----|--------------|---------------|------------|--------|
| R19 | Sophisticated Attacker | DE.1: Security monitoring is not adequately performed to detect unauthorized/suspicious activities. | 4 | 5 |
| R20 | Sophisticated Attacker | DE.2: Security incidents are not adequately logged and reported for investigations. | 3 | 5 |
| R21 | Sophisticated Attacker | DE.3: A defined logging process is not in place. | 4 | 5 |
| R22 | Sophisticated Attacker | DE.4: A process to collect logs in a centralized location does not exist. | 4 | 5 |
| R23 | Sophisticated Attackers | RE.1: Security incidents do not incorporate challenges and lessons learned. | 3 | 4 |
| R24 | Malicious Insider | RE.2: Availability requirements to support the business are not defined. | 3 | 3 |
| R25 | Sophisticated Attacker | RE.3: An incident response plan has not been documented or tested. | 3 | 3 |
| R26 | Sophisticated Attacker | RC.1: Recovery strategies are not updated annually. | 3 | 2 |
| R27 | Sophisticated Attacker | RC.2: Recovery plans do not incorporate lessons learned. | 2 | 2 |

The risk analysis identified 14 moderate risks to ePHI in the environment. Actual healthcare entities have more than 27 risks.

# Graphical Representation of Risks

In Figure 7-3, the 27 identified risks are posted in the heat map, to provide a graphical representation of the risks to patient information. In this initial version of the risk analysis, 11 high risks, 14 moderate, and two low risks are identified. The heat map format shown in Figure 7-3, by using the color scheme outlined previously, draws business leaders' attention to the number of high risks in the pink- and yellow-shaded boxes, showing most of the risks within the entity as high or moderate.

| | | **Risk Matrix** | | | | |
|---|---|---|---|---|---|---|
| **Impact** | Very High 5 | Very Low | Low | Moderate R17, R20 | High R9, R10, R12, R13, R18, R19, R21, R22 | Very High |
| | High 4 | Very Low | Low | Moderate R2, R8, R16, R23 | High R3, R5, R14, R15 | Very High |
| | Moderate 3 | Very Low | Low | Moderate R1, R6, R7, R11, R14, R24, R25 | Moderate R4 | High |
| | Low 2 | Very Low | Low R27 | Low R26 | Low | Moderate |
| | Very Low 1 | Very Low | Very Low | Very Low | Low | Low |
| | | Very Low 1 | Low 2 | Moderate 3 | High 4 | Very High 5 |
| | | | | **Likelihood** | | |

**Figure 7-3.** *Version one of the risk heat map, showing the risk profile of the entity required to protect ePHI*

Before moving onto the risk remediation discussion, further analysis of the risks is required. Next, risks are analyzed in the context of how each is connected in the kill chain.

# Reevaluation of Risks Based on a Chaining of Events

In reviewing the list of risks, three stood out as events that can be chained together during an attack. Exploiting end users is a very popular way for sophisticated attackers to execute an initial compromise of the target, to gain a foothold. Lack of training and awareness is a weakness of high concern, because of the sophistication of phishing e-mails. Social media risks also present threats, as adversaries utilize information available from social media to craft spear-phishing e-mails. These messages are very detailed and specific to the recipient. The clues indicating the illegitimacy of e-mails are so minute that it is difficult for end users to identify them. A weak training and awareness program makes it highly unlikely that end users will be able to detect e-mails designed to create an initial compromise. Monitoring of the environment by security teams is also not adequate, and logs are not aggregated in a central location. The entity does not have the capability to correlate details to detect an attack or review logs during a forensic review. This means the entity cannot detect outsiders moving through the network looking for ePHI. To put it more bluntly, very little in the way of detective measures exist to alert the entity that malicious activity is occurring. Based on this, Risk 15 was reassessed, and the values for likelihood and impact were increased for Risks 15, 19, and 22. Table 7-5 highlights the changes made to these risks. Once a sophisticated attacker learns of the missing capabilities, a lengthy campaign and significant loss of data can ensue.

***Table 7-5.*** *Updated Risk Register for Risks R15, R19, and R22 After a Review of the Original Analysis*

| No. | Threat Actor | Risk | Likelihood | Impact |
|-----|-------------|------|-----------|--------|
| R15 | Sophisticated Attacker | PV.11: Security education and awareness training is not adequate for workforce members to understand threats posed to ePHI. | 4 → 5 | 4 → 5 |
| R19 | Sophisticated Attacker | DE.1: Security monitoring is not adequately performed to detect unauthorized/suspicious activities. | 4 → 5 | 5 |
| R22 | Sophisticated Attacker | DE.4: A process to collect logs in a centralized location does not exist. | 4 → 5 | 5 |

The updated heat map, Figure 7-4, now has three risks in the very high category. Eight high, 14 moderate and two low risks appear on the heat map. The biggest change to the risk profile was increasing R15, R19 and R22 from the high to very high risk category.

| | | Risk Matrix | | | |
|---|---|---|---|---|---|
| | **Very High** 5 | Very Low | Low | Moderate R17, R20 | High R9, R10, R12, R13, R18, R21 | Very High R15, R19, R22 |
| | **High** 4 | Very Low | Low | Moderate R2, R8, R16, R23 | High R3, R5, R14 | Very High |
| **Impact** | **Moderate** 3 | Very Low | Low | Moderate R1, R6, R7, R11, R14, R24, R25 | Moderate R4 | High |
| | **Low** 2 | Very Low | Low R27 | Low R26 | Low | Moderate |
| | **Very Low** 1 | Very Low | Very Low | Very Low | Low | Low |
| | | **Very Low** 1 | **Low** 2 | **Moderate** 3 | **High** 4 | **Very High** 5 |
| | | | | **Likelihood** | | |

***Figure 7-4.*** *Version two of the risk heat map, with three risks moved to the very high level*

This exercise illustrates why it is good practice to either have a committee or, at least, additional levels of review for the risk analysis, before the analysis is finalized. A new perspective or questioning exercise to evaluate how risk ratings have been applied ensures that the risks and severity levels are not just the opinions of a small subset of the organization.

## Very High Risks

The risks documented in Figure 7-5 are of concern, owing to the attack path leading to patient information. Once inside the network, very little detection and alerting capabilities exist to stop the attacker from making it all the way to the sensitive data being targeted. While technology should never be a crutch, or assumed to hold all the answers, there are capabilities foundational to cybersecurity rooted in technology. Without these investments, very little chance exists to detect attacks and limit the damage resulting from unwanted access to the network.

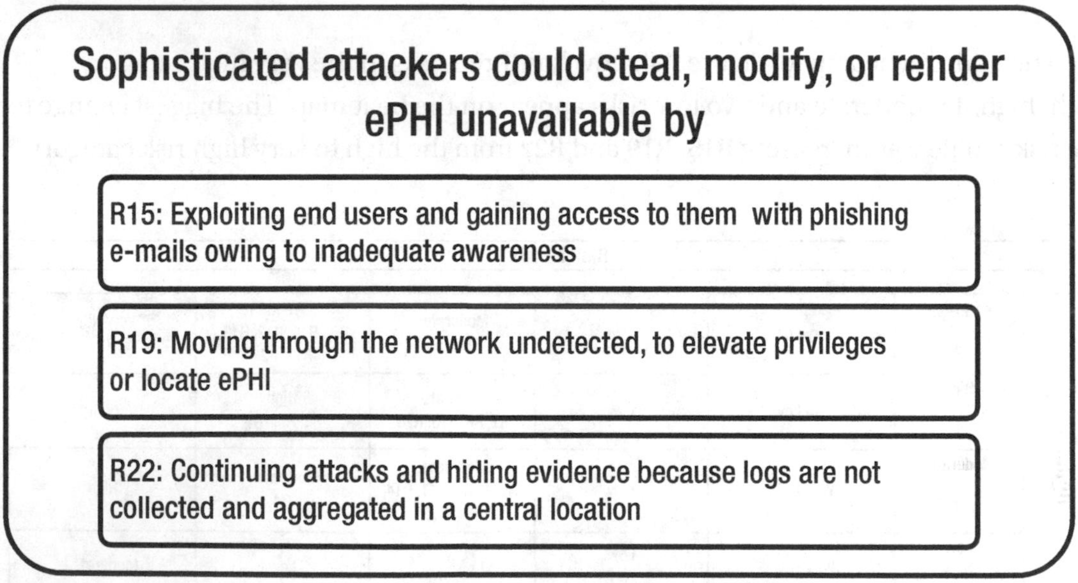

---

**Sophisticated attackers could steal, modify, or render ePHI unavailable by**

R15: Exploiting end users and gaining access to them  with phishing e-mails owing to inadequate awareness

R19: Moving through the network undetected, to elevate privileges or locate ePHI

R22: Continuing attacks and hiding evidence because logs are not collected and aggregated in a central location

---

***Figure 7-5.*** *The very high risks identified are concerning, because the first risk, once exploited, could cause significant damage, as remaining risks show that very little defense-in-depth exists to limit damage to the entity*

# High Risks

A combination of risk types and threats is shown in Figure 7-6, constituting the high risks to ePHI. Sophisticated attackers are the most common threat, but two scenarios exist whereby malicious insiders can exploit weaknesses, leading to a breach of ePHI. These weaknesses include a lack of segregation of duties and improper disposal of IT assets.

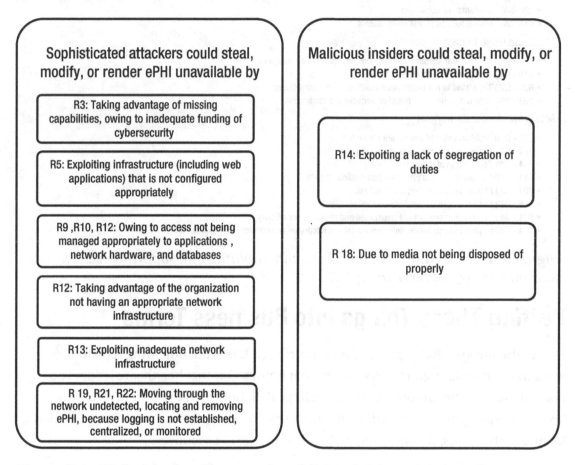

*Figure 7-6.* *High risks that illustrate the additional risks sophisticated attackers pose and scenarios where malicious insiders can cause damage to the organization*

# Moderate

In most cases, moderate risks can have a longer time line for remediation than the very high and high risks. Six months or longer is a reasonable time, unless the moderate risks in question are certain to be targeted in specific attack scenarios or commitments to stakeholders require shorter remediation times.

To prioritize these risks, Figure 7-7 displays the breakdown of moderate risks, grouped in categories: very high, high, and moderate impact vulnerabilities; a single moderate likelihood of exploitation; and one highly likely vulnerability with a moderate impact associated.

**Moderate (Very High Impact)**
- R20 (SA) - Incidents are not logged
- R17 (SA) - ePHI is located in test environments

**Moderate (High Impact)**
- R23 - (SA) Incident Management process does not include lessons learned
- R16 - (SA) Data at rest is not encrypted
- R08 - (SA) Time lines to remediate vulnerabilities are not established
- R02 - (SA) Data is not managed based on sensitivity classification

**Moderate (Moderate Impact)**
- R25 - (SA)  Incident Response plans are not tested
- R24 - (MI) Availability requirements are not defined
- R14 - (MI) Segregation of duties are not enforced
- R11 - (SA) End points are not protected from malicious code
- R07 - (MI) Access to source code is not enforced
- R06 - (MI) Code changes are not tested for vulnerabilities
- R01 - (MI) Hardware assets are not inventoried and reviewed periodically
- R04 - (MI) Legal and compliance requirements are not integrated into policies and procedures

***Figure 7-7.*** *Moderate risks, based on vulnerabilities that sophisticated attackers and malicious insiders can exploit*

# Putting These Things into Business Terms

One of the biggest challenges for cybersecurity leaders is documenting risks in ways that are meaningful to executives. That is not to say that healthcare leaders do not understand the importance of protecting ePHI, but when discussing risks and investments required to remediate them, the more closely these risk items can be tied to business objectives, the more impactful the message to executives.

## Operational Impacts

Breaches require the attention of key members from business and IT, which forces attention away from business priorities. Anyone with a role on an incident response or management team knows that investigating the simplest of incidents can eat up a single day. Responding to a breach, which requires reporting to HHS, can account for the loss of nearly 100 days of productivity for multiple people during the incident response. How likely is it for an organization to hit operational goals when key executives are not fully engaged?

Entities may also experience less favorable terms when negotiating contracts with new clients[2] or, worse yet, if intellectual property is breached, some entities may struggle to continue operating.

## Financial Statement Impacts

In addition to lost productivity, costs, including attorney's fees, consultants, and other expenses, impact financial results. Larger organizations can absorb financial impacts better than small and mid-size companies, but the impacts are felt at entities of all sizes.

- Reduced operational focus can lead to reduced net income, highlighted on the income statement and the balance sheet.

- Cash outlays for expenses are reflected in the statement of cash flows as changes in cash owing to operating activities.

- Long term, cash used to pay breach expenses and not invested in the business has an impact, based on the expected organizational rate of return.

- Many entities experience downgrades in credit rating once a breach is announced, which causes increased expense related to financing activities and impacts earned income.

## Summary

The purpose of this chapter, including its name, is to level set what should be expected from risk analysis output. Most executives assume that their organization is okay and that sufficient security capabilities exist. There is often shock and disbelief at the number of risks documented when a thorough analysis is completed. The preceding sample analysis identified 27 risks, and, realistically, risk assessments can yield three times as many when executed properly. This does not signify failures on the part of the entity, or that the challenge of protecting ePHI is so great that failure is inevitable. It means that in

---

[2]Neil Amato, "The hidden costs of data breaches," Journal of Accountancy, www.journalofaccountancy.com/news/2016/jul/hidden-costs-of-data-breach-201614870.html, July 25, 2016.

today's interconnected world, in which everything is digitized, there are many details to be considered when building security programs.

Tracking risks and remediation plans does not have to be high-tech to be effective. Figure 7-8 displays a snippet of a risk register documented in an Excel spreadsheet. The full version of the risk register appears in Appendix C of this book.

| Risk No | Risk | Severity |
|---------|------|----------|
| 15 | Sophisticated attackers could steal, modify, or render ePHI unavailable by exploiting end users and gain access | Very High |
| 19 | Sophisticated Attackers could steal, modify, or render ePHI unavailable by moving through the network | Very High |
| 22 | Sophisticated Attackers could steal, modify, or render ePHI unavailable by continuing attacks and hiding evidence because logs are not collected and aggregated in a central location | Very High |

**Figure 7-8.**  *A sample of very high risks details how each would appear on a risk register created using Excel*

Many risks are moderate—not severe enough to sound alarms, but not small enough to ignore, which forces consideration of resource plans and document intentions. Then, there are the low and very low risks. Usually, these risks are not remediated, unless remediated with other vulnerabilities that are patched. Very low and low risks are often tracked and monitored, to confirm that these risks do not increase over time.

# CHAPTER 8

# Increasing Program Maturity

The process of reducing risk is achieved by mapping each risk to a security measure meant to mitigate or reduce the risk and focusing on increasing the maturity and capabilities of the cybersecurity control. Earlier, each of the NIST cybersecurity subcategories had an internal cybersecurity control designed to meet the subcategory objective. The program as discussed in Chapter 3 is in its infancy and, therefore, on the low end of the maturity scale. Initially, the focus is on getting the cybersecurity control maturity of each subcategory to a 3, on the 1-to-5 scale. A 3 represents a control that is operational, which is good enough to comply with the HIPAA Security Rule Standards and protect ePHI. Once each subcategory is operational, focus can turn to reaching higher levels, 4s and 5s, where resource investment makes sense, based on the risk landscape and objectives of the cybersecurity program.

## Moving from Ad Hoc to Operational

The first things to consider are the low-hanging fruit, easy things to correct with little effort, and very high and high-risk areas. First things first, the cybersecurity policy must be addressed. This is highlighted in subcategory ID.GV-1. All the control statements aligned to NIST subcategories, the how statements for each objective, must be documented in the cybersecurity policy. There is no standard template, but part of the monitoring process must confirm that each control is documented and supported by a policy statement. At this point, the assumption is that all cybersecurity controls identified earlier are documented in the policy.

© Eric C. Thompson 2017
E. C. Thompson, *Building a HIPAA-Compliant Cybersecurity Program*,
https://doi.org/10.1007/978-1-4842-3060-2_8

# Identify

The identify function focuses on the foundational aspects of developing a cybersecurity program. To be effective, entities must identify the assets requiring protection, in this case, what the hardware and software assets used to process ePHI are and how this data flows through the IT systems. Risks must be identified and managed, and governance mechanisms have to be established and enforced (see Table 8-1).

***Table 8-1.*** *Capabilities Required to Make Subcategories Within Identify Achieve an Operational Level*

| Subcategory | Processes and Capabilities to Achieve Level 3 |
| --- | --- |
| ID.AM-1: Physical devices and systems within the organization are inventoried. | A complete list of hardware assets is maintained and reviewed periodically to confirm the list is complete. |
| ID.AM-2: Software platforms and applications within the organization are inventoried. | A complete list of software assets and licensing agreements in use at the entity is compiled and maintained and reviewed periodically. |
| ID.AM-3: Organizational communication and data flows are mapped. | A diagram illustrating ePHI flows through the entity, highlighting movement between systems, exists and is updated periodically. |
| ID.AM-4: External information systems are cataloged. | Assessment is made of all vendors supporting information systems requiring outside connections to IT systems, to ensure that the vendor and the connection are secure. |
| ID.AM-5: Resources (e.g., hardware, devices, data, and software) are prioritized, based on their classification, criticality, and business value. | Assets tracked at ID.AM-1 and ID.AM-2 are classified, based on whether ePHI or other sensitive data is processed by the assets in question. |
| ID.AM-6: Cybersecurity roles and responsibilities for the entire workforce and third-party stakeholders (e.g., suppliers, customers, partners) are established. | Job descriptions include cybersecurity responsibilities. Understanding of these responsibilities is acknowledged by members of the workforce. These requirements apply to employees and nonemployees. |

*(continued)*

*Table 8-1*  (*continued*)

| Subcategory | Processes and Capabilities to Achieve Level 3 |
| --- | --- |
| ID.BE-1: The organization's role in the supply chain is identified and communicated. | When management presents organizational goals and objectives to the workforce, the role the entity plays in the ecosystem is emphasized, and if an incident occurs, the effects to other healthcare organizations are understood. |
| ID.BE-2: The organization's place in critical infrastructure and its industry sector is identified and communicated. | Dependencies, other healthcare entities, and members of the community, highlighting reliance placed on protecting patient information, are emphasized and documented in steering or cybersecurity operating charters. |
| ID.BE-3: Priorities for organizational mission, objectives, and activities are established and communicated. | Members of the workforce consistently receive updates on management's goals and the progress to date. |
| ID.BE-4: Dependencies and critical functions for delivery of critical services are established. | Business impact analysis is completed, and the entity understands what processes require priority focus for confidentiality, integrity, and availability of ePHI. |
| ID.BE-5: Resilience requirements to support delivery of critical services are established. | Members of management understand the resilience requirements, impacts of unavailability, of systems to stakeholders. These stakeholders include patients and/or clients. |
| ID.GV-1: Organizational information security policy is established. | A policy document outlining all expected behaviors, conduct, and use of IT resources of the workforce is communicated, and cybersecurity controls are established, enforcing such behavior. |
| ID.GV-2: Information security roles and responsibilities are coordinated and aligned with internal roles and external partners. | Resource plans are established to meet the capabilities required to make each subcategory and control operational. If necessary, partnerships are established with outside firms to fill these roles. |

(*continued*)

*Table 8-1* (*continued*)

| Subcategory | Processes and Capabilities to Achieve Level 3 |
| --- | --- |
| ID.GV-3: Legal and regulatory requirements regarding cybersecurity, including privacy and civil liberties obligations, are understood and managed. | Awareness and security updates include reinforcement of regulatory and third-party compliance requirements at regular intervals and when changes to the external environment occur. |
| ID.GV-4: Governance and risk management processes address cybersecurity risks. | Cybersecurity program objectives are aligned with cyber risks. Management controls designed to achieve cyber program objectives are present and documented in the cybersecurity policy. |
| ID.RA-1: Asset vulnerabilities are identified and documented. | A comprehensive list of vulnerabilities to all assets that interact with ePHI are documented and used in the analysis of risk. |
| ID.RA-2: Threat and vulnerability information is received from information sharing forums and sources. | The entity subscribes to threat and vulnerability intelligence feeds, which are utilized during cybersecurity operations and risks management activities. |
| ID.RA-3: Threats, both internal and external, are identified and documented. | The process of developing and reassessing the risk analysis discussed in this book is required to meet this objective. |
| ID.RA-4: Potential business impacts and likelihoods are identified. | The process of developing and reassessing the risk analysis discussed in this book is required to meet this objective. |
| ID.RA-5: Threats, vulnerabilities, likelihoods, and impacts are used to determine risk. | The process of developing and reassessing the risk analysis discussed in this book is required to meet this objective. |
| ID.RA-6: Risk responses are identified and prioritized. | The risk register documents management's approach to either remediating the risk or mitigating the risk and accepting any residual risks. |

(*continued*)

***Table 8-1***  (*continued*)

| Subcategory | Processes and Capabilities to Achieve Level 3 |
|---|---|
| ID.RM-1: Risk management processes are established, managed, and agreed to by organizational stakeholders. | Risk management processes and procedures outlined by the business are presented to management or to a risk management committee and approved. |
| ID.RM-2: Organizational risk tolerance is determined and clearly expressed. | Management has expressed a risk tolerance, which is used in part to determine how to address risk. |
| ID.RM-3: The organization's determination of risk tolerance is informed by its role in critical infrastructure and sector-specific risk analysis. | Risk tolerance is communicated to the workforce. Tolerance levels are established by senior management or a security committee and take into account impacts to the business. |

# Protect

The protect function's objectives focus on various access requirements, training and awareness, data integrity, maintenance, and availability (see Table 8-2).

***Table 8-2.***  *Capabilities Required to Mature the Subcategories in the Protect Function to Achieve an Operational Level*

| | |
|---|---|
| PR.AC-1: Identities and credentials are managed for authorized devices and users. | A process to request, approve, and provision access is documented and operating effectively. Segregation of approval and provisioning of access is enforced. |
| PR.AC-2: Physical access to assets is managed and protected. | Physical access to office space and data centers is restricted via badge access or other identified physical controls. |
| PR.AC-3: Remote access is managed. | Remote access is limited to users who require this privilege and have approval granted. Two factors authentications are required. |
| PR.AC-4: Access permissions are managed, incorporating the principles of least privilege and separation of duties. | Same as capabilities outlined in PR.AC-1. |

(*continued*)

*Table 8-2*  (*continued*)

| | |
|---|---|
| PR.AC-5: Network integrity is protected, incorporating network segregation, where appropriate. | All network hardware is configured, based on an accepted hardening standard. Deviations are tracked by the exception management process and reviewed annually. |
| PR.AT-1: All users are informed and trained. | New hire and annual cybersecurity awareness and compliance training is delivered, and completion is tracked. |
| PR.AT-2: Privileged users understand roles and responsibilities. | On a periodic basis, users with privileged access undergo training specific to these roles. |
| PR.AT-3: Third-party stakeholders (e.g., suppliers, customers, partners) understand roles and responsibilities. | A process for obtaining security questionnaires or third-party assessments outlining information security controls is established. Security gaps at third-parties are discussed, and issues are remediated prior to engaging with the third party. |
| PR.AT-4: Senior executives understand roles and responsibilities. | Cybersecurity responsibilities for members of senior management are documented in position descriptions and performance expectation documents. |
| PR.AT-5: Physical and information security personnel understand roles and responsibilities. | Job descriptions and performance criteria for cybersecurity professionals are documented and acknowledged. |
| PR.DS-1: Data at rest is protected. | Encryption technology is utilized to protect data at rest internally and on portable devices. If encryption is not maintained, alternate controls have been identified and operate effectively. |
| PR.DS-2: Data-in-transit is protected. | Secure communications methods are established when data is transmitted outside of the organization. Examples include SSH or TLS. |
| PR.DS-3: Assets are formally managed throughout removal, transfers, and disposition. | A process to track assets in production and retired assets is established and includes retention of certificates of destruction. |

(*continued*)

*Table 8-2* (*continued*)

| | |
|---|---|
| PR.DS-4: Adequate capacity to ensure availability is maintained. | Systems administrators established computing capacity baselines, receive alerts when thresholds are reached, and planned corrective actions are taken. |
| PR.DS-5: Protections against data leaks are implemented. | A solution that captures attempts to transmit sensitive data outside organizational boundaries using insecure means of communication is implemented and monitored. |
| PR.DS-6: Integrity checking mechanisms are used to verify software, firmware, and information integrity. | IT systems alert administrators when errors are detected due to faulty input or data processing. |
| PR.IP-1: A baseline configuration of information technology/industrial control systems is created and maintained. | Hardening standards are adopted and monitored. Changes to those standards are detected by periodic scans or technology solutions that block attempts to change configurations. |
| PR.IP-2: A System Development Life Cycle to manage systems is implemented. | Changes to applications and supporting infrastructure require change control procedures, authorization to develop, quality assurance/user-acceptance testing and approval, to be followed prior to any change implementations into production. |
| PR.IP-3: Configuration change control processes are in place. | Changes to configurations, especially those governed by hardening standards, must go through a change control process and be approved prior to implementing the change. These changes are also tracked by the exception process and reviewed at least annually. |
| PR.IP-4: Backups of information are conducted, maintained, and tested periodically. | A process is in place to back up all systems, and periodic tests of those backups ensure they are operating effectively. |
| PR.IP-5: Policy and regulations regarding the physical operating environment for organizational assets are met. | Policy documents address the need for physical security within the data centers and include requirements for environmental controls (A/C, fire suppression, and moisture sensors). |

(*continued*)

***Table 8-2***  (*continued*)

| | |
|---|---|
| PR.IP-6: Data is destroyed according to policy. | A process to destroy hard drives or storage devices taken out of production must be operating effectively, and records maintained for periodic review. |
| PR.IP-7: Protection processes are continuously improved. | Annual assessments of the information security program are conducted, and findings delivered to management, to determine if corrective actions are required. |
| PR.IP-8: Effectiveness of protection technologies is shared with appropriate parties. | Management, or a committee overseeing the cybersecurity function, receive regular updates and notifications when urgent matters must be addressed. |
| PR.IP-9: Response plans (incident response and business continuity) and recovery plans (incident recovery and disaster recovery) are in place and managed. | Response plans are documented and training provided to relevant team members. Any lessons learned are reviewed by the team and incorporated into the plan. |
| PR.IP-10: Response and recovery plans are tested. | Response plans are tested annually, and lessons learned are incorporated into the plan. |
| PR.IP-11: Cybersecurity is included in human resources practices (e.g., deprovisioning, personnel screening). | HR conducts background checks on new hires, has established criteria and qualifications for each job posting. HR also enforces policy requirements and communicates terminations timely for access deprovisioning. |
| PR.IP-12: A vulnerability management plan is developed and implemented. | Regular scans of the environment are completed or vulnerability information is communicated to the entity by a third party. Remediation time lines based on severity of the vulnerability are established and monitored. |
| PR.MA-1: Maintenance and repair of organizational assets are performed and logged in a timely manner, with approved and controlled tools. | Maintenance performed is approved by appropriate individuals and monitoring of third parties performing maintenance is conducted. Confirmation that only approved work was completed, and no other changes were made is confirmed. |

(*continued*)

***Table 8-2*** (*continued*)

| | |
|---|---|
| PR.MA-2: Remote maintenance of organizational assets is approved, logged, and performed in a manner that prevents unauthorized access. | A process to approve and grant remote access for maintenance is established, and remote connections are disabled once maintenance is completed. |
| PR.PT-1: Audit/log records are determined, documented, implemented, and reviewed in accordance with policy. | A logging strategy is documented and operating effectively. Logs are reviewed periodically, retained based on regulatory and third-party requirements, considering available resources to comply with expectations. |
| PR.PT-2: Removable media is protected, and its use restricted, according to policy. | The use of external drives and other portable storage is limited by restricting access to those functions. |
| PR.PT-3: Access to systems and assets is controlled, incorporating the principle of least functionality. | User access is reviewed periodically to confirm that users, especially privileged users and administrators, still require access based on job function. |
| PR.PT-4: Communications and control networks are protected. | Firewalls and other perimeter protection technologies that define the network boundary are in place. |

# Detect

The detect function guides entities in implementing controls and capabilities to detect anomalies and other behaviors that indicate compromise to the system or potential attacks (see Table 8-3).

***Table 8-3.*** *Capabilities Required to Mature the Subcategories Within the Detect Function to Achieve an Operational Level*

| | |
|---|---|
| DE.AE-1: A baseline of network operations and expected data flows for users and systems is established and managed. | Baselines for traffic and data flow are established to detect anomalies in the network. |
| DE.AE-2: Detected events are analyzed to understand attack targets and methods. | Technology capable of aggregating and correlating logs to facilitate detection and forensic investigations are implemented. |
| DE.AE-3: Event data are aggregated and correlated from multiple sources and sensors. | A SIEM or similar technology is implemented and fed relevant log data from servers, firewalls, and other network equipment processing ePHI traffic. |
| DE.AE-4: Impact of events is determined. | Events are correlated with assets processing ePHI and the risk analysis, to understand potential impacts of events. |
| DE.AE-5: Incident alert thresholds are established. | An incident response plan is created and identifies thresholds for differentiating events and incidents. |
| DE.CM-1: The network is monitored to detect potential cybersecurity events. | Firewalls, IDS/IPS, and logging at end points is enabled, collected, and analyzed centrally. |
| DE.CM-2: The physical environment is monitored to detect potential cybersecurity events. | Cameras and/or security guards are utilized to monitor access to locations where sensitive assets reside. |
| DE.CM-3: Personnel activity is monitored to detect potential cybersecurity events. | Host-based monitoring tools are implemented at end points to detect suspect behavior. |
| DE.CM-4: Malicious code is detected. | End-point protection solutions are implemented. A process to test that updates and effective operation are conducted periodically. |
| DE.CM-5: Unauthorized mobile code is detected. | End-point protection solutions are implemented. A process to test that updates and effective operation are conducted periodically is in place. |
| DE.CM-6: External service provider activity is monitored to detect potential cybersecurity events. | External connections are logged during active access periods, to confirm that only expected activities are performed by vendors. |

(*continued*)

*Table 8-3*  (*continued*)

| | |
|---|---|
| DE.CM-7: Monitoring for unauthorized personnel, connections, devices, and software is performed. | Network monitoring solutions that detect unauthorized devices are implemented and monitored. |
| DE.CM-8: Vulnerability scans are performed. | Scans are performed regularly, either monthly or quarterly, and results are monitored to confirm that remediation occurs within established time frames. |
| DE.DP-1: Roles and responsibilities for detection are well-defined to ensure accountability. | Cybersecurity personnel who are part of the primary response team are given documented descriptions of expected activity. |
| DE.DP-2: Detection activities comply with all applicable requirements. | Annual monitoring of detection activities confirms each is compliant with cybersecurity policies. |
| DE.DP-3: Detection processes are tested. | Attack and penetration or red team assessments are conducted to confirm cyber capabilities can detect attacks. |
| DE.DP-4: Event detection information is communicated to appropriate parties. | Incident response plans must contain documented escalation parameters. |
| DE.DP-5: Detection processes are continuously improved. | Results of assessments are reviewed, and changes are made to the program, to remediate assessment findings. |

# Respond

The respond function is focused on ensuring that entities identify and categorize events and incidents, respond appropriately, and communicate with appropriate stakeholders, internally and externally (see Table 8-4).

***Table 8-4.*** *Capabilities Required to Mature the Subcategories Within the Response Function to Achieve an Operational Level*

| | |
|---|---|
| RS.CO-1: Personnel know their roles and order of operations when a response is needed. | An incident response plan is developed and tested regularly. |
| RS.CO-2: Events are reported consistent with established criteria. | Metrics and key milestones are documented and monitored during actual incidents and tabletop exercises. These metrics include end user reporting of incidents/events and communication to other stakeholders. |
| RS.CO-3: Information is shared consistent with response plans. | Response plans dictate who should be contacted and when communications must occur during an event or exercise. |
| RS.CO-4: Coordination with stakeholders occurs consistent with response plans. | Tracking of communication and coordination requirements is assigned to a member of the team and tracked. |
| RS.CO-5: Voluntary information sharing occurs with external stakeholders to achieve broader cybersecurity situational awareness. | The entity proactively joins other organizations to share data gathered and lessons learned from events. |
| RS.AN-1: Notifications from detection systems are investigated. | A process exists and is outlined in the response plans to guide the team in investigation events and concluding whether an incident has occurred. |
| RS.AN-2: The impact of the incident is understood. | Responders are able to trace the occurrence and location of incidents to the risk analysis and understand the impact of systems affected. |
| RS.AN-3: Forensics are performed. | Thresholds are established, dictating when it is necessary to engage forensic teams. |
| RS.AN-4: Incidents are categorized consistent with response plans. | Post event/incident reviews confirm correct classification of the incident that has occurred. If not, understanding of required improvements are identified and incorporated into the response plan. |
| RS.MI-1: Incidents are contained. | Internal or external capabilities exist to contain incidents, once identified. |

*(continued)*

***Table 8-4*** (*continued*)

| | |
|---|---|
| RS.MI-2: Incidents are mitigated. | Internal or external capabilities exist to mitigate incidents, once identified. |
| RS.MI-3: Newly identified vulnerabilities are mitigated or documented as accepted risks. | A process exists for regularly identifying vulnerabilities, and remediation efforts are measured against documented time lines, based on severity. |
| RS.IM-1: Response plans incorporate lessons learned. | Incident responses are reviewed, and documented improvement opportunities are integrated into the plan going forward. |
| RS.IM-2: Response strategies are updated. | The response plan is reviewed and updated annually. |

# Recover

The recover function guides entities through the process of developing capabilities to recover from incidents (see Table 8-5).

***Table 8-5.*** *Capabilities Required to Mature the Subcategories Within the Recover Function to Achieve an Operational Level*

| | |
|---|---|
| RC.RP-1: Recovery plan is executed during or after an event. | Recovery plans are established, tested, and available when events occur. |
| RC.IM-1: Recovery plans incorporate lessons learned. | All recovery plans (business continuity/ disaster recovery and incident response) include examination for lessons learned post event. |
| RC.IM-2: Recovery strategies are updated. | Plans are reviewed annually by the team and updated accordingly. |
| RC.CO-1: Public relations are managed. | Internal or external capabilities exist to manage public perception, when necessary. |
| RC.CO-2: Reputation after an event is repaired. | Internal or external capabilities exist to repair the entities image, when necessary. |
| RC.CO-3: Recovery activities are communicated to internal stakeholders and executive and management teams. | The response and recovery plans include regular communication to necessary stakeholders during and after the event. |

# Addressing Very High and High Risks

The next step is to review the very high and high risks. All risks are important, but resource management dictates action be taken toward the most severe risks to ePHI. Figure 8-1 is the heat map developed during the analysis of the risks in the previous step, before considering the selection of security measures.

## Risk Matrix

| | | Very Low 1 | Low 2 | Moderate 3 | High 4 | Very High 5 |
|---|---|---|---|---|---|---|
| **Impact** | **Very High** 5 | Very Low | Low | Moderate R17, R20 | High R9,  R10, R12, R13, R18, R21 | Very High R15, R19, R22 |
| | **High** 4 | Very Low | Low | Moderate R2, R8, R16, R23 | High R3, R5, R14 | Very High |
| | **Moderate** 3 | Very Low | Low | Moderate R1, R6, R7, R11, R14, R24, R25 | Moderate R4 | High |
| | **Low** 2 | Very Low | Low R27 | Low R26 | Low | Moderate |
| | **Very Low** 1 | Very Low | Very Low | Very Low | Low | Low |
| | | **Very Low** 1 | **Low** 2 | **Moderate** 3 | **High** 4 | **Very High** 5 |
| | | | | **Likelihood** | | |

*Figure 8-1.* *The heat map created during the analysis of risks created previously in the risk assessment process*

# Very High Risks

Three very high risks were identified during the analysis. These were

- *R15*: Sophisticated attackers could steal, modify, or render ePHI unavailable, by exploiting end users, gaining access to the network via phishing e-mails through inadequate awareness of end users to identify and report these types of e-mails.

- *R19*: Sophisticated attackers could steal, modify, or render ePHI unavailable, by moving through the network undetected, elevating privileges, and accessing IT resources in which ePHI is in use, motion, and rest.

- *R22*: Sophisticated attackers could steal, modify, or render ePHI unavailable, by hiding evidence of the intrusion, because logs are not collated and aggregated in a central location.

Each risk is mapped to NIST CSF subcategories and internal controls designed to reduce risk and protect ePHI. Now, it is possible to calculate the risk reduction, based on planned improvements. Table 8-6 presents the high risks discussed in this section and the reassessed likelihood and impact ratings.

*Table 8-6. High Risks Identified During the Risk Analysis*

| No. | NIST Subcategory | Likelihood | Impact |
|-----|------------------|------------|--------|
| R15: | PR.AT-1. New hire and annual cybersecurity awareness and compliance training is delivered and completion is tracked. | 4 | 5 |
| R19: | Sophisticated attackers could steal, modify, or render ePHI unavailable, by moving through the network undetected, elevating privileges, and accessing IT resources in which ePHI is in use, motion, and rest. | 4 | 4 |
| R22: | Sophisticated attackers could steal, modify, or render ePHI unavailable, by hiding evidence of the intrusion, because logs are not collated and aggregated in a central location. | 4 | 4 |

Figure 8-2 graphically displays the movement of each risk on the heat map, highlighting the risk reduction achieved by maturing the subcategory to an operational level.

| Risk Matrix | | | | | |
|---|---|---|---|---|---|
| **Impact** | **Very High** 5 | Very Low | Low | Moderate | High R9,  R10, R12, R13, R18, R19, R21, R22 | Very High R15, R19, R22 |
| | **High** 4 | Very Low | Low | *Moderate* ↖ *R9,  R10, R12, R13, R18, R19,* | High *R15, R19, R22,* R3, R5, R14 | Very High |
| | **Moderate** 3 | Very Low | Low | *Moderate* ↖ *R3, R5, R14* | Moderate | High |
| | **Low** 2 | Very Low | Low | Low | Low | Moderate |
| | **Very Low** 1 | Very Low | Very Low | Very Low | Low | Low |
| | | **Very Low** 1 | **Low** 2 | **Moderate** 3 | **High** 4 | **Very High** 5 |
| | | **Likelihood** | | | | |

*Figure 8-2.   Increasing the maturity of cybersecurity controls aligned and selected to reduce risk levels is depicted in this heat map. Predicted risk reductions are shown in bold, with arrows displaying the directional changes to the risks.*

Based on the projects planned for the cybersecurity program, all three very high risks moved to high risks, and all the previously stated high risks are reduced to moderate level risks. The key is to ensure that the projects designed to improve the cybersecurity program controls are successfully completed.

# Summary

This chapter covered improvements required to enhance the cybersecurity program. Because HHS guidance suggest identifying and selecting security measures to reduce risk and protect ePHI, the NIST CSF framework was adopted to demonstrate this objective. "Reasonable" means achieving what is cost-effective and makes sense for risk mitigation. This means having each subcategory of the framework and internal controls aligned with these subcategories, at a maturity level equal to three out of five scales. Whichever term is used to describe this level, anything less is not adequate, and in many cases, what the preceding graphics illustrate is the need for subcategories to operate at a higher maturity level. One factor considered when measuring likelihood earlier was the role maturity of controls plays. To some degree, controls that are less mature will have vulnerabilities more likely to be exploited. That is a function of missing governance requirements, which dictate employee actions, processes not operating as needed, and a lack of management oversight. If management is not monitoring the control environment, there is a higher likelihood that vulnerabilities can continue to remain unmitigated and be exploited.

Long term, the goal of the cybersecurity program is not to stop at operational subcategories. This is a baseline level desired for all subcategories and controls to comply with HIPAA. Many will not be required to rise above this level, while others must be more mature, to keep pace with continued sophistication of new threats. To protect patient information properly, continued investment in the program is required, especially in the focus areas of detect and response functions. Those considerations are covered in Chapters 12 and 13, when strategy, roadmaps and cybersecurity investment are discussed.

# CHAPTER 9

# Targeted Nontechnical Testing

To this point, the risk analysis was executed by conducting through inquiry and the examination documents such as policies, previous assessment results, and audit reports. A limited amount of current, tangible information derived through direct testing was incorporated into the analysis thus far. This is not atypical for the initial phase of the analysis and assessment. Establishing baseline risks, as shown in Figure 9-1, through documenting and correlating current information and known capabilities into a list of risks needing treatment, is the first step. As the chapter title states, the nontechnical testing executed is chosen based on the value the test brings to the risk assessment and analysis. These specific tests are chosen because there is confirmation necessary to ensure that the risks as documented are accurately reflected.

© Eric C. Thompson 2017
E. C. Thompson, *Building a HIPAA-Compliant Cybersecurity Program*,
https://doi.org/10.1007/978-1-4842-3060-2_9

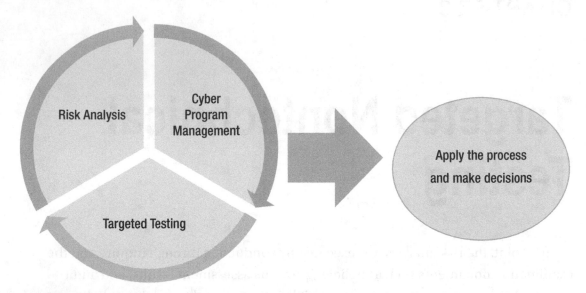

**Figure 9-1.**  *The wheel on the left highlights the establishment and enhancement of the cybersecurity program through analysis of risks, establishing the cybersecurity program and controls, and testing the program through nontechnical and technical evaluations.*

# The Nontechnical "Eye Test"

The goal of testing specific areas of the cybersecurity program is to understand whether the vulnerabilities and risks established to this point are the same, worse, or better than originally thought. Some of the most valuable tests of cybersecurity programs do not involve highly technical individuals attempting to breach an environment; rather, each focuses on processes and the people expected to execute IT governance controls. Access management, especially privileged access, change control, training and awareness, incident management, and vendor risk management are important areas of concern. These tests provide detailed information about cybersecurity program maturity and allow the entity to specifically target areas of the program for process improvement and risk reduction.

# Access Management

Access management is a source of significant risk to organizations, and one that can come with a bit of difficulty. Effective access controls are about integrating the process of provisioning and de-provisioning access into everyday business operations. Privileged access management is at the center of many articles and leading practices focused on reducing cybersecurity risk. Compromising privileged accounts can open the door to large-scale breaches. But access across all logical access layers within systems processing ePHI requires tight control, to achieve cybersecurity goals, including risk reduction and treatment.

# Privileged Access

Privileged access refers to users with access to ePHI who are not required to authenticate through an application layer or some type of front-end portal. Rather, these individuals can access data directly at the local server through operating systems, databases, and data warehouses. More concerning are shared or generic administrator accounts that are not named to an individual. Often, the changes these individuals can make to data are not logged, making it difficult to understand if any changes were made.

Windows and Linux operating systems have enough logging capabilities designed to detect changes to file systems. Databases are not always configured to track every table or data change. Consistently performing periodic reviews of privileged access has become more important than ever, because restricting access to a limited number of individuals, based on job function, is the one review every entity can implement to reduce the risk of inappropriate access to, or modification of, data.

Network infrastructure is the third area in which privilege access requires examination. Anyone who can change firewall rules, update routing tables, or manipulate and capture traffic as it moves through the environment should require frequent confirmation. These types of users, if allowed to keep access that is not necessary, are risky when credentials become compromised unexpectedly.

## Reviewing Privileged Access

Testing privileged access can be done manually by executing test scripts or generating canned reports from the system in question. For Linux servers, administrators execute scripts at the command line interface, to generate display accounts with specific types of access under audit. Some common privileges to review include

- Users with the ability to sudo to the root account

- Any users with access to directories and folders considered sensitive

Windows servers use PowerShell scripts to produce output showing access to specific privileges. Privileges are also displayed through analysis of Active Directory, by viewing users in groups and folders considered sensitive. At the operating-system level, it is important to test

- Domain administrators on domain controller

- Local administrators on servers with ePHI

- Database administrators on local SQL servers

- Anyone placed into security groups within Active Directory that access sensitive files and folders.

Producing a test or review of access sufficient to satisfy auditors and regulators requires several important components. User lists cannot be manual; rather, each must be generated via the system. Manual lists are not reliable. The first attribute tested is the reviewer, documenting how he or she is comfortable the list of privileged users generated is complete. Next, the reviewer must document what characteristics were analyzed to conclude access is appropriate for each privileged user. Examples include

- Is the user still in the same role since the last review?

- Does this role require the level of access currently granted?

Any no answers to these questions require further investigation, to confirm whether access is still required.

Once all the production environments are reviewed, results of the testing should be compared to the risk analysis, to determine if any updates are required. For instance, if a pervasive number of examples of inappropriate access to ePHI exist, the risk analysis must reflect this current state, until control remediation efforts are implemented.

## Application Access

Access at the application layer is often overlooked in applications other than the EMR or other enterprise applications processing ePHI. To confirm access to any applications with patient information is appropriate, testing access to each application by reviewing all users is an important step. Depending on the size of the organization, this test might take a few weeks or several months. Either way, understanding how effective access is controlled to applications with ePHI is important.

Depending on the example, the user lists required for testing are shown in Figure 9-2, which serves as a reminder of the applications identified at the healthcare provider, the insurance plan, and business associate that are in scope for the risk analysis.

**Healthcare Provider**

- EMR 1
- EMR 2
- Laboratory Application
- Radiology Application

**Health Plan**

- Claims processing system
- Insurance Contract Repository
- Insurance Payer Rules Repository

**Business Associate**

- Billing Application

*Figure 9-2.* *The applications that must be tested for access are listed under each sample entity*

# Change Control

There are several types of changes that must be considered for testing. Code and configuration changes that result in a change to the functionality of the system are critical. The patch management process also requires testing. Patches are used to fix or remediate bugs and vulnerabilities in the applications, database, or underlying operating system. These patches, despite being supplied by vendors normally, must follow the change control process and undergo QA testing and receive approval from a change approval board (CAB) prior to migration into production. Application teams should be able to generate a list of patches applied to the system during the period under audit and supply documentation demonstrating adherence to the process.

## Code and Other Changes to Functionality

End users and entities using applications to conduct business are continually updating functionality to meet the needs of the business. These changes are either developed in-house or a request is made to the vendor to develop the necessary changes. Code changes require modification of the source code to allow the application to function in a new way. Examples include changes to how calculations are made or how data is processed. Configuration changes also change functionality but may not affect sources. Settings within the application are changed to allow for the new functionality.

## Patches

Patching needs serious attention in today's cyber landscape. There are no excuses for not patching all environments, to mitigate vulnerabilities known to the outside world. Production is very important, because since that is where ePHI often resides, but all environments must be patched. Leaving vulnerabilities unmanaged inside the entity is not a good practice.

## How to Test the Change Management Process

Change control is a critical area that has to be assessed on an annual basis. Entities should have controls in place that are operating effectively, preventing the following risky behaviors:

- At any given point in time, the entity must demonstrate the ability to produce a list of all changes moved into production and generated from the system in question. Relying solely on a ticketing system to produce changes leaves the organization at risk for changes to be moved into production without the change following the processes outlined.

- No one person should be developing, approving, and migrating changes into production. At the very least, the same person should not develop and approve changes for production, and, if the developer and migrator must be the same, owing to a lack of available resources, a monitoring/review control must be implemented and executed no less often than every month.

- All changes have to be tested and approved prior to movement into production. This approval should be in the form of a CAB, which reviews each change for impact to the system and potential issues related to privacy and security prior to release to the production environment.

Testing must be executed against a sample of changes made to each application processing ePHI; confirming that all were tested and approved prior to release and that segregation of duties was maintained. Deviations from the expected process have to be analyzed for pervasiveness and additional risks.

# Training and Awareness

Training and awareness are interesting topics related to cybersecurity risk. Not often are these thought of as a capability or input to risk analysis and risk reduction, but, rather, as a compliance check box. HIPAA requires training and security reminders and other third-party compliance requirements, such as the criteria found in security objectives of the SOC 2 framework, and HITRUST requires regular delivery of training and awareness to the workforce.

Security and awareness training all too often consists of end users launching computer-based training, skipping to the final exam as quickly as possible, and repeatedly taking the test until a passing score is reached. Understanding and retaining key details is not achieved, and end users do not identify and report threats. That is why end users are categorized as vulnerabilities waiting to be exploited, especially by sophisticated threats. To be effective and generate a return on the training and awareness budget, training and awareness require measurable components that are actionable and provide input into the risk analysis and risk management process.

Training should be broken up into more frequent modules of shorter duration. These must be targeted topics, focusing on topics such as phishing scams, social engineering, social media risks, and so on. Reinforcement through reminder e-mails, videos, screensavers and login banners, and real-time learning are more effective. To be effective in this current landscape, training must also include consistent exposure, so end users become more familiar with the types of malicious e-mails used to launch attacks. Many vendors offer products that allow entities to conduct regular phishing simulations. This allows the entity to measure several key indicators, such as how many end users clicked on the e-mail, the number of clicks each user completed, and the reporting of suspicious e-mails. These metrics become leading indicators of how vulnerable the workforce is to exploits and how likely it is that attacks will go undetected.

When assessing the training and awareness function, the program should be assessed against the key activities outlined in the previous paragraphs. Providers, health plans, and business associates still relying on traditional training delivered once a year have vulnerabilities in end users waiting to be exploited. These individuals connect to the network every day. Regular phishing exercises used to test the workforce are no longer a nice-to-have but a key component of awareness. Consistent reinforcement is required to keep potential threats at the forefront of users who are busy and taking on more every day. Finally, tracking data enables cybersecurity leaders and members of the steering committee to make better risk-analysis and security-investment decisions.

# Incident Management

Documenting and communicating an incident response plan to members of the executive and incident response team is a key requirement of the NIST Cybersecurity Framework. These plans must be tested regularly and monitored as events occur, to confirm that the plan is operating in a way that meets the entity's data protection needs. Testing these plans and reviewing the results to understand what went well and what could be done better is necessary to improve the entity's ability to identify, contain, and eradicate any intrusions that threaten ePHI. There are several important pieces of the response process that, if not executed correctly, can increase the severity of an incident.

- An alert not being classified properly as an event or an incident, which leads to an inappropriate response

- Important steps of the plan not executed in a timely manner or properly, such as escalation to upper management and external communications

- Response times lagging expectations for identifying and invoking the incident response process

If a test has never been conducted, unknown issues go undetected until an actual event occurs. Plans require regular testing to reinforce responsibilities of team members. Consider engaging a third party with experience, to facilitate the exercise the first few times, then consider facilitating the exercises internally.

# Third-Party (Vendor) Risk Management

Third-party risk management is another area of vital importance that is often overlooked. One reason is that organizations struggle with purchases occurring in a silo, classifying data and building governance requirements into the procurement process. These factors lead to access of sensitive data, including ePHI, when carrying out contracted services, without having gone through any due diligence procedures to understand how ePHI is protected When business units work in these silos, procurement, contracting, and cybersecurity are not aligned with established procedures required before engaging with any entities that can access patient data. The root cause can be traced to overlooking fundamental pieces of governance, not identifying what is considered sensitive, business-critical data and documenting requirements for assessing risks related to engaging third parties who have access to, or are in possession of, ePHI. Instances exist at covered entities and business associates in which the required BAAs were not secured prior to engaging third parties' processing, maintaining, or storing ePHI. Even so, BAA agreements are not enough when allowing third parties to interact with ePHI. Specific due diligence requirements must be established and completed prior to engaging any third party with access to patient data, and the process monitored by management.

There are two ways to identify a population of vendor agreements for testing. First, there are probably several vendors known to the cybersecurity team, with agreements in place. More likely than not, these are the vendors used by IT, network service providers, data center, and application hosting services. Another way to gather a population of vendors is to obtain a list of vendors paid through the accounts payable (AP) system. The laborious part of the process will be reviewing the list and trying to understand if the third party has access to ePHI. Hopefully, a description of the service offered will shed enough light to make the determination. Once the list of third parties with access to ePHI is created, interview the individuals involved in the procurement process and business agreements, to understand what measures were taken to assess the risk to ePHI.

# Updating the Risk Analysis and Risk Register

Once testing is complete for each of these areas described, the risk analysis must be updated, based on the findings identified. As one might assume, because this entity has an immature cybersecurity program, it is logical to predict that a fair number of findings will exist, some of which could be significant. To refresh, the following bullet points highlight the risks identified in these categories prior to testing, and Table 9-1 lists the likelihood and impacts assigned to each corresponding risk associated with the control testing executed.

***Table 9-1.*** *Risks Related to Change Mangement, Access Control, and Training and Awareness, with Initial Likelihood and Impact Ratings*

| No. | Risk | Likelihood | Impact |
|-----|------|------------|--------|
| R6 | Code changes are not tested for vulnerabilities and other bugs. | 3 | 3 |
| R7 | Access to source code is not effectively controlled. | 3 | 3 |
| R9 | Application access management is ineffectively managed. | 4 | 5 |
| R10 | Database access management is ineffectively managed. | 4 | 5 |
| R12 | Network access management is ineffectively managed. | 4 | 5 |
| R14 | Responsibilities are not segregated within the organization. | 3 | 3 |
| R15 | Security education and awareness training is not adequate for workforce members to understand threats posed to ePHI. | 5 | 5 |
| R19 | Security monitoring is not adequately performed to detect unauthorized/suspicious activities. | 5 | 5 |
| R25 | An incident response plan has not been documented or tested. | 3 | 3 |
| R28 | Third parties with access to ePHI are not vetted through due diligence processes, including reviews of independent reports, security questionnaires, and onsite visits to analyze potential risks to ePHI. | 4 | 4 |

- Application, database, and network access management are very high risks, however, because access management is not mature enough to prevent or detect inappropriate access, the likelihood of a successful attack increases.

- Access to source code, testing source code for vulnerabilities, and segregation of duties are moderate risks, but the conclusions of testing performed demonstrate that access to source code is not restricted, and because segregation of duties is not enforced, inappropriate and harmful code can be placed into production without detection.

- Training and awareness are a very high risk, and the findings of testing show that the program is ineffective at equipping end users with the ability to identify and report any attempts made by sophisticated attackers to infiltrate the network via e-mail and other social-engineering vectors.

- Incident management is a moderate risk, but testing of the plan shows the team is not prepared to identify an incident in a timely manner and communicate to necessary individuals the next steps in containing and eradicating the attack.

- Third-party risk management does not appear on the risk register. It is possible that through inquiry and document review no evidence of any issues existed prior to testing the process, the likelihood of third parties being breached is high, and the impact depends on the amount of ePHI accessible.

Table 9-1 outlines the likelihood and impact ratings for risk categories tested. Several, including R9, R10, R12, R15, and R19 were already rated as very high risks.

The testing performed leads to the conclusion that risks aligned with this testing must be updated to show the higher level of severity. Figure 9-3 illustrates where these risks lie on the heat map prior to the testing, and Figure 9-4 displays the movement of the risks to higher levels of severity once the testing is complete.

**Risk Matrix**

| Impact | | Very Low 1 | Low 2 | Moderate 3 | High 4 | Very High 5 |
|---|---|---|---|---|---|---|
| | Very High 5 | Very Low | Low | Moderate | Very High R9, R10, R12, R19 | Very High |
| | High 4 | Very Low | Low | Moderate | Very High R14,R28** | Very High |
| | Moderate 3 | Very Low | Low | Moderate R6, R7, R14,R25 | Moderate | High |
| | Low 2 | Very Low | Low | Low | Low | Moderate |
| | Very Low 1 | Very Low | Very Low | Very Low | Low | Low |
| | | Very Low 1 | Low 2 | Moderate 3 | High 4 | Very High 5 |
| | | | | **Likelihood** | | |

***Figure 9-3.*** *The risks tested during targeted nontechnical testing, as rated prior to the performance of the testing. **Note: R28 is a new risk identified during testing*

**Risk Matrix**

| Impact | | Very Low 1 | Low 2 | Moderate 3 | High 4 | Very High 5 |
|---|---|---|---|---|---|---|
| | Very High 5 | Very Low | Low | Moderate | Very High R9, R10, R12,R15,R19 | Very High |
| | High 4 | Very Low | Low | Moderate | Very High R25,R28 | Very High |
| | Moderate 3 | Very Low | Low | Moderate R6, R7, R14 | Moderate | High |
| | Low 2 | Very Low | Low | Low | Low | Moderate |
| | Very Low 1 | Very Low | Very Low | Very Low | Low | Low |
| | | Very Low 1 | Low 2 | Moderate 3 | High 4 | Very High 5 |
| | | | | **Likelihood** | | |

***Figure 9-4.*** *The testing resulted in updating the severity of several risks; R9, R10, R12 and R25.*

Owing to the nature of the test results highlighted in the preceding bullet points, it is necessary to move the risks tested into quadrants of the heat map, to more accurately reflect the severity. Access controls for applications, databases, and network devices processing ePHI are major deficiencies in the environment and were moved to the Very High Risk quadrant reserved for risks with likelihood and impact values of 5. These must be addressed quickly. Risks such as these can be exploited quickly by sophisticated external threats as well as internal threats. Incident response and management risk, R25, rose to a high risk based on conclusions drawn from testing results.

## Summary

The process of assessing and analyzing risks to ePHI begins with documenting the known elements of the environment in which ePHI is in use, motion, and rest, interviewing key individuals, and reviewing relevant documentation. This allows the process to get off to the right start, but more needs to be done so that the analysis is actionable, by providing additional details. The tests performed in this phase focus on process, not technical capabilities or configuration settings. Cybersecurity programs consist of people, processes, and technology. It can be argued that the first two—people and process—are more important than the technology aspect. If fundamental pieces, such as access control, change control, segregation of duties, third-party risk management, and the ability to respond to incidents, are not operating effectively, then technology can be rendered ineffective.

# CHAPTER 10

# Targeted Technical Testing

The execution of the risk analysis thus far was based on inquiry and examination of methods, including policies, previous assessment results, and audit reports. Additionally, nontechnical testing of several key risk areas was also executed. This generated more current and tangible information to incorporate into the risk analysis. Solidifying the risk analysis, as shown in Figure 10-1, through cybersecurity program and control management and targeted testing, enriches the risk information used in decision making. Technical tests were chosen based on the need for detailed context regarding the risks identified.

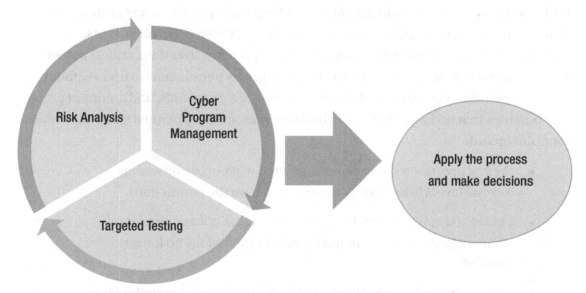

***Figure 10-1.*** *The wheel on the left highlights the establishment and enhancement of the cybersecurity program through analysis of risks, establishing the cyber security program and controls and testing the program through nontechnical and technical testing*

© Eric C. Thompson 2017
E. C. Thompson, *Building a HIPAA-Compliant Cybersecurity Program,*
https://doi.org/10.1007/978-1-4842-3060-2_10

# The Technical "Eye Test"

Technical testing is an important component of risk and cybersecurity program management. Technical testing aids risk and cybersecurity leaders' efforts to accurately assess whether security capabilities are effective in reducing risk or have known vulnerabilities that require further analysis in terms of risk to ePHI. One other important test is the attack and penetration, or red team, assessment. These tests measure the effectiveness of protection controls, or, if red team assessments are executed, detect and response controls are also tested.

# Assessing Directory Services

Directory services are a common way assets, people, and hardware are managed by IT. The Lightweight Directory Access Protocol (LDAP), a term often used interchangeably with Active Directory (AD), the directory service offered by Microsoft, is in use at many covered entities and business associates. Reliance is placed on directory services to provision and de-provision user access. In some environments, users must be members of specific groups to access applications, databases, and other repositories in which ePHI is in use, motion, and at rest. This scenario requires users to authenticate via the directory prior to gaining access to other resources wherein ePHI exists. When access management has not been managed properly, over time, critical access issues manifest through access creep, via providing new permissions to users without removing permissions related to their previous role, stale accounts, and groups or group memberships that no longer have valid business reasons for continued existence. Other examples include

- *Nested permissions*: Permissions granted to group membership several layers below the group meant to have the permissions

- *Access creep*: When additional permissions are granted to users changing roles, without removing older permissions no longer needed

- *Stale users and groups*: Users and groups idle for long periods of time

- *Empty groups*: Groups created with no members in them

- *Groups with one member*: Self-explanatory

If these issues have persisted for some time, usually the only feasible method for untangling the mess is engaging a third party with the capability of harvesting all the directory credentials. The analysis outlines the critical issues and assists in remediating the problematic conditions. Even if access control has been effectively managed, it does not hurt to engage a third party, to assess the directory environment and confirm that unknown issues do not exist.

# Data Loss Prevention

Data loss, or data leakage, depending on who you talk to, prevention (DLP) is a security capability/assessment in a similar vein as vulnerability scanning. The objective is to uncover instances of end users, malicious insiders, and, possibly, outsiders who have gained access to the network, sending ePHI outside network boundaries by e-mail or to the Internet via ports 80 or 443. These solutions also uncover instances of ePHI at rest in unsecured environments. DLP is not cutting-edge cybersecurity but a fundamental requirement. Earlier chapters highlighted the explosion of digital health records and how this phenomenon increased the challenge of protecting health information. With such a large amount of data collected and stored by healthcare providers, payers, and business associates, information begins to creep into unintended and unauthorized areas of an entity. Gradually it slips outside the boundaries of the network and into the hands of unknown outsiders. These outsiders are not necessarily malicious types stealing records, but vendors, consultants, and other third parties unknown to the cybersecurity team. DLP capabilities are supposed to provide alerts when sensitive data is transmitted outside the network. Many players exist in this space, and all offer very similar services.

- Monitoring of egress points, the doorway through which data enters and leaves the organization, to prevent sensitive information from leaving the entity by either blocking the transmission or ensuring that any sensitive data is encrypted prior to leaving the organizational boundary.

- Discovery of data within boundaries but not in use or at rest within policy.

- Monitoring use of cloud services (discussed in the following "Cloud Discovery and Governance" section).

Actions taken by DLP solutions depend on the rules created within the solution. Those rules are based on entity expectations and resource bandwidth. Some do not allow ePHI to ever be e-mailed or sent in attachments. Others require ePHI to be encrypted if transmitted via e-mail. Based on these rules, the DLP solution acts accordingly when detecting the presence of ePHI or any sensitive data the entity is concerned about. The transmission is either blocked and an alert sent to the cybersecurity team, or it is automatically encrypted, and alerts may or may not be generated. Usually, that depends on whether enough resources exist to investigate each alert.

Other important features provided by DLP include data discovery, scanning the environment to look for ePHI in use or at rest in unexpected places. Common use cases for this capability are outlined in Table 10-1.

***Table 10-1.*** *Examples of Use Cases Commonly Identified When Implementing DLP Capabilities*

| Use Case | Capability Required |
|---|---|
| ePHI stored on laptops | End points are scanned, instances of patient information are captured, and alerts are sent to the security team. |
| Transferring ePHI to thumb drives | DLP solutions on end points include disabling the ability to transfer data to drives plugged in to USB ports. |
| ePHI exists in testing and development environments | Allowing patient information into non-production environments is not a leading practice, and monitoring capabilities are necessary to detect these occurrences. |

# Cloud Discovery and Governance

Establishing governance and discovery capabilities to monitor usage of cloud services can be incorporated into DLP solutions. Many of the vendors providing DLP solutions offer cloud detection capabilities. This solution is necessary when entities utilize products such as Box. If Box is made available to end users for collaboration, proper governance dictates that ePHI not be stored in these environments. These DLP solutions scan the cloud environment to detect instances of data improperly stored there. Now, if collaboration tools such as Dropbox, Box, Google Docs, and Slack, as examples, are not authorized for use, other solutions are available to detect these occurrences. If ePHI is sent to these types of hosted sites, risks unknown to cybersecurity and compliance teams exist. These are common in university-based health systems and at other research organizations where teaming globally is a benefit. Payers and business associates must also address similar problems. The volume of data now available, and services offered by specialists assisting organizations with developing new services or ways to reduce costs, increase the number of outsiders with access to data. The danger grows through perceptions that cybersecurity and compliance teams slow down the pace of business, and the visibility of how users behave with ePHI is lost.

# Vulnerability Identification and Management

If the WannaCry episode in May 2017 taught us anything, it is that vulnerabilities long forgotten can be revived to create havoc. Not having a defined patch management program leaves an entity exposed to attacks using vulnerabilities that should have been remediated. A process for discovering, remediating, and tracking reportable metrics is the only effective way to handle vulnerabilities. This is another area of cybersecurity that lacks the intrigue most desire, but managing vulnerabilities requires thoughtful analysis. For instance, many common tools used to scan devices for weaknesses rate the findings as high, medium, and low. It's easy for those in charge of remediation to focus on the highest findings and leave the medium and low issues for another time. After a while, those mediums and lows are forgotten about. What happens when resources such as ExploitDB's web site or Metasploit have exploits available to the public? Is that low-rated vulnerability still low if it exists on a web server used as a front end to a database storing ePHI? This is just one example of what to consider in developing a threat- and vulnerability-management program.

Vulnerability assessments are executed by scanning hardware and software assets, to identify known vulnerabilities. Tenable and Qualys are two examples of vendors that offer vulnerability-scanning solutions. These scans typically produce reports outlining the known vulnerabilities and missing patches affecting the targeted assets. This fundamental process must be implemented and operating effectively for any cybersecurity program to realize a level of maturity capable of reducing risks to ePHI. An effective threat- and vulnerability-management program includes elements such as the following:

- Policies requiring scanning to be conducted at regular intervals

- Procedures for conducting the scans, reviewing results, and documenting remediation plans

- Consistent operations of the documented processes

- Gathering of metrics, such as the number of vulnerabilities by severity and average time to resolve

- Management review of the results and potential program adjustments, if the results are not satisfactory

Some scanning solutions can scan hardware and software assets for adherence to configuration standards. Another key component of cybersecurity programs includes adopting hardened configurations for devices in the environment. One popular standard available is published by the Center for Internet Security.[1] Standards are available for several platforms, including those listed in Table 10-2, which are in scope for this risk analysis.

***Table 10-2.*** *Examples of CIS Hardening Standards Available for an Enterprise*

| Windows | Linux |
| --- | --- |
| Server 2012 and 2012 R2 | Red Hat 7 |
| Server 2008 | Red Hat 6 |
| Windows 10 | Red Hat 5 |
| | OpenSUSE |
| | CentOS |

Entities must adopt the appropriate standards and implement policies and procedures requiring all hardware in these categories to adhere to these standards. Requiring the technology implementation team to use a hardened image when deploying new assets is one element that requires documentation of formal controls. The second element is periodically scanning the infrastructure, to confirm all components are compliant. If an exception is required, it must be documented and tracked in the same manner as policy exceptions and reviewed annually.

---

[1]Center for Internet Security, "Center for Internet Security Microsoft Windows 2012 R2 Benchmark", Verson 2.2, https://www.cisecurity.org/cis-benchmarks, April 28, 2016.

# Attack and Penetration/Red Team Testing

Traditional attack and penetration is an exercise by which internal or external teams probe the network, discovering any existing weaknesses in the defenses and exploiting them. These assessments focus more on the protect function of the NIST CSF.

To assess the protect, detect, and respond capabilities, entities may choose to have a red team assessment. The red team approach also differs in that the objective is not to document and test all vulnerabilities in network defenses. Instead, these teams gain entry the fastest way possible. For example, if the simulated attackers can penetrate the network through phishing attacks, then no other vulnerabilities are sought or exploited during the test. Once inside the entity's information systems, the goal is to move as quietly as possible, until the team attacks the trophies and data sources agreed to at the outset of the assessment, or the entity detects and responds to the attack. These assessments are planned with limited members of the entity, so that the assessment is as real as possible.

The CIS (Critical Cyber Security Controls)[2] point to these tests as important in understanding the strengths and weaknesses of the cybersecurity program. Attack and penetration tests are valuable for understanding all the technical weaknesses that exist. Red team assessments test a broader set of functions that make up the cybersecurity program. Which test to conduct depends on what the entity hopes to learn about its cybersecurity program.

# Testing Results and Risk Updates

The goal of the assessment described are to obtain reports and, with enough insight, add value to the risk analysis. If that is the case, the next step is to update the appropriate risks, based on the assessment results.

# Access Management Testing

Access management was tested in the nontechnical testing phase and again during the technical phase. The technical testing reconfirmed the conclusions of those tests and

---

[2]Center for Internet Security, "Center for Internet Security Critical Security Controls for Cybersecurity," Version 6.1, www.tml.org/p/TheCISCriticalSecurityControlsEffectiveCyberDefense.pdf, August 31, 2016.

pinpointed key areas in need of remediation. Figure 10-2 describes examples of issues uncovered, specifically those related to LDAP/AD.

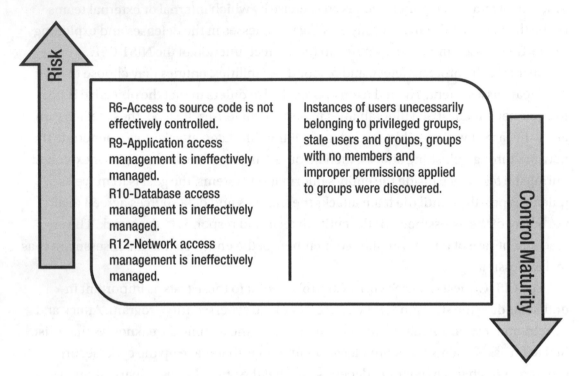

***Figure 10-2.***  *As issues demonstrating decreased maturity of the control are understood, risks associated to these controls increase*

## Data Protection Testing

Data does not appear to be protected adequately, as data is resting in unstructured and unencrypted internal share drives and in cloud-collaboration sites. This situation leaves data exposed to internal threats and/or sophisticated outsiders. It appears the security controls are not as mature as initially thought, and, therefore, these risks must be updated to reflect the actual increased severity (see Figure 10-3).

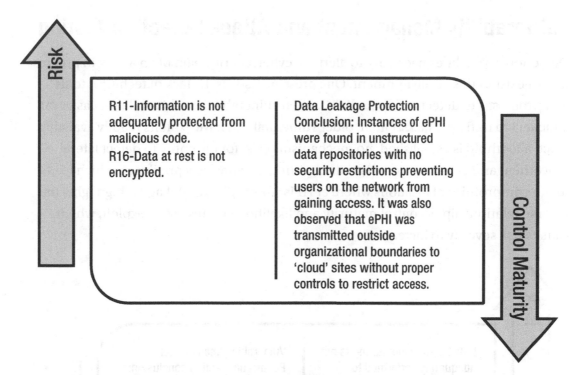

*Figure 10-3.* *The risks of sophisticated attackers stealing, modifying, or rendering ePHI unavailable, because data is stored in insecure locations, internally and externally. These locations can be exploited by sophisticated outsiders as well as insiders.*

Having data at rest in unsecure locations increases the likelihood that any sophisticated attacker or insider threat can successfully exploit vulnerabilities and cause a breach. Even though these risks are measured based on the abilities of sophisticated attackers, the risk treatment activities mitigate the risks of insider threats through implementation of access restriction controls. As indicated in Table 10-3, the likelihood measures for R11 and R16 were increased to level 4. The impact of R11 was also increased to level 4, because of the increased impact to ePHI posed by these insecure practices.

*Table 10-3.* *Likelihood and Impact Factors Were Increased After Testing Results Were Analyzed, with the Exception of Impact to R16, Which Was Already at Level 4*

| Risk | Likelihood | Impact |
| --- | --- | --- |
| R11: Information is not adequately protected from malicious code. | 3 → 4 | 3 → 4 |
| R16: Data at rest is not encrypted. | 3 → 4 | 4 No change |

# Vulnerability Management and Attack Detection Testing

Detection capabilities necessary to alert the cybersecurity team of an attack in progress do not exist in this IT environment. One pressing issue is the lack of technical tools and processes to detect and remediate known vulnerabilities. This makes it easier for attackers to initiate attacks. Often, older vulnerabilities have exploits readily available. Once a foothold is established, no mechanisms exist for the entity to detect lateral movement and changes to credentials elevating the attacker's privileges, which leads to the compromise of locations where ePHI is stored. Figure 10-4 again highlights the inverse relationship of control maturity and likelihood of successful exploit, which causes risk severity to increase.

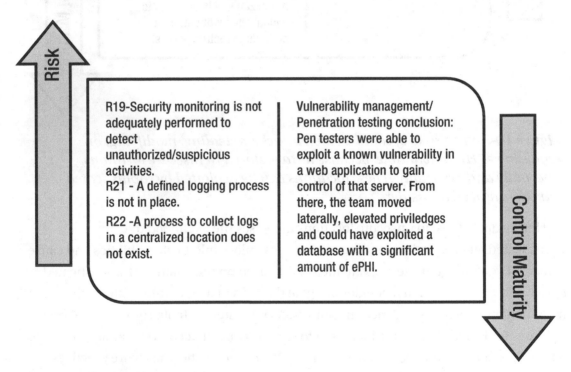

**Figure 10-4.** *The inability of the entity to detect and/or remediate known vulnerabilities decreased the maturity of the detect-and-respond cybersecurity controls. This increases the risks to ePHI*

Based on the testing and increased understanding of cybersecurity capabilities, all three of these risks must be increased to level 5 for likelihood and impact. This results in each risk moving closer to the upper right-hand quadrant of the heat map in the grid reserved for high risks. Figure 10-4 displays the risks prior to the testing performed, and Figure 10-5 shows the risks moving from moderate to high grids on the heat map after the testing is complete and results are analyzed.

| Risk Matrix | | | | | | | |
|---|---|---|---|---|---|---|---|
| | Very High 5 | | | | | R9, R10, R12, R21 | R19,R22 |
| **Impact** | High 4 | | | | R16 | R15, R28 | |
| | Moderate 3 | | | | R6,R11 | | |
| | | 1 | 2 | 3 | 4 | 5 | |
| | | | | **Likelihood** | | | |

**Figure 10-5.** *The risk categories tested include three in the moderate category, six high risks, and two very high risks*

The access issues, lack of monitoring controls, and risks related to data not protected at rest lead to the conclusion that risks R11 and R16 should be assessed as high risks, and R6, R9, R10, R12, and R21 should be re-measured and moved from high risk grids on the heat map to very high risk grids. The ease attackers would have in infiltrating the network and moving without any detection capabilities alerting the entity to an attack warrant these conclusions (see Figure 10-6).

| Risk Matrix | | | | | | |
|---|---|---|---|---|---|---|
| | Very High 5 | | | | | R6, R9,R10,R12,R19,R21, R22 |
| **Impact** | High | | | | R11, R16 | |
| | | Very Low 1 | Low 2 | Moderate 3 | High 4 | Very High 5 |
| | | | | **Likelihood** | | |

**Figure 10-6.** *After testing is completed, two risks are identified as high and seven are moved into the very high category*

137

# Summary

Technical testing is an important part of the risk analysis, risk assessment, and cybersecurity program. Placing tight controls around access, especially privileged access, is important. The cybersecurity kill chain highlights privilege escalation as the key step in successfully breaching sensitive data. Another basic element of cybersecurity program management is managing vulnerabilities. The WannaCry outbreak showcased what happens when older vulnerabilities are not identified and patched. Establishing a process to address this necessity is a prerequisite to implementing any sophisticated cyber-defense capabilities. Sophisticated attackers are smart and focus on the path of least resistance into a network. Many times, those are end users, but if vulnerabilities with published and available exploits exist, these examples might be lower cost ways to breach a network. When the organization is ready for real-life test scenarios, testing the capabilities of the cybersecurity program via red team assessments delivers insights into the ways attackers can avoid detection once inside an entity's system. With so many avenues available to intrude on a network, it is important to focus attention on detecting and responding to these intrusions.

# PART III

# Applying the Results to Everyday Needs

# CHAPTER 11

# Refreshing the Risk Register

After everything completed thus far, it is a good time to pause and update the risk analysis. At this point, several circumstances have changed, based on what was learned during the testing phase. Most of the initial iteration was completed using what is known about the environment. This was followed by testing several key areas, to understand deeper characteristics of the IT systems. This means that several adjustments to risk severity are required. This is the process outlined from the beginning. As new details are learned about the environment and IT systems processing ePHI, risk analysis updates are required. The cycles for this process can be annual, continuous, or in whatever manner fits the entity's needs. The key is to establish a process and consistently follow the documented process.

## Updating the Risk Register

Each of the following functional areas lists risks to ePHI. Several changes were made to risks in the protect and detect functions, and risks in the other functions did not change. The status of all the risks are displayed in Tables 11-1 through 11-5.

## Identify

No changes were made to the risks in this function. Several require attention, and details of those specific activities are outlined in Chapter 17. Two examples are data not being managed, based on its classification, and cybersecurity not being funded to effectively achieve its objectives.

© Eric C. Thompson 2017
E. C. Thompson, *Building a HIPAA-Compliant Cybersecurity Program*,
https://doi.org/10.1007/978-1-4842-3060-2_11

***Table 11-1.*** *Identified Risks That Are Aligned to Gaps in Cybersecurity Capabilities Found in the Identify Function*

| No. | Threat Actor | Vulnerability | Likelihood | Impact |
|-----|--------------|---------------|------------|--------|
| R1 | Malicious Insider | ID.1: An up-to-date inventory of physical assets does not exist. IT ownership and accountability for information assets is not clearly defined and documented. | 3 | 3 |
| R2 | Sophisticated Attackers | ID.2: Data is not managed based on its classification requirements. | 3 | 4 |
| R3 | Sophisticated Attackers | ID.3: Cybersecurity is not appropriately funded to effectively maintain and support business objectives. Compliance gaps are not monitored or resolved in a timely manner. | 4 | 4 |
| R4 | Malicious Insider | ID.4: Legal and regulatory compliance requirements are not adequately integrated into policies and procedures. | 4 | 3 |

# Protect

Five risks were elevated in this function. The key ingredient missing was proper access management. Access to applications, database, and network devices that have ePHI in motion, in use, and at rest must be controlled. If access is not restricted to as few individuals as necessary, risk of a breach increases.

*Table 11-2.* *Risks in Boldface Increased, Based on Results of Testing Performed*

| No. | Threat Actor | Vulnerability | Likelihood | Impact |
|-----|--------------|---------------|------------|--------|
| R5 | Sophisticated Attackers | PV.1: Infrastructure and applications are inappropriately configured. | 4 | 4 |
| R6 | Malicious Insider | PV.2: Code changes are not tested for vulnerabilities and other bugs. | 3 | 3 |
| R7 | Malicious Insider | PV.3: Access to source code is not effectively controlled. | 3 | 3 |
| R8 | Malicious Insider | PV.4: Standard time lines to remediate vulnerabilities are not established. | 3 | 4 |
| **R9** | **Sophisticated Attackers** | **PV.5: Application access management is ineffectively managed.** | **5** | **5\*** |
| **R10** | **Sophisticated Attackers** | **PV.6: Database access management is ineffectively managed.** | **5** | **5\*** |
| **R11** | **Sophisticated Attackers** | **PV.7: Information is not adequately protected from malicious code.** | **4** | **4** |
| **R12** | **Sophisticated Attackers** | **PV.8: Network access management is ineffectively managed.** | **5** | **5\*** |
| R13 | Sophisticated Attackers | PV.9: The organization does not have an up-to-date network security infrastructure. | 4 | 5 |
| R14 | Malicious Insider | PV.10: Responsibilities are not segregated within the organization. | 3 | 3 |

(*continued*)

*Table 11-2.* (*continued*)

| No. | Threat Actor | Vulnerability | Likelihood | Impact |
|-----|--------------|---------------|------------|--------|
| **R15** | **Sophisticated Attacker** | **PV.11: Security education and awareness training is not adequate for workforce members to understand threats posed to ePHI.** | **4\*** | **5** |
| **R16** | **Sophisticated Attacker** | **PV.12: Data at rest is not encrypted.** | **4** | **4\*** |
| R17 | Sophisticated Attacker | PV.13: Protected health information is used in development and testing environments. | 3 | 5 |
| R18 | Malicious Insider | PV.14: Secure disposal of media is not adequately performed. | 4 | 5 |
| R28 | Sophisticated Attacker/ Malicious Insider | PV.12: Due diligence is not conducted on vendors with access to ePHI prior to executing business agreements. | 4 | 4 |

*\*Value did not change due to testing performed.*

# Detect

The ability to detect an intrusion is a significant capability necessary to reduce risk. Developing policies and procedures outlining what must be logged, where logs are kept, and how to utilize logs for detection purposes are key elements of this capability. The risks in boldface highlight these missing functions, which are all rated at the highest level possible.

*Table 11-3.* *Risks in Boldface Increased, Based on Results of Testing Performed*

| No. | Threat Actor | Vulnerability | Likelihood | Impact |
|-----|--------------|---------------|------------|--------|
| **R19** | **Sophisticated Attacker** | **DE.1: Security monitoring is not adequately performed to detect unauthorized/suspicious activities.** | **5** | **5\*** |
| R20 | Sophisticated Attacker | DE.2: Security incidents are not adequately logged and reported for investigations. | 3 | 5 |
| **R21** | **Sophisticated Attacker** | **DE.3: A defined logging process is not in place.** | **5** | **5\*** |
| **R22** | **Sophisticated Attacker** | **DE.4: A process to collect logs in a centralized location does not exist.** | **5** | **5\*** |

*\*Value did not change, owing due to testing performed.*

# Respond

Changes to the risks in this functional domain were documented after testing was performed. This is attributed to the monitoring capabilities missing, which, if not present, do not generate necessary alerts to trigger the response process. An argument can be made to increase the risk rating for R25, because an incident response plan is not documented. A risk practitioner conducting the analysis for another entity might conclude that this missing capability leads to increased risk to the confidentiality, integrity, and availability of ePHI. If an attack occurred, an inappropriate response might allow the attack to do more damage. This illustrates how decisions made during the risk analysis by one practitioner lead to conclusions different from those of another practitioner conducting the analysis with the same information. Neither choice is necessarily right or wrong. It is an entity-level decision, which is why this risk remains moderate for now.

***Table 11-4.*** *Identified Risks That Are Aligned to Gaps in Cybersecurity Capabilities Found in the Respond Function. Risks in Boldface Increased, Based on Results of Testing Performed*

| No. | Threat Actor | Vulnerability | Likelihood | Impact |
|-----|-------------|---------------|------------|--------|
| R23 | Sophisticated Attackers | RE.1: Security incidents do not incorporate challenges and lessons learned. | 3 | 4 |
| R24 | Malicious Insider | RE.2: Availability requirements to support the business are not defined. | 3 | 3 |
| **R25** | **Sophisticated Attacker** | **RE.3: An incident response plan has not been documented or tested.** | **4** | **4** |

# Recover

No adjustments were made in this domain, because none of the capabilities aligned with these risks were tested.

***Table 11-5.*** *Identified Risks That Are Aligned to Gaps in Cybersecurity Capabilities Found in the Respond Function*

| No. | Threat Actor | Vulnerability | Likelihood | Impact |
|-----|-------------|---------------|------------|--------|
| R26 | Sophisticated Attacker | RC.1: Recovery strategies are not updated annually. | 3 | 2 |
| R27 | Sophisticated Attacker | RC.2: Recover plans do not incorporate lessons learned. | 2 | 2 |

# Risk Heat Map Updated

Now that the nontechnical and technical testing is complete, the risk register is updated, and an updated heat map is created. Figure 11-1, when compared to the heat map shown in Chapter 8, shows a significant shift in risks to the upper-rightmost quadrant, where the high and very high risks are located. These risks are the most damaging to the entity and patients whose information was not protected, if exploited. When considering risk remediation projects, these risks require immediate consideration.

| Risk Matrix | | | | | |
|---|---|---|---|---|---|
| **Impact** | **Very High**<br>5 | Very Low | Low | R17, R20 | **High**<br>R13, R18 | **Very High**<br>R9,R10,R12,R15,<br>R19,R21,R22 |
| | **High**<br>4 | Very Low | Low | R2, R8,R23 | **High**<br>R3, R5,<br>R15,R16,R28 | Very High |
| | **Moderate**<br>3 | Very Low | Low | R1, R6, R7, R11,<br>R14, R24, R25 | Moderate<br>R4 | High |
| | **Low**<br>2 | Very Low | Low<br>R27 | Low | Low | Moderate |
| | **Very Low**<br>1 | Very Low | Very Low | Very Low | Low | Low |
| | | **Very Low**<br>1 | **Low**<br>2 | **Moderate**<br>3 | **High**<br>4 | **Very High**<br>5 |
| | | **Likelihood** | | | | |

***Figure 11-1.***  *The final version of the heat map, with risks displayed after technical and nontechnical testing was performed*

# Summary

A key point stated throughout this book is that risk analysis does not end. At any point, new information must be ingested, and the risk analysis updated. In this case, pulling all available information together to assess the risks to ePHI that was created in Chapter 8 gets the process off to the right start. Once the initial analysis is complete, additional work is required to enhance the value of the risk analysis. If a hypothesis is formed that access management is not controlled, a prudent next action is testing the process, to understand how pervasive the lack of control is in the systems that interact with ePHI. It is also difficult to communicate expected remediation activities without quantitative information.

The testing results led to increases in the severity of several risks. These increases are the result of detailed information gleaned from completed tests, which otherwise would go unnoticed.

# CHAPTER 12

# The Cybersecurity Road Map

After focusing on identifying and measuring risks to ePHI, the next two chapters focus on laying out short- and long-term plans for the cybersecurity program. Risk analysis and assessment guides cybersecurity leaders toward protecting the most sensitive and important assets and gives clarity to the current state of the program. The key objective of cybersecurity leaders inside healthcare providers, payers, and business associates is protecting ePHI. This is accomplished by reducing cyber risk, assisting the organization in complying with the HIPAA Security Rule, and identifying new risks. To set the program up for success, those in charge of cybersecurity need a clear idea of what the program should ultimately look like. In *The 7 Habits of Highly Effective People* (Free Press, 1989), Stephen R. Covey refers to this as to "beginning with the end in mind," and David Allen, in his book *Getting Things Done* (Penguin, 2001), describes it as outcome-focused thinking. It is nearly impossible to be successful without some idea of what the program should look like in three to five years; however, thinking five years out in the cybersecurity world is nearly impossible. Effective road maps focus on a balance of best-in-class capabilities, combined with investments focused on the greatest amount of risk reduction.

## Defining the Cybersecurity Strategy

The cybersecurity strategy, the "what will be accomplished" and "how it will be accomplished," is defined here based on protecting ePHI from unauthorized use and disclosure. Figure 12-1 highlights the objectives of the cybersecurity program to increase maturity and capabilities that reduce risk, protect ePHI, and achieve regulatory compliance.

149

© Eric C. Thompson 2017
E. C. Thompson, *Building a HIPAA-Compliant Cybersecurity Program*,
https://doi.org/10.1007/978-1-4842-3060-2_12

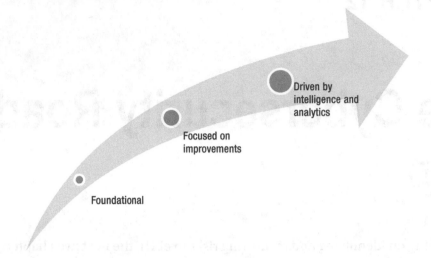

**Figure 12-1.** *These sample high-level objectives represent graphically the objectives of the cybersecurity program to improve the program, in order to reduce risk to ePHI*

The key success factors needed to reach each objective in the road map are outlined in Figure 12-2. The first step requires establishing a solid foundation of cybersecurity capabilities. These are measured by reaching specific targets in each subcategory of the NIST CSF, the framework chosen here. These targets include documenting expectations of each subcategory in the cybersecurity policy and associated procedure documents and that the processes established operate effectively.

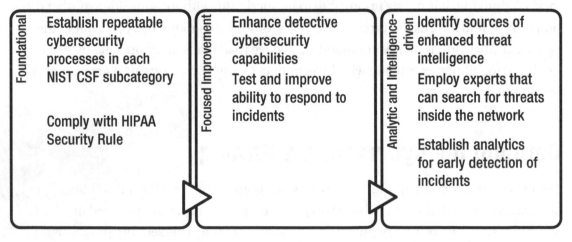

**Figure 12-2.** *The objectives of the cybersecurity program include three milestones, with key indicators of success targeted for each objective*

Eventually, the cybersecurity program must focus on specific functions in which the most significant investment is made. Until the program is established to a point where this focus can be achieved, balance is required. Investing in world-class protection technology while allowing detect and respond capabilities to remain subpar does not enhance, but likely diminishes, the program's ability to protect ePHI. The same concept holds true for focusing solely on detecting or responding to attacks. If protection mechanisms are not operating at an acceptable level, allowing very basic exploits to breach the IT systems, the detection capabilities are never going to provide the expected benefits. Management must ensure that compliance requirements are baked into this milestone. As the key capabilities necessary for building foundational cybersecurity capabilities are designed, the necessary safeguards of the HIPAA Security Rule must stay top of mind.

Once the first milestone is reached, the second, which is focused improvement, is launched. This program intends to establish and improve detective and response capabilities, taking specific subcategories beyond the operational level. Objectives differ across entities. This objective might be improving governance or protection. It is based on the cybersecurity program goals, objectives, and strategy and the milestones that must be reached.

Finally, in this three-year road map, the final objective, analytic and intelligence-driven, requires building a team to incorporate threat intelligence into security processes and building analytics profiles to detect potential incidents earlier than the current standard.

Milestones are important. These indicators communicate to the cybersecurity team and business leaders the progress at a point in time. Governance items, such as creating policies and procedures, require a stake in the ground at the 90-day mark. Basic cybersecurity capabilities require implementation goals at the end of year one. Examples include vulnerability scanning, virus and malware defense, and hardening IT assets. Gaining lift from these initial priorities generates momentum heading into the second year and more complex projects.

# The Three-Year Road Map

The three-year road map defines the vision of the cybersecurity program, which is to protect ePHI by surrounding it with world-class detection and response capabilities, comply with HIPAA, and meet the expectations of other third-party stakeholders. The milestones necessary to achieve this outcome include

- Establishing and maintaining fundamental capabilities by investing in people, processes, and technology required to meet baseline protections regulators would expect

- Investing in specific enhancements, targeting areas of the cybersecurity program to achieve the highest level of risk reduction possible

- Upgrading and investing further into people, processes, and technology, enabling proactive deployment of resources through analytics and intelligence-gathering

This three-year road map focuses on these milestones to one day become an intelligence-driven program. The third milestone, if incomplete at the end of year three, does not mean failure of the road map and the projects within it. Unforeseen events and shifting priorities cause milestone adjustment, so it is important to view the road map as a fluid plan that is flexible enough to absorb change while keeping efforts and resources pointed toward the entities objectives.

# Foundational

What does a foundational cybersecurity program look like? For this purpose, "foundational" means meeting the objectives defined when creating the cybersecurity function. If the cybersecurity program must protect the confidentiality, integrity, and availability of ePHI, then foundational refers to the entity having in place the capabilities any reasonable person would expect to see in that environment. Each subcategory has unique criteria to meet this milestone, but it is expected that each has policy statements, procedures outlined, and owners identified to carry out the expected processes.

## How to Measure Cybersecurity Capabilities Against Foundational Requirements?

Earlier, *foundational* was defined based on the PRISMA model created by NIST. As a reminder, this scale is used to measure each subcategory of the NIST CSF, more specifically, the controls documented and put into operation to meet the purpose of each subcategory, to place a value on the maturity of the control. The scale requires documentation of each control in the cybersecurity policy, and procedures outlining how each control is placed into operation. On the cybersecurity road map, the milestones for these measures ideally are met within the first 90 days.

## Identify

The NIST CSF is intuitive and encourages entities to build cybersecurity programs and potentially think of cybersecurity sequentially. The identify function seeks to accomplish the following:

- Identify and prioritize all hardware and software assets, which is completed with the risk analysis. Entities must know where ePHI is stored, processed, and transmitted by hardware and software and document each example.

- Policies are written, reviewed, and approved by management through a cybersecurity governance or steering committee.

- Risk analysis and management standards are established, risks and remediation steps are reviewed, and risk tolerances are created by the governance committee.

- Cybersecurity objectives are aligned with business objectives to enhance the function's ability to meet the needs of the organization.

The last bullet point is often overlooked when building cybersecurity programs. This happens when IT, cybersecurity, and the business operate in silos. This prevents the sharing of business objectives with cybersecurity. It is impossible for cybersecurity to meet the business's needs. One way to illustrate how business objectives and cybersecurity work together is illustrated in Figure 12-3. This concept is taught sometimes when introducing enterprise risk management (ERM), most common when introducing the COSO framework.

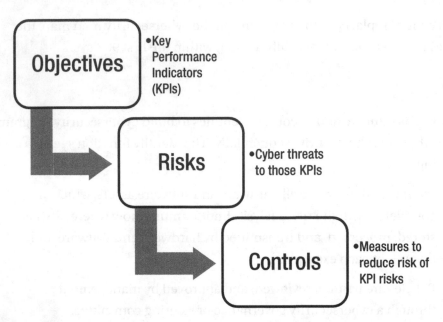

**Figure 12-3.** *This step-down figure shows the flow of risks in an entity, from business objectives to controls from a cybersecurity perspective*

---

**Note**    The Committee of Sponsoring Organizations (COSO) of the Treadway Commission developed a framework to assist organizations, their boards of directors, and other stakeholders to develop, manage, and monitor internal controls designed to mitigate the potential for adverse outcomes related to organizational objectives.

---

To be most effective, management at healthcare providers, payers, and business associates must share short-term and long-term business objectives with their cybersecurity teams. Examples might include those in Table 12-1. These are very high-level examples of missions and objectives each type of entity may focus on to meet revenue and profit targets.

---

[1]James DeLoach and Jeff Thomson (Committee of Sponsoring Organizations of the Treadway Commission), "Improving Organizational Performance and Governance," www.coso.org/Documents/2014-2-10-COSO-Thought-Paper.pdf, February 10, 2014.

***Table 12-1.*** *Examples of Business Objectives Each Type of Entity Has Toward Protecting ePHI That Need to Be Met*

| Entity Type | Objective |
| --- | --- |
| Healthcare Provider | Provide high-quality care to all in the community while reducing costs of care. |
| Health Insurance Payer | Deliver responsive and timely service to all insured families. |
| Business Associate | Uphold the trust of our clients while ensuring that each receives the services expected of a trusted business adviser. |

In the preceding examples, not taking proper precautions to secure ePHI is not in alignment with each mission and may cause the entities in question not to meet financial targets. Suffering a breach and exposing health information is counter to providing high-quality care or being responsive to members' needs or a trusted business partner.

## Protect

The protect function is the largest in the NIST that is focused on the necessary protections to keep unauthorized users from viewing, changing, or destroying ePHI. The spectrum of controls covered in this function include

- *Access controls*: For security and compliance purposes, access must be controlled at all layers.

  - *Network*: The firewalls, routers, and switches from which ePHI flows

  - *Operating system*: Administrators with group access and local accounts

  - *Database*: ePHI at rest makes this critical.

  - *Application*: ePHI is in use.

  - *Remote access*: This privilege should be granted sparingly.

Access control is a must, and its importance cannot be understated. Any environments with ePHI require strict procedures to be followed, before provisioning access to systems with ePHI. The more users with access to a system with ePHI, the higher the risk of a breach. The severity of the risk depends on how effectively the controls governing access are operating.

- Training and Awareness

  - All employees and nonemployees must complete awareness training geared toward handling ePHI and complying with the HIPAA Security and Privacy Rules.

  - Reminders enforcing topics the entity considers high-risk have to be sent.

  - Nonemployees, contractors, and vendors must complete the same training and awareness requirements as employees.

  - Compliance with required training is tracked and enforced for all categories of workforce members, employees, and nonemployees.

- Data Protection

  - Data in use, motion, and at rest is protected.

  - Data in use requires a mechanism such as end point protection, to prevent users from moving data to portable devices, cut-and-pasting data, or printing data.

  - Data in motion requires that monitoring capabilities, such as DLP, are used to detect ePHI traversing the network or attempting to leave the entity in unsecured manners. These solutions allow the entity either to stop the traffic from leaving, alert the cybersecurity team, and/or automatically encrypt the data, to prevent unauthorized use.

  - Data at rest requires encryption to provide the highest level of assurance that it is protected, in addition to encrypting laptops and other mobile devices through end point solutions or an add-on to a DLP solution. Encryption controls are often lacking in databases, data warehouses, or other repositories where data is at rest. Cost and performance are common issues preventing these controls.

- Information protection

  - Configuration management

  - Data backup

  - Change management/change control

  - Vulnerability management

  - Data destruction

  - Human resources role in cybersecurity

- Maintenance

- Protective Technology

  - Securing communication networks

  - Implementing logging

# Detect

- Anomalies and Events

  - Detect events are analyzed, and data is aggregated, thresholds to identify incidents are established, and impacts of events are known.

- Security Monitoring

  - Network and physical environments are monitored to detect events and cyber intrusions. This includes security event log monitoring.

  - Personal activity is monitored and malware detected, mobile code is detected, vulnerability scans are performed and monitored, and vendors' access from outside is monitored. The network can detect unauthorized connections of rogue devices.

- Detection process

  - Roles, responsibilities, and accountability are outlined, processes are tested, detections are communicated, and the process is continually improved.

## Respond

- Response plans are executed, and communications plans include roles, responsibilities, and appropriate communications to stakeholders.

- Information is shared, and coordination with shareholders occurs.

- Notification of events occurs, events are analyzed, and impacts are understood.

- Forensics are performed.

- Incidents are categorized, contained, and mitigated.

## Recover

- Recovery plans exist and are tested, and the lessons learned are incorporated.

# Focused Improvement

This next phase focuses the cybersecurity program on capabilities it desires to excel at. It is not possible to achieve best-in-class capabilities in every subcategory or function of the NIST CSF framework. Entities need a defensive game plan. The plan here is to focus on detection and response capabilities to protect health information. The subjects discussed in this section highlight some areas entities can focus monitoring activities on when improving these functions.

## Revisiting the Kill Chain

During the risk analysis, adjustments are made to risks caused by inadequate training, awareness, monitoring and response processes and capabilities, and because attackers can easily move from initial exploit to exfiltrating ePHI. This is outlined in the cyber kill chain developed by Mandiant (now FireEye). Figure 12-4 displays how vulnerabilities chained together and downstream from one another in the attack vector are riskier than stand-alone vulnerabilities and risks. The same approach is useful when focusing on improving the program.

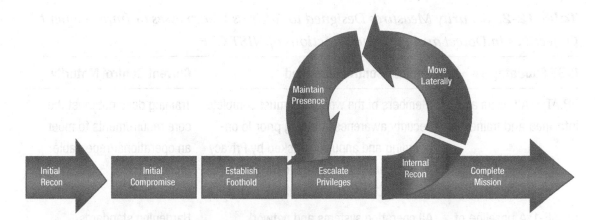

**Figure 12-4.** *The figure developed by Mandiant (now FireEye) highlights the vectors many intrusions take when attackers gain entry and move through the network, until the objectives are completed*

How would an improvement plan be created using this diagram, and the risks identified? Several improvements that should be made stand out.

- Immaturity of the training and awareness function

- Nonexistence of baseline configuration standards

- Insufficient vulnerability management

- Missing capabilities to monitor users and the network for anomalous behavior

- No process for collecting, storing, or correlating logs to generate security alerts

Recalling the risks identified during the analysis, Table 12-2 highlights the NIST subcategory, control, and current maturity of process.

***Table 12-2.*** *Security Measures Designed to Address Weaknesses or Improvement Objectives in Detect and Respond Functions of NIST CSF*

| NIST Subcategory | Internal Control Identified | Current Control Maturity |
|---|---|---|
| PR.AT-1: All users are informed and trained. | Members of the workforce must complete security awareness training prior to on-boarding and annually, tracked by Privacy Department and reported to the InfoSec Steering Committee annually. | Training does not meet the core requirements to meet an operational/repeatable process. |
| DE.AE-1: A baseline of network operations and expected data flows for users and systems is established and managed. | All operating systems and network hardware are configured in alignment with the Center for Internet Security (CIS) Standards and monitored monthly by the network security engineer to detect noncompliance. | Hardening standards, baseline configurations, and normalized traffic patterns are not established, documented, and understood. |
| PR.AC-4: Access permissions are managed, incorporating the principles of least privilege and separation of duties. | Access to system resources requires approval from the system owner, must be provisioned by a member of the information security team, and reviewed periodically for appropriateness. | Access management is very immature at this point and represents a very high risk to ePHI. |
| DE.CM-1: The network is monitored to detect potential cybersecurity events. | The network boundary is protected by appropriate technology (firewalls, IDS) that is monitored by the security administration team for anomalous indicators. | Monitoring of network traffic and monitoring for anomalous behavior are not established. |
| DE.CM-3: Personnel activity is monitored to detect potential cybersecurity events. | Monitoring capabilities are identified and implemented by the security administrator, to monitor end-user behavior and potential threats to the organization. | User behavior is not monitored, and risky behaviors or understanding of typical operations are not present and monitored. |

The purpose of identifying these five controls and capabilities is to focus the cybersecurity program on tipping points in the kill chain. These are the points at which there is potential to detect and stop an attack. Most successful attacks follow the pattern laid out in Figure 12-4, and state-sponsored and criminal organizations carrying out attacks against computer networks are concerning to government officials, security practitioners, and business leaders, because these groups are good at very simple things.

- They can trick end users into opening documents and links laced with malware or designed to entice them to give up network credentials.

- They discover network devices accessible via the Internet.

- They find devices with unpatched vulnerabilities.

- They find accounts belonging to terminated users that are either active or disabled that can be leveraged during a breach.

- They conduct internal reconnaissance, mapping the network, because basic tools, if present, are not monitored or fully utilized.

- They exfiltrate data via usual ports 80 or 443, which are never detected.

These examples are not meant to imply that protecting ePHI is easy or predictable but that the idea of how sophisticated these attackers can be requires a disclaimer, which is that they work smart, and if entities want to make it easy for them, they will seize this opportunity.

## Training and Awareness

Transforming end users from a vulnerability to a detection capability requires moving away from traditional security awareness training. Typically, this annual exercise is characterized by users clicking through a presentation and taking a test to check a box. This adds no value to end users or the organization. Building awareness requires consistent and frequent interaction to transform users to early detectors of attacks.

Building awareness is accomplished by utilizing focused training, centered on a key topic, such as phishing or social media. To balance the increased frequency, duration of each training module must decrease. Cybersecurity leaders cannot expect the business to support multiple training sessions lasting more than an hour. That is too much time and not an efficient use of it. The SANS Institute, in its Securing the Human guidance, states that once the 15-minute duration is reached, the level of retention and effectiveness diminishes.

Testing users with real-life examples also drives key points home. Phishing is a popular topic, making it easier to test end users' ability to identify phishing attempts and report them. Conducting regular exercises, either monthly or bimonthly, develops the following skills and capabilities:

- *Increased prevention*: One benefit is that members of the workforce are less likely to open and click anything inside a suspicious e-mail.

- End users learn where to report suspicious e-mails, as alerting the cybersecurity team that users could be targets of an attack is better than deleting the e-mail and saying nothing.

- *Reduction in reporting time*: The quicker suspected phishing is reported, the quicker mitigating actions are taken.

To be effective, metrics must be identified and tracked to measure user behaviors the entity seeks to correct. SANS Securing the Human[2] offers many resources assisting organizations to identify metrics that measure effectiveness. If a phishing simulation tool is used as a teaching tool, metrics concerning the numbers of users failing the test should be collected. Other behaviors should also be tracked, such as the following:

- Incidents identifying data at rest that are not in compliance with security standards

- Data blocked by e-mail gateway preventing ePHI or other sensitive information from leaving the network

- Number of policy violations investigated

Reaching the highest levels of the detect function requires a training and awareness program focused on teaching end users how to be the first lines of defense. End users have an ability to discover suspicious activity and alert security professionals when things out of the ordinary occur.

---

[2]SANS: Securing the Human, https://securingthehuman.sans.org, 2010–2017.

## Baseline Configurations

Adopting hardening standards is key, because the potential for misconfiguration can lead to vulnerable situations. Without comprehensive scanning, these situations are not known to cybersecurity, unless it happens to stumble across them, or an exploit occurs. The CIS created standards for many Windows and Linux platforms, firewalls, and other network equipment. Documenting hardening requirements in policy and procedure documents is the first step, but regular monitoring of configurations is also required. Vulnerability solutions, such as Tenable's Nessus scanner, can complete hardening scans regularly.

Besides regular scanning, solutions exist that alert cybersecurity teams to changes in configurations, so that those changes can be investigated.

## Boundary Security

Network boundaries are protected by firewalls, intrusion detection systems, web proxy filters, e-mail gateways, and more. These are foundational capabilities and technologies. Creating a cybersecurity program approaching an intelligence-driven program, outlined in phase 3 of the road map, requires these capabilities to exist. During focused improvement, the objective is to analyze the people, process, and technology behind these subcategories for two things. Is this current capability reducing the risks to ePHI sufficiently? Technical tools are required, but people and process considerations should be understood before any investments are made. Implementing a new intrusion detection system (IDS) or a security incident and event management (SIEM) solution will not make a difference if cybersecurity analysts do not understand why alerts are generated or what to do with alerts when they come to the analyst. Analysts must understand that they require sufficient investigation and should be closed, once it is concluded no risk exists. Closing the alert means documentation of the investigation steps, and details examined must be documented and archived. If applicable, lessons learned must be included. Finally, a process for reviewing the effectiveness of changes is also worth consideration. Otherwise, the entity may not be aware when changes to a process are not implemented properly. These characteristics assist the cybersecurity program in its mission to reduce risk to ePHI and ensure that investments made in monitoring the network boundary are fully utilized.

## Monitoring End-User Activity

Insider threats, the malicious employees and nonemployees in the organization, require as much attention as threats looming outside the network. These individuals ignore policies and view governance requirements as a hindrance to getting things done. Other insider threats include disgruntled end users, hidden inside cubicles, who feel the entity owes them something, and they decide to take it.

# Intelligence and Analytics-Driven Security

Using intelligence and analytics to drive the cybersecurity program can mean many things. The outcomes desired are reducing the time it takes to detect intrusions and limiting the potential impact. Here the objective is that during the third year, the cybersecurity team can identify and search for indicators of compromise (IOCs) in the IT environment, understand what assets are most at risk, and if an incident does occur, quickly understand what happened and what is the impact to the organization. Key activities required at this level include:

- Continuously monitoring traffic, user behavior, and establishing a baseline for the environment

- Obtaining contextual intelligence, which elevates to real-life information seen at other entities

- Using sandbox environments to learn attackers' tactics, techniques, and procedures to better deploy defensive resources.

- Placing decoys in the network designed to gather better intelligence about an attacker's methods.

## Threat Intelligence

The number of vendors offering actionable threat intelligence, designed to enhance protection, detection and response capabilities, has grown the last few years. These solutions are costly, either requiring significant capital investments or annual subscription expenses. It is still unclear whether these solutions deliver returns that justify the associated investments and costs.

## Machine Learning and Artificial Intelligence

Machine learning comes in two forms: supervised and unsupervised. Unsupervised machine learning and artificial intelligence allow for the security tools—normally, behavior-based-analytics and anomaly detection—to learn the IT environment on its own. These solutions are supposed to be more effective than signature-based ones, because it is more difficult for attackers to obfuscate malware to avoid detection. These solutions are beginning to gain a foothold in cybersecurity, with a significant number of vendors offering products and solutions in this space. Transitioning toward machine learning and AI solutions should be gradual and based on risk-reduction efforts.

## Threat Analysis and Reverse Engineering

Threat analysis is a full-time job, and being able to reverse engineer malware and extract indicators of compromise requires talent and experience. There is intelligence to be gathered and benefits gained when an entity can immediately isolate an e-mail that got past solutions meant to stop it and learn how the malware acts once launched. Those details are useful for searching the IT systems for other incidents. The problem is that this can be a full-time activity, and most organizations cannot spare full-time resources to focus solely on this task. Before an organization can consider implementing this function in-house, many capabilities must be operating effectively and there must be staff who can absorb the workload. The most practical way to establish this process is to engage with a third party that executes the necessary steps and reports on developments when necessary.

## Decoys

Decoys are another way for mature entities to collect actionable intelligence on their own. Honeypots and honeynets are two of the most common examples. Architecting honeypots can take several forms. Entities can place a web server outside of the DMZ, with an adjacent IP address, and when configured properly, record the actions of attackers, to understand how adversaries launch attacks. In VM environments, decoy servers can be placed between production servers, to capture intelligence as well. The intelligence gathered is meant to supplement other intelligence feeds and capabilities designed to enhance the detect and respond functions. Again, vendors offering these types of services are increasing and ready. It might be worth investigating if any product offerings meet the organization's needs.

## Addressing HIPAA Security Rule Requirements

Addressing people, process, and technology needs for each subcategory, meaning that policies and controls exist for each subcategory and the controls are operating as expected, ultimately contributes to addressing the requirements of the HIPAA Security Rule.

# Summary

The road map conveys a narrative, describing what the cybersecurity team wants the program to look like at a point in time. Vision, mission, strategy, or other synonyms are used to describe the creation of this document and the role it plays. Rather than focus on the form, the substance is what is important. The road map verbally, graphically, and pictorially describes what the program intends to accomplish, and to be effective, it must be outcome-focused. This is done by following principles of execution, such as those put forward by Chris McChesney and Sean Covey in *The 4 Disciplines of Execution* (FranklinCovey, 2012). In the book, the authors describe four key components to successful execution. Planning a cybersecurity program means

- Clearly defining what success looks like in the road map

  - Ensure that all subcategories have defined policies and procedures and that the processes are implemented effectively.

  - Identify key subcategories for improvement by the end of the second year.

  - Make sure that the detect and response functions are near best-in-class. Additional investment in people, process, and technology must be made, and management must identify metrics to measure success and review the operation of the functions annually, to define additional objectives for improvement.

- Measuring the program annually, not in the third year of the road map

  - The preceding key objectives listed must be assessed annually, to ensure that the required improvements are on pace to meet objective dates.

- If investments and changes in either the fundamental requirements or targeted improvements are not on pace to meet the deadlines, adjustments must be made to ensure that objectives are met.

- Reporting regularly

  - Dashboards outlining the objectives and metrics that determine success should be shared regularly with team members, management, and other stakeholders.

- Integrating success factors into performance

  - Control and process owners must be held accountable for effective operation; otherwise, the processes break down and objectives are not met.

The road map is important because, to be successful, a cybersecurity program leader must know where he or she wants to take the program. This is not something consultants or colleagues can provide; it comes from within the leader. The specific details of people, process, and technology can be leveraged from others, once the picture of what success looks like is painted by the leader.

# PART IV

# Continuous Improvement

# CHAPTER 13

# Investing for Risk Reduction

Limited resources are a fundamental concept of economics, and tough decisions about how to deploy those resources must be made. Examples can include choosing one technology over another, or choosing between technology and head count. This is especially true for cybersecurity programs at healthcare providers, insurance payers, and business associates, where budgets and resources are often limited. This shines a light on why conducting regular risk analysis and assessment exercises is important. Decisions on how to utilize limited resources must focus risk-based deployment. Some choices are made because of the effect on reducing multiple risks, others because a significant risk is reduced by the investment.

## Arbitrary Benchmarks and Other Budget Fallacies

Examples exist of entities measuring spending on cybersecurity against peers in the same sector, based on a percentage of the IT budget. Executives also like to understand what cybersecurity should cost and at what point the spending on new technology or increased staff ends, because the program is sufficient to protect ePHI. Spending may not always continue at the same rate, especially if the program has to rapidly mature some subcategories, but spending on cybersecurity never has an end date. Finally, when funds are allocated for cybersecurity needs, purchasing technology-based solutions require thoughtful consideration and understanding of other budgetary impacts besides the capital investment. Basic solutions go underutilized when purchased without consideration for additional head count or staff augmentation.

© Eric C. Thompson 2017
E. C. Thompson, *Building a HIPAA-Compliant Cybersecurity Program*,
https://doi.org/10.1007/978-1-4842-3060-2_13

## Cybersecurity As a Percentage of Total IT Spend

A popular topic debated among cybersecurity professionals is what comparative benchmarks should be used to analyze cybersecurity spend. A popular one focuses on the percentage of total IT spend that is earmarked for cybersecurity. The most common percentage is 10%. So, for every $1 million spent on IT, $100,000 goes toward cybersecurity. The problem with arbitrary metrics when quoting them or trying to align the budget process to them is that no consideration for risk and program maturity is accounted for in the metric. Less mature programs require more spending initially, to catch up, but the drop-off after the initial thrust of budget dollars may not be as much as originally expected, because investments and expenses required to keep ePHI protected in a compliant environment are significant.

## How Much Does Cybersecurity Cost?

The answer to this question, which has little traction in executive suites, is that the cost of cybersecurity is whatever it takes to protect ePHI, which depends on many considerations including

- How mature is the program?
    - Are additional investments required just to meet baseline standards?
    - Do personnel with the right skills exist to operate, monitor, and measure the program?
- What is the risk profile?
    - Is the entity a confirmed target?
    - How much data is at risk?

One thing to consider is, no matter how large or small an entity is, if ePHI is at risk, certain protections standards must be met, and those standards cost money. Best-in-class technology is always feasible, but entities should not cut off spending on cybersecurity needs just because a percentage of the total IT budget has been exceeded.

# Remembering the Human Factor of Budgeting

Chapter 1 discussed a common occurrence among board members at entities that experience a breach or who worry when a high-profile breach occurs elsewhere. Money is earmarked for cybersecurity and directed at solutions executives prioritize. When this occurs, additional funding for staff or outsourcing operations is not included, which causes solutions not to be implemented properly. What is not understood in these situations is that further regulatory and reputational risks may develop when incidents occur and investigations reveal that solutions were in place but not funded to operate properly. The cybersecurity team does not just need money for new and improved solutions to keep pace with threat actors but also people with the skills necessary to effectively protect patient records.

# A Risk-Based Approach to Cyber Budgeting

The approach here is developing the capital budgeting and operating expense budgets after the risk analysis, risk assessment, and as much testing as possible are completed. That way, thoughtful allocation of resources in the areas with the most risk is achieved. Because the road map illustrates the desired direction of the cybersecurity program and the amount of risk reduction desired over a three-year period, budgetary considerations must consider the desired future state of the cybersecurity program's necessary outlays in subsequent years. Reduced financial impacts owing to risk reduction should also be included in the budget analysis.

## The Updated Risk Analysis

The final version of the risk analysis revealed significant risks requiring changes and additional capabilities in all categories and most subcategories of the NIST CSF. In reviewing the risk analysis, some key risks require attention, including training and awareness, monitoring for anomalous user behavior and traffic patterns, and unusual connections that increase the risk of data exfiltration. Improvements are also necessary in access control.

# Cybersecurity Objectives and Road Map

There are several investments required to meet the milestones established in the cybersecurity road map. Initially, the focus is on fundamental people, process, and technology enhancements.

## Investing in the Fundamentals

It takes more technology than one might think to build a fundamental cybersecurity program designed to establish the safeguards required by the HIPAA Security Rule. Today entities must have

- Firewalls

- Web proxy

- E-mail gateway/proxy

- Data loss prevention

- Intrusion detection systems

- Privileged account management

- Privileged session management

- Security incident and event management (SIEM) or other log correlation capability

- Automated vulnerability scanning

- Automated access-control mechanisms

This list represents investments in technology, backed by mature processes, which are required before moving to the next phase of the road map. This phase is the most inflexible of the three, because it focuses on ensuring that each subcategory is in line with expectations under the HIPAA Security Rule and operating effectively as part of the cybersecurity program. These improvements and investments must be made as soon as possible, ideally, in the first six months, but no later than the first year. Arguably, these requirements must be funded without budget consideration. These weaknesses pose risks that cannot be put off to another budget cycle. It is reasonable, though, that solutions are purchased are good enough to do the job at present and to plan to implement more advanced capabilities later. None of the preceding requirements outlined requires top-shelf solutions.

Automated access-control solutions are not cheap either, and many would argue that access control can be improved through process improvement alone. In today's business environment, especially for healthcare providers and business associates, consolidation and acquisition have caused increased complexity within IT systems and the directory services meant to organize user access and control permissions. Fully integrating two entities and organizing each's resources under one umbrella often takes time. Automated solutions are valuable to security and compliance teams, by reducing the time necessary to add users to default groups, cleaning up vulnerable issues in the directories, and confirming that users and permissions stay current and alert to potential unauthorized changes.

## Targeted Improvements of the Program

Here, targeted improvements focus on subcategories and processes to protect from and detect attacks. The focal points of the targeted improvements are derived from thinking about how attacks unfold, based on the kill chain highlighted several times already. Specifically, the events and behaviors that lead key in this phase are

- End-user training designed to protect the environment against risky employees who are significantly vulnerable

- Tools to monitor end-user behavior and prevent each from visiting risky web sites and downloading suspicious payloads

- Establishing baseline hardening standards for hardware assets and monitoring the environment for deviations from these standards

- Upgrading boundary defenses, firewalls, and IDS solutions, selecting ones geared toward preventing and detecting advanced attacks

- Improving automated access control measures

Investments and increases in expenditures during this phase achieve further reductions to the entity's risk profile. It also prepares the program for the next phase: intelligence and analytics enhancements. Ideally, the second phase milestones are complete by the end of year two, but the ability to remain flexible and adjust is necessary.

## Intelligence and Analytic-Driven Program

This final phase is planned for year three. Budgeting for the capabilities here include enhancing the detect and response functions. Sandboxing is a key component of this phase. These environments allow the detonation of malicious software and URLs to understand the behaviors of an attacker's exploit. These behaviors become the indicators left behind that analysts can hunt for in the environment. Decoys are also placed through the network, designed to trick attackers into revealing their tools, techniques, and procedures. The cybersecurity team gathers real-time intelligence useful for searching other systems. These two enhancements enrich the contextual information present in threat feeds and are used in SIEM and other correlation tools. Here, fewer investments are planned, but each could be significant. The hope is that once cybersecurity program maturity increases, fewer investments are required, but each is significant for the advancements made by the program.

# Summary

Previously, the execution of a risk analysis and several comprehensive tests of the entity and its IT systems and creation of a three-year cybersecurity road map uncovered a number or priorities that require funding by the organization. The funds required to reduce risk, meet regulatory requirements, and achieve the milestones outlined in the road map require increases in capital investments and operating expenses. The first set of priorities, those necessary to ensure that fundamental capabilities exist and ePHI is safeguarded, are nonnegotiable and must be funded. Once the fundamental capabilities exist, the plan is to move forward on reaching the targeted enhancement milestones, prior to becoming an analytics and intelligence-driven cybersecurity program.

# CHAPTER 14

# Third-Party Risk: Beyond the BAA

Of all the ways to apply risk-based cybersecurity principles, analyzing risks to ePHI related to engaging third parties is very important. Failing to evaluate cyber risk at service providers is dangerous, and recent examples, such as the breach reported by Anthem in August of 2017, and risks to ePHI resulting from these relationships must be included on the risk register as well. In terms of patient data, business associates (BAs) are entities that perform services on behalf of covered entities and have access to ePHI. Business associates also engage third parties, establishing downstream BA arrangements. Regulations require that business associate agreements (BAAs) be executed for all such arrangements, establishing requirements for BAs to operate under. Included are permissible uses and disclosures of PHI and the expectation to protect PHI by adhering to safeguards required under the HIPAA Security Rule. BAAs also include provisions for notification when breaches occur. BAAs, however, should not be relied on for due diligence and information protection assurance. Managing third-party risk is not the sexiest aspect of cybersecurity; however, mismanaging third-party risk can be very damaging and lead to headlines. It is understood that BAAs are obtained any time a third party has access to, or is in possession of, ePHI. The focus of this chapter is to analyze and either accept or address the cyber risks to ePHI, prior to executing a business agreement and in addition to obtaining the signed BAA.

## Analyzing Third-Party Risk

Third-party risk management is an often-overlooked aspect of the cybersecurity program. Allowing outsider access to, or possession of, sensitive information extends the organizational defense boundaries and requires an assessment of the risks to ePHI in the same manner as data held on-premise. To put it another way, when allowing third

© Eric C. Thompson 2017
E. C. Thompson, *Building a HIPAA-Compliant Cybersecurity Program*,
https://doi.org/10.1007/978-1-4842-3060-2_14

parties access to ePHI, risks must be measured using the NIST 800-30 methodology. What causes this analysis to be overlooked is missing governance requirements outlining due diligence expectations prior to allowing access to ePHI. This process is iterative as well and includes the following steps:

- *Organizational objectives*: Understanding and communicating the benefits the engagement creates

- *Governance requirements*: Based on the classification of data, in this case ePHI, what due diligence requirements must be completed prior to engagement (in this case, a risk analysis based on NIST 800-30)?

- *Risk analysis*: Are the risks posed by this engagement acceptable?

- *Monitoring*: What is the process for reevaluating the arrangement and accepting the risks year over year?

The challenge to ensuring that these steps are followed is establishing the oversight function. The most effective way to establish governance and oversight is by placing ownership of the process with someone responsible for reporting to the cybersecurity steering committee. Whoever this person is, he or she must be responsible for reporting on whether the proper procedures are implemented and followed.

## Governing Third-Party Risk Management

Governance begins with data classification backed by policies dictating requirements for handling each data type. At the very least, healthcare providers, payers, and business associates require a classification for ePHI. Most entities have other data types, such as PII, confidential, and public. Strict requirements, beyond obtaining the signed BAA, must be enforced for engagements affecting ePHI. The list of key activities in Table 14-1 is an example of the required steps necessary to assess third parties. Each unique arrangement dictates whether one of these actions is sufficient or a combination is necessary to assess and analyze all the risks to ePHI.

***Table 14-1.***  *Sample Due Diligence Activities That Can Be Used to Assess Risks of Using Third Parties to Render Services Involving ePHI*

| Due Diligence Requirements | Documentation and Assessments |
| --- | --- |
| Independent reports | Reports provided by external assessors that evaluate elements of the third party's security program |
| Questionnaires | Most common activity undertaken. Third parties are required to fill out these documents, which are reviewed by IT or privacy departments. |
| Phone interviews | If questions persist after the security questionnaire is returned, security teams can discuss them with potential third parties. |
| On-site visits | Not as common as others. Member(s) of the security team visit the third party to observe cybersecurity controls in action. |

# Evaluating Security Controls

The key task when evaluating third parties with access to ePHI is understanding the risks to ePHI at the third party and if security controls implemented provide sufficient protection to reduce those risks. The process of analyzing risk at third parties is the same as the processes entities should follow when analyzing risks internally.

## Gathering Relevant Information

The purpose of gathering information about the third-party cybersecurity program, no matter which of the activities discussed earlier is utilized, is to answer the same question. Does this entity's cybersecurity program protect ePHI in the same manner expected of ePHI on-premise? Information must be gathered through review of documentation, interviews, and inspection of premises. Several mechanisms exist by which independent audit reports can be obtained and reviewed during due diligence. A common vehicle includes reports issued under the guidance of the American Institute of Certified Public Accountants (AICPA). It is responsible for governing the process of issuing Service Organization and Control (SOC) reports, commonly referred to as SOC 2s, which provide details useful for due diligence activities. The International Standards Organization (ISO) and HITRUST also offer third-party certification options. Questionnaires, phone interviews, and on-site visits are also common when independent reports are not available.

## SOC 2—Common Criteria

A SOC 2 report is issued by an entity performing a service and responsible for protecting data of its client. These reports are conducted against a set of criteria known as the Trust Service Principles (TSPs). TSPs exist for security, availability, processing integrity, confidentiality, and privacy. Many refer to TSPs as the common criteria, because these trust principles must be in scope for any SOC 2 audit report that includes the other trust principles. For example, a SOC 2 cannot be issued on the availability, processing integrity, confidentiality, or privacy criteria unless security is also included. These reports are issued to customers by service organizations, to demonstrate the security controls adopted and placed in operation that are meant to protect customer data.

---

**Note**   In addition to SOC 2, there are also SOC 1 and SOC 3 reports. A SOC 1 is typically utilized for financial audit purposes, covering internal controls over financial reporting. SOC 3 reports are general-use reports that can be distributed by the auditee.

---

- *Independence*: The standards under which SOC reports are issued are governed by the AICPA, which means only CPA firms registered with that body can perform audits and issue opinions related to a service provider's controls. This also means the auditor must be independent, that is, it has had no part in designing or implementing the controls being audited, and the firm, its leaders, and key members of the audit team have had no financial interest in the service provider being audited.

- *System and controls in-scope*: SOC 2 reports contain, among other things, a description of the system that performs the service. This includes all infrastructure components in which data is ingested, flows, and either leaves the entity or is stored. Applications, databases, operating systems, and other key network components are documented, and controls placed into operation with the intention of protecting data are tested. These are the security controls designed to protect customer data in use, motion, and at rest within the system. The scope of SOC 2 reports can also include criteria supporting availability, processing integrity, confidentiality, and/or privacy, depending on the needs of an entity's customers.

These two elements make SOC 2 reports desirable to service-provider customers. The scope of the report focuses on the areas that matter to customers concerned with data protection. Independent assessments used as a basis for the report opinion and SOC 2 reports come not only with an opinion written by the independent auditor but Section IV of the report includes descriptions of the controls tested, types of tests performed, and the conclusions of those tests.

Seven criteria are considered, each with its own set of principles. Third-party service providers design and place into operation controls intended to meet each principle.

---

**Note**   Normally, more than one control is required to meet objectives under the common criteria, and controls can be mapped to more than one objective. This control mapping is documented in Section IV of a SOC 2 report, along with a description of the test performed and the conclusion reached by the auditor conducting the test procedures.

---

The following tables provide descriptions of each of the seven criteria, the principles found within each of the criteria, and examples of controls, test descriptions, and conclusions for each test. Emphasis is placed on reviewing and understanding how to review a SOC 2 report, because it is very often a misunderstood vehicle. Checking the report opinion by skimming the testing section to check for exceptions is not sufficient. Deeper analysis, to understand the context of the report in relation to the business, is necessary.

## CC 1.0: Common Criteria Related to Organization and Management

These criteria, listed in Table 14-2, focus on the structure of the security organization, reporting lines, defined security responsibilities, and workforce standards and evaluating the competency of those responsible for implementing security.

***Table 14-2.*** *Criteria Related to Organization and Management, Sample Elements That Each Control Designed to Meet These Criteria May Contain, Examples of Testing Procedures, and Conclusions*

| Criteria | Criteria Description | Control Characteristics | Test Description | Conclusion |
|---|---|---|---|---|
| CC 1.1 | The entity has defined organizational structures, reporting lines, authorities, and responsibilities for the design, development, implementation, operation, maintenance, and monitoring of the system, enabling it to meet its commitments and requirements as they relate to security. | An organization chart, with job titles and reporting lines, exists and is made available to the workforce. | The organizational chart is obtained and examined for the required attributes. | No exceptions |
| CC 1.2 | Responsibility and accountability for designing, developing, implementing, operating, maintaining, monitoring, and approving the entity's system controls are assigned to individuals within the entity with the authority to ensure that policies and other system requirements are effectively promulgated and placed in operation. | Job descriptions include responsibilities for cybersecurity procedures. | For a sample of job descriptions, review each for the required attributes. | No exceptions |
| CC 1.3 | Personnel responsible for designing, developing, implementing, operating, maintaining, and monitoring the system affecting security have the qualifications and resources to fulfill their responsibilities. | Job descriptions include responsibilities for cybersecurity procedures. | For a sample of job descriptions, review each for the required attributes. | No exceptions |

*(continued)*

***Table 14-2.*** (*continued*)

| Criteria | Criteria Description | Control Characteristics | Test Description | Conclusion |
|---|---|---|---|---|
| CC 1.4 | The entity has established workforce conduct standards, implemented workforce candidate background screening procedures, and conducts enforcement procedures to enable it to meet its commitments and requirements as they relate to security. | Cybersecurity policies and employee code of conduct documents exist, are made available to the workforce, and are reviewed annually by management. | Cybersecurity policy and code of conduct documents are obtained and examined for required attributes. | No exceptions |

Cybersecurity must be an established part of the organization, with clearly defined job descriptions for members of the team, the leaders of the program, and business leaders. Members of the team must know who oversees the program, and the workforce must know who to contact when issues arise.

## CC 2.0: Common Criteria Related to Communications

These criteria, listed in Table 14-3, are designed to establish lines of communication regarding the boundaries of the system assessed and expectations for internal and external security communications.

***Table 14-3.*** *Criteria Related to Communications, Sample Elements That Each Control Designed to Meet These Criteria May Contain, Examples of Testing Procedures, and Conclusions*

| Criteria | Criteria Description | Control Characteristics | Test Description | Conclusion |
|---|---|---|---|---|
| CC 2.1 | Information regarding the design and operation of the system and its boundaries has been prepared and communicated to authorized internal and external system users, to permit users to understand their role in the system and the results of system operation. | System descriptions are documented by management and made available to appropriate personnel. | The auditor obtains a copy of the system description and observes that it is made available to appropriate personnel. | No exceptions |
| CC 2.2 | The entity's security commitments are communicated to external users, as appropriate, and those commitments and the associated system requirements are communicated to internal system users, to enable them to carry out their responsibilities. | Documentation of security commitments are communicated to external and internal users. | Auditor obtained and examined documents provided for appropriate attributes. | No exceptions |
| CC 2.3 | The entity communicates the responsibilities of internal and external users and others whose roles affect system operation. | A process for providing and tracking security commitments is maintained by the entity. | The auditor obtains and examines the related documents to confirm that necessary attributes exist. | No exceptions |

*(continued)*

***Table 14-3.*** (*continued*)

| Criteria | Criteria Description | Control Characteristics | Test Description | Conclusion |
|---|---|---|---|---|
| CC 2.4 | Internal and external personnel with responsibility for designing, developing, implementing, operating, maintaining, and monitoring controls relevant to the security of the system have the information necessary to carry out those responsibilities. | | | |
| CC 2.5 | Internal and external system users have been provided with information on how to report security failures, incidents, concerns, and other complaints to appropriate personnel. | | | |
| CC 2.6 | System changes that affect internal and external system user responsibilities or the entity's commitments and requirements relevant to security are communicated to those users in a timely manner. | | | |

To be effective, expectations required under the cybersecurity program must be communicated internally and externally. End users must know their duties, to keep ePHI secure; business and IT leaders must have defined expectations; and, if applicable, external stakeholders, such as customers, must also be aware of cybersecurity expectations. Expectations must be clearly communicated.

## CC 3.0: Common Criteria Related to Risk Management and Design and Implementation of Controls

These criteria, listed in Table 14-4, focus on risk assessment, risk management, and management's review of controls designed to reduce risk.

*Table 14-4.* *Criteria Related to Risk Management Design and Implementation of Controls, Sample Elements That Each Control Designed to Meet These Criteria May Contain, Examples of Testing Procedures, and Conclusions*

| Criteria | Criteria Description | Control Characteristics | Test Description | Conclusion |
|---|---|---|---|---|
| CC 3.1 | The entity (1) identifies potential threats that would impair system security commitments and requirements, (2) analyzes the significance of risks associated with the identified threats, and (3) determines mitigation strategies for those risks (including controls and other mitigation strategies). | A risk assessment is completed and reviewed annually by management, including the threats, vulnerabilities, likelihood, and impacts of risks to the system. | The auditor obtains and reviews the risk assessment and annual review to conclude that all attributes are present. | No exceptions |
| CC 3.2 | The entity designs, develops, and implements controls, including policies and procedures, to implement its risk mitigation strategy. | Internal controls, policies, and procedures are developed to reduce risks to the system in scope. | The auditor obtains copies of policy and procedure documents, reviewing each for risk management and mitigation coverage. | No exceptions |

(*continued*)

*Table 14-4.* (*continued*)

| Criteria | Criteria Description | Control Characteristics | Test Description | Conclusion |
|---|---|---|---|---|
| CC 3.3 | The entity (1) identifies and assesses changes (for example, environmental, regulatory, and technological changes) that could significantly affect the system of internal control for security and reassesses risks and mitigation strategies based on the changes, and (2) reassesses the suitability of the design and deployment of control activities, based on the operation and monitoring of those activities, and updates them as necessary. | Internal controls, policies, and procedures are developed to reduce risks to the system in scope. | The auditor obtains copies of policy and procedure documents, reviewing each for risk management and mitigation coverage. | No exceptions |

Risk assessment and management cannot be left up to a single person or group of persons. Recommendations of risk severity and mitigation options can be made to management by practitioners, but management must agree that risk exists and be willing to adopt mitigation strategies. These mitigation decisions should be made, based on management's risk tolerance.

## CC 4.0: Common Criteria Related to Monitoring Controls

These criteria, listed in Table 14-5, are meant to establish the need for management to monitor the implementation and operation of controls key to meeting the security criteria of the system in question.

*Table 14-5.*  *Criteria Related to Monitoring Controls, Sample Elements That Each Control Designed to Meet These Criteria May Contain, Examples of Testing Procedures, and Conclusions*

| Criteria | Criteria Description | Control Characteristics | Test Description | Conclusion |
|---|---|---|---|---|
| CC 4.1 | The design and operating effectiveness of controls are periodically evaluated against security commitments and requirements. Corrections and other necessary actions relating to identified deficiencies are taken in a timely manner. | The cybersecurity and compliance programs are assessed annually, either by internal audit or an external firm. | The auditor obtains and reviews the assessment completed during the audit period. Documentation of remediation activities recommended by the assessor is reviewed to confirm that time lines for completion are monitored. | Exception noted: Evidence of remediation activities was not present. |

Monitoring the control environment is best achieved by independent or objective assessors and not by those operating the controls in question. Engaging the internal audit department or an external firm is best for meeting this objective. In this example, the entity in question does not monitor the control owner's progress toward remediating findings during internal and external control assessments.

## CC 5.0: Common Criteria Related to Logical and Physical Access Controls

These criteria, listed in Table 14-6, focus on logical and physical access to the system. For logical access, this means each segment in the logical access path: application, operating system, database, and network access. Network access refers to initial authentication, usually Active Directory or LDAP.

*Table 14-6.* *Criteria Related to Logical and Physical Access Controls, Sample Elements That Each Control Designed to Meet These Criteria May Contain, Examples of Testing Procedures, and Conclusions*

| Criteria | Criteria Description | Control Characteristics | Test Description | Conclusion |
|---|---|---|---|---|
| CC 5.1 | Logical access security software, infrastructure, and architectures have been implemented to support (1) identification and authentication of authorized internal and external users; (2) restriction of authorized internal and external user access to system components, or portions thereof, authorized by management, including hardware, data, software, mobile devices, output, and offline elements; and (3) prevention and detection of unauthorized access to meet the entity's commitments and system requirements, as they relate to security. | System controls, such as Active Directory and unique user IDs, control authentication and authorization to system resources, forcing each user to have a unique user ID. | For a sample of users, new or existing, each is tested to confirm that access is appropriate for job responsibilities, and each user is given a unique user ID. | No exceptions |

(*continued*)

*Table 14-6.* (*continued*)

| Criteria | Criteria Description | Control Characteristics | Test Description | Conclusion |
|---|---|---|---|---|
| CC 5.2 | New internal and external users, whose access is administered by the entity, are registered and authorized prior to being issued system credentials and granted the ability to access the system to meet the entity's commitments and system requirements, as they relate to security. For those users whose access is administered by the entity, user system credentials are removed when user access is no longer authorized. | Prior to granting new user access, system owners must approve access, and system administrators allow access only after approval is granted. Access is also reviewed semiannually by system owners, to confirm that access to system resources is still appropriate. | For a sample of new users during the audit period, confirm that user access was approved by the proper system owner and that access granted was appropriate. Semiannual access reviews are performed, and any changes to access notated are executed in a timely manner. | Exceptions noted: Three users in the test sample did not have approvals obtained prior to access being granted. |
| CC 5.3 | Internal and external users are identified and authenticated when accessing the system components (for example, infrastructure, software, and data), to meet the entity's commitments and system requirements, as they relate to security. | Prior to granting new user access, system owners must approve access, and system administrators allow access only after approval is granted. Access is also reviewed semiannually by system owners, to confirm that access to system resources is still appropriate. | For a sample of new users during the audit period, confirm that user access was approved by the proper system owner and that access granted was appropriate. Semiannual access reviews are performed, and any changes to access notated are executed in a timely manner. | Exceptions noted: Three users in the test sample did not have approvals obtained prior to access being granted. |

(*continued*)

***Table 14-6.*** (*continued*)

| Criteria | Criteria Description | Control Characteristics | Test Description | Conclusion |
|---|---|---|---|---|
| CC 5.4 | Access to data, software, functions, and other IT resources is authorized and modified or removed, based on roles, responsibilities, or the system design, and is changed to meet the entity's commitments and system requirements, as they relate to security. | Prior to granting new user access, system owners must approve access, and system administrators allow access only after approval is granted. Access is also reviewed semiannually by system owners, to confirm access to system resources is still appropriate. | For a sample of new users during the audit period, confirm that user access was approved by the proper system owner and that access granted was appropriate. Semiannual access reviews are performed, and any changes to access notated are executed in a timely manner. | No exceptions |
| CC 5.5 | Physical access to facilities housing the system (for example, data centers, backup media storage, and other sensitive locations, as well as sensitive system components within those locations) is restricted to authorized personnel, to meet the entity's commitments and system requirements, as they relate to security. | Access to data centers, backups, and other storage devices and media is restricted to administrators requiring access for job functions, including computing and environmental support. | Review list of users with access to the data centers and confirm that all require access for job duties. | No exceptions |

(*continued*)

*Table 14-6.* (*continued*)

| Criteria | Criteria Description | Control Characteristics | Test Description | Conclusion |
|---|---|---|---|---|
| CC 5.6 | Logical access security measures have been implemented to protect against security threats from sources outside the boundaries of the system, to meet the entity's commitments and system requirements. | Traffic is restricted from external sources to that approved for business reasons. All external traffic is encrypted, and server hardware standards are adopted and monitored to keep devices processing ePHI secure. | Auditor obtains firewall rules, system evidence, and scanning evidence confirming that the standards outlined in the control are in place. | No exceptions |
| CC 5.7 | The transmission, movement, and removal of information is restricted to authorized internal and external users and processes and is protected during transmission, movement, or removal, enabling the entity to meet its commitments and system requirements, as they relate to security. | Only privileged users/administrators can transfer data outside the entity's boundaries for processes approved by the CIO and leader of the cybersecurity program. Transfers must be executed via secure communication methods. | The auditor obtains and reviews the list of users with the ability to transfer data and confirms that the users on the list are appropriate. System evidence confirms that data transfers are completed via encrypted methods. | No exceptions |

(*continued*)

***Table 14-6.*** (*continued*)

| Criteria | Criteria Description | Control Characteristics | Test Description | Conclusion |
|---|---|---|---|---|
| CC 5.8 | Controls have been implemented to prevent or detect and act upon the introduction of unauthorized or malicious software to meet the entity's commitments and system requirements, as they relate to security. | End points have detective capabilities that prevent end users from downloading unauthorized executables from the Internet and warn when users attempt to download from known malicious sites. | Auditors obtain and confirm that all end points are secured by capabilities preventing and detecting and receive updates periodically to stay current with evolving threats. | No exceptions |

Evaluating the controls governing logical and physical access is important to understand at the service provider. In this example, the service provider appears to grant access to users without either obtaining or retaining the documented approvals. When exceptions are documented, management responses are included in the SOC 2 report explaining why the issue occurred and how management is addressing it. Here, we can infer that the access granted is not inappropriate for the job functions performed, but evidence that the control process was followed did not get retained. These items must be further evaluated for risks to ePHI.

## CC 6.0: Common Criteria Related to System Operations

These criteria, listed in Table 14-7, focus on how entities identify and track the resolution of vulnerabilities within the system in scope.

*Table 14-7.* *Criteria Related to System Operations, Sample Elements That Each Control Designed to Meet These Criteria May Contain, Examples of Testing Procedures, and Conclusions*

| Criteria | Criteria Description | Control Characteristics | Test Description | Conclusion |
|---|---|---|---|---|
| CC 6.1 | Vulnerabilities of system components to security breaches and incidents owing to malicious acts, natural disasters, or errors are identified, monitored, and evaluated, and countermeasures are designed, implemented, and operated to compensate for known and newly identified vulnerabilities, to meet the entity's commitments and system requirements, as they relate to security. | The entity has a process for identifying and tracking the resolution of vulnerabilities affecting servers and other hardware processing ePHI. | The auditor obtains and reviews tracking documents displaying the process of identification and tracking vulnerabilities affecting ePHI. | No exceptions |
| CC 6.2 | Security incidents, including logical and physical security breaches, failures, and identified vulnerabilities, are identified and reported to appropriate personnel and acted on in accordance with established incident response procedures, to meet the entity's commitments and system requirements. | Incidents follow a documented incident response process, which includes post-incident reviews, to understand lessons learned related to incidents investigated and resolved. | The auditor obtains incident response reports for all incidents occurring during the audit period and selects a sample to review for all required attributes. | No exceptions |

This criterion requires entities to manage and work through remediating vulnerabilities. Management can choose to place static time lines on when vulnerabilities have to be remediated, or the controls can state that vulnerabilities are tracked, and remediation processes are worked to confirm that all are resolved.

## CC 7.0: Common Criteria Related to Change Management

These criteria, listed in Table 14-8, focus on the elements of change control, whether there is a process for changes to be made to in-scope systems, and security considerations that are evaluated and approved.

***Table 14-8.*** *Criteria Related to Change Management, Sample Elements That Each Control Designed to Meet These Criteria May Contain, Examples of Testing Procedures, and Conclusions*

| Criteria | Criteria Description | Control Characteristics | Test Description | Conclusion |
|---|---|---|---|---|
| CC 7.1 | The entity's commitments and system requirements, as they relate to security, are addressed during the system development life cycle, including the authorization, design, acquisition, implementation, configuration, testing, modification, approval, and maintenance of system components. | Changes to the production system require authorization by the system owner, to begin development, testing of the changes in a QA environment, and approval by the change advisory board, before the change is migrated into production. | The auditor reviewed a list of all changes made to the system during the audit period, selecting a sample to test for all required attributes | Exceptions noted: For five of the changes selected, testing and change advisory approval prior to migration into production was not obtained. |

(*continued*)

*Table 14-8.* (*continued*)

| Criteria | Criteria Description | Control Characteristics | Test Description | Conclusion |
|---|---|---|---|---|
| CC 7.2 | Infrastructure, data, software, and policies and procedures are updated, as necessary, to remain consistent with the entity's commitments and system requirements, as they relate to security. | Cybersecurity policies and employee code of conduct documents exist, are made available to the workforce, and are reviewed annually by management. | Cybersecurity policy and code of conduct documents are obtained and examined for required attributes. | No exceptions |
| CC 7.3 | Change management processes are initiated when deficiencies in the design or operating effectiveness of controls are identified during system operation and are monitored to meet the entity's commitments and system requirements, as they relate to security. | Changes to the production system require authorization by the system owner, to begin development, testing of the changes in a QA environment, and approval by the change advisory board, before the change is migrated into production. | The auditor reviewed a list of all changes made to the system during the audit period, selecting a sample to test for all required attributes | Exceptions noted: For five of the changes selected, testing and change advisory approval prior to migration into production was not obtained. |
| CC 7.4 | Changes to system components are authorized, designed, developed, configured, documented, tested, approved, and implemented to meet the entity's security commitments and system requirements. | Changes to the production system require authorization by the system owner, to begin development, testing of the changes in a QA environment, and approval by the change advisory board, before the change is migrated into production. | The auditor reviewed a list of all changes made to the system during the audit period, selecting a sample to test for all required attributes | Exceptions noted: For five of the changes selected, testing and change advisory approval prior to migration into production was not obtained. |

This criterion focuses on assessment and reporting of controls related to change control, whether the entity controls how changes are made to the system, and if cybersecurity considerations are part of the process. These focus is on key concepts, such as having input from cybersecurity during the development process through all stages of change control.

This walk-through of a partial SOC 2 example is meant to give readers a flavor of what information is contained in these reports and how entities should use this information. In an actual report, multiple controls will likely be mapped to each of the criteria to meet the objectives.

# ISO Certification

ISO certification[1] is available to entities of all sizes. The most common certification is ISO 27001. The 27000 family focuses on the Information Security Management System (ISMS) and associated controls. The goal of the ISMS is to assist entities required to protect sensitive assets, such as ePHI. When entities get certified, proof of the certification is available so that those entities can provide it to customers and potential customers. The only drawback is that documentation for the ISO certification does not include the details of controls and testing results. Entities will have to infer what controls are in place to meet the ISO criteria. Any significant concerns related to the control environment must be addressed via questionnaire, telephone interviews, or during on-site visits.

# HITRUST Certification

Earlier, HITRUST CSF was discussed as a framework that can be utilized to assess and analyze risks to ePHI. HITRUST also offers users of its framework the opportunity to get certified. Administrative factors, the unique elements of the entity seeking certification, determine the controls required for certification. The reports generated for entities meeting HITRUST certification requirements include descriptions of the system in scope, the controls tested, whether the controls meet certification requirements, and details regarding gaps in the control environment. Any controls not meeting maturity requirements must have a corrective action plan (CAP). This information is available to customers and potential customers who need to understand how data is protected.

---

[1]International Organization for Standardization, `www.iso.org/isoiec-27001-information-security.html`.

# Cybersecurity Questionnaire

When independent certification or reports are not available from the service provider, entities often turn to the use of questionnaires to assess the entity and determine risks to ePHI. The problem with this approach is the false sense of security perceived satisfactory answers provide. Table 14-9 displays examples of questions that can be used to understand the key components of a third party's cybersecurity program. Security questionnaires are much longer and ask for more detail than in this example. Each can also be customized, based on the third party and the type of services contracted. These nuances can be adopted once the process for evaluation of third parties is established.

***Table 14-9.*** *Security Questionnaires Similar to This Are Used in Lieu of, or in Conjunction with, Audit Reports, to Evaluate Potential Third-Party Service Providers Prior to Engagement*

| Cybersecurity Questions to Assist in Understanding How ePHI Is Protected |
| --- |
| 1. How are hardware and software assets inventoried and tracked? |
| 2. Are external connections to the system by vendors and other support providers tracked and monitored? |
| 3. Are data flows through the system documented? |
| 4. How are security roles and responsibilities established? |
| 5. Describe the process for identifying, assessing, and managing risk. |
| 6. How is access to the system controlled at all layers (application, database, operating system)? |
| 7. Describe the training and awareness program. |
| 8. How is data in motion, at rest, and use protected? |
| 9. What role do human resources play in cybersecurity? |
| 10. How is change control managed, and please describe the process for integrating cybersecurity into the change process? |
| 11. Describe processes for receiving and responding to alerts related to system maintenance requirements (disk space, memory issues, etc.). |
| 12. How are perimeter security capabilities managed and maintained? |

*(continued)*

*Table 14-9.* (*continued*)

| Cybersecurity Questions to Assist in Understanding How ePHI Is Protected |
|---|
| 13. Describe how the network is baselined (traffic, device connections, and types of communications) and how monitoring capabilities allow for identification of anomalous traffic and behaviors. |
| 14. Describe the overall monitoring of the system for security events and incidents and formal processes for investigating abnormal events. |
| 15. Outline the incident response process, including identification, escalation, communication, and resolution. |
| 16. How often is the incident response plan tested? |
| 17. Describe the process for establishing the recovery plan, including identification of business-critical processes, testing, and post-recovery review and lessons learned. |

The goal is to get a sense of what cybersecurity controls are in operation and how closely each matches what is expected by the entity to protect ePHI. The questions that make up the questionnaire allow for inquiries shown here to be removed or modified while also adding others. The key is to craft the questionnaire to meet the needs of the business.

## Gathering Additional Details

Despite the fact that these reports are marketed to third-party service providers to eliminate customer questions, it is rare that reviewing a SOC 2 report, ISO certificate, HITRUST report, or cybersecurity questionnaire yields all the information required to evaluate cybersecurity controls and analyze risk. To gather the additional information, supplemental questions, phone interviews, and sometime on-site visits are required to properly assess risk. The key is not stopping until enough information is gathered.

# Evaluate Security Controls and Identify Risks

Once all the holes are filled and no questions linger, it is time to evaluate the security controls at the third party and measure the risks. This is done by using the same process to analyze risks internally.

- Document ePHI affected, by engaging the service provider.

- Consider threat actors and threat scenarios.

- Identify vulnerabilities.

- Measure likelihood and impact.

- Calculate level of risk.

Outsourcing a service does not outsource the risk; therefore, it is important to document the level of risk and the rationale for risk acceptance.

# Evaluating Threats to ePHI Held at the Third Party

The threat actors, events, and scenarios to ePHI at service providers are no different than those faced by the entity outsourcing services. Sophisticated actors, state-sponsored groups, and organized cybercriminals attack third parties if they think something of value can be gained. They also target third parties as a vector into the desired entity as well. If a system gets breached at a third party, a trusted connection to a client can be targeted next. Third-party service providers also have malicious insiders and hacktivists posing threats. Environmental issues, such as natural disasters, fires, catastrophic accidents, or terrorism, require consideration. Some considerations regarding threats include what might differentiate the threats to the ePHI at third parties and whether it can be expected that the adversary will naturally target the service provider because it is in possession of ePHI.

# Identifying Vulnerabilities at the Third Party

The guidance in Appendix F[2] of NIST 800-30 is the place to start identifying potential vulnerabilities at the third party. Broad categories to consider include access management, change control, security operations, and governance. In Figure 14-1, vulnerabilities that could affect data held by the service provider are identified by category.

---

[2]NIST, "Guide for Conducting Risk Assessments," NIST Special Publication 800-30, Revision 1, `http://nvlpubs.nist.gov/nistpubs/Legacy/SP/nistspecialpublication800-30r1.pdf`, September 2012.

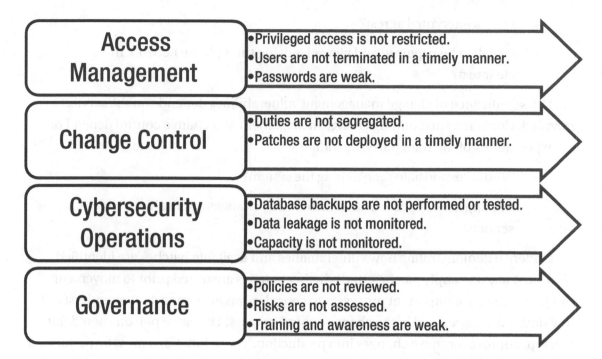

*Figure 14-1.* *Four cybersecurity domains in which vulnerabilities may exist, allowing threats to affect the confidentiality, integrity, and availability of ePHI held by a third-party service provider*

Access management is very important when transmitting ePHI to service providers. This includes all types of access—update and read-only. Understanding how users are restricted from seeing ePHI and how these restrictions are continuously monitored is important. Privileged access is particularly concerning, because excessive access by a user, especially privileged types of access, often is exploited during an attack. This is prominent in FireEye's kill chain. Finally, even though passwords are not a significant defense, weak password settings make it too easy for attackers to view, steal, modify, or render ePHI unavailable.

Cybersecurity operations are important, based on the services performed. If the service provider is hosting data, capabilities guarding against the risk of data being unavailable or lost must be present. If capacity becomes an issue or an environmental disaster occurs, the service provider must be prepared to keep operations from being interrupted. Controls monitoring data in motion, in use, and at rest are necessary.

- How does the service provider confirm that data is not stored in unauthorized locations, such as file shares, thumb drives, or outside the entity's network?

- Is data encrypted at rest?

- Can data be captured and viewed moving through the network in clear text?

The significance of change management vulnerabilities depends on the service provided. Concerns surrounding change management and change control depend on the expectations of the third party, including

- Who is responsible for patching the system?

- Are upgrades, updates, and custom code changes applicable to the service?

Evidence demonstrating how vulnerabilities and available patches are identified, the time it takes to apply patches, and whether patches are tested prior to movement into production are important processes to consider. It is also important to understand how duties are segregated in the change control process. The same person should not develop, approve, or move changes into production. Those functions must be performed by different individuals.

Last, but not least, governance is very important. Understanding the tone at the top, how seriously management at the third party takes cybersecurity and risk management, is required. If policies and procedures are not current and reviewed annually, training and awareness lack or risk identification, and management is not a key function, engaging with such a third party is questionable. If management does not take cybersecurity seriously, it is unlikely that members of the business take it seriously. Governance vulnerabilities are significant. This cannot be understated.

# Measuring Risk at the Third Party

Measuring the risks at the third party takes the same form as internal risks. Pairing the threats and vulnerabilities, concluding on the likelihood and impact to measure risk, is how it's done.

## Risk Statements

The first step in this portion of the risk analysis is to choose which vulnerabilities apply to this engagement. For the purposes of this analysis, the ones identified earlier will apply here. Figure 14-2 displays those once again.

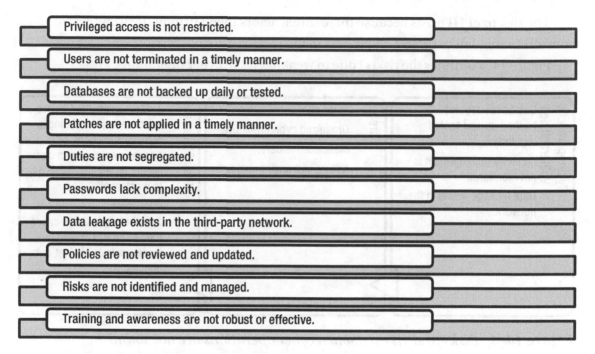

Privileged access is not restricted.

Users are not terminated in a timely manner.

Databases are not backed up daily or tested.

Patches are not applied in a timely manner.

Duties are not segregated.

Passwords lack complexity.

Data leakage exists in the third-party network.

Policies are not reviewed and updated.

Risks are not identified and managed.

Training and awareness are not robust or effective.

*Figure 14-2.* *Vulnerabilities identified in the third-party network*

With the vulnerabilities documented, it is time to analyze which actors or situations can exploit each and affect the confidentiality, integrity, and/or availability of the ePHI at the third party. Each of these vulnerabilities must be evaluated in terms of risk.

Figure 14-3 illustrates the process for developing a risk statement, based on the access vulnerabilities at the service provider.

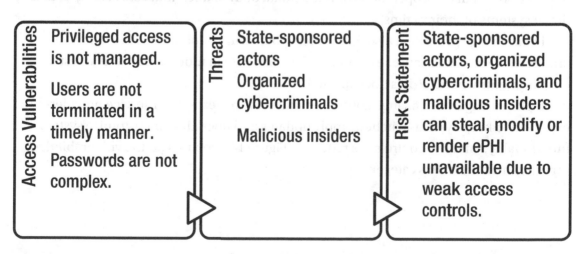

**Access Vulnerabilities**
Privileged access is not managed.

Users are not terminated in a timely manner.

Passwords are not complex.

**Threats**
State-sponsored actors

Organized cybercriminals

Malicious insiders

**Risk Statement**
State-sponsored actors, organized cybercriminals, and malicious insiders can steal, modify or render ePHI unavailable due to weak access controls.

*Figure 14-3.* *Weak access controls can be exploited by three threat actors affecting the confidentiality, integrity, and availability of ePHI*

The risk to ePHI exists because three threat actors might exploit the weak access controls to that fail to protect client data in the third-party's possession.

Figure 14-4 outlines the risk(s) due to weaknesses in cyber operations.

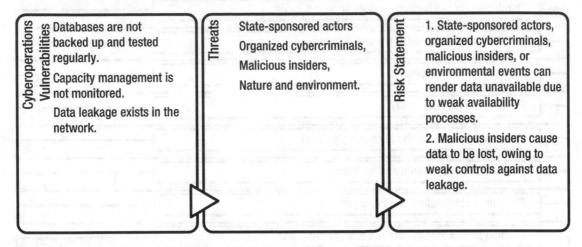

*Figure 14-4. Risks to ePHI exist when cyber operations are not sound*

Risks identified owing to cybersecurity operations include several threats that could render ePHI unavailable because of weak availability processes. Those include backups, which must be tested, and capacity management. Environmental issues include risky businesses, such as chemical plants or nuclear power plants, which can cause issues with business continuity. Floods, hurricanes, tornadoes, and other events that occur in nature also can disrupt operations or render data unavailable. Attackers also try to take down systems of their victims.

Data leakage protection also falls under cybersecurity operations. Preventative and detective controls must be established against data in motion, use, and at rest in environments where ePHI is not expected.

Risks arising due to change control weaknesses are next. When service providers are expected to keep systems patched, apply updates and upgrades, or customize system functionality, effective controls are required. Figure 14-5 focuses on the vulnerabilities, threats, and risks in this category.

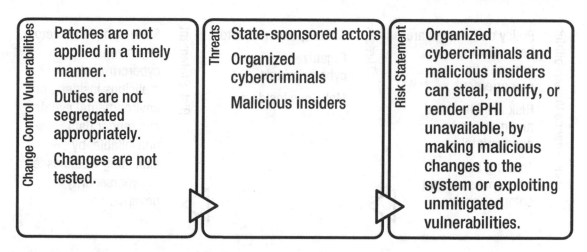

**Figure 14-5.** *Risks owing to change control weaknesses can lead to unpatched vulnerabilities not being mitigated or inappropriate changes being placed into production*

Change control issues lead to risks related to vulnerabilities not being mitigated and adversaries exploiting them. Entities often get caught in a trap of focusing on vulnerabilities with critical or high labels. And when vulnerabilities, even those considered to be low or medium by the scanners or organizations supplying intelligence, go unmitigated for long periods of time, exploits are developed and made available in open source locations, such as Exploit DB,[3] or in the Metasploit framework.[4]

Finally, the risks related to governance weaknesses need to be evaluated. Figure 14-6, outlines the vulnerabilities and the threats that can exploit them.

---

[3]Exploit Database, www.exploit-db.com/.

[4]Metasploit, www.metasploit.com/.

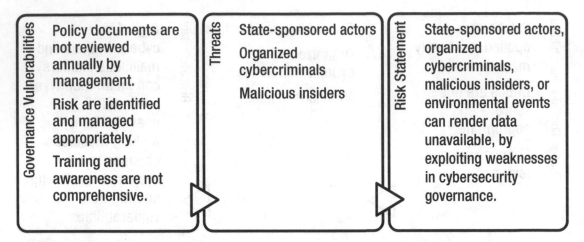

**Governance Vulnerabilities**

Policy documents are not reviewed annually by management.

Risk are identified and managed appropriately.

Training and awareness are not comprehensive.

**Threats**

State-sponsored actors

Organized cybercriminals

Malicious insiders

**Risk Statement**

State-sponsored actors, organized cybercriminals, malicious insiders, or environmental events can render data unavailable, by exploiting weaknesses in cybersecurity governance.

***Figure 14-6.*** *Governance vulnerabilities highlight weaknesses in cybersecurity, owing to management not setting the proper tone regarding the importance of protecting ePHI*

Governance is foundational in a cybersecurity program, and when vulnerabilities exist, other functions are weak. Access management, change control, and cyber operations do not receive proper attention. When investigation breaches with governance root causes occur, it is not surprising to learn that these exploits were not sophisticated at all, for example, breach occurrences in which large amounts of ePHI are posted in clear text on the Web.

# Third-Party Risk Integration

Once the risks are identified to ePHI at the third-party service provider, it is time to incorporate those risks into the assessment and risk register, before finalizing the analysis. This is as simple as placing a new header in the current analysis, delineating these risks from the risks identified internally and adding the third-party risks.

This section of the risk analysis, illustrated in Table 14-10, is the third-party risk (TPR) section, and the risks are numbered accordingly.

***Table 14-10.*** *Risks Associated with Engaging the Third-Party Provider Evaluated in This Chapter*

| Risk | Risk Statement | Likelihood | Impact |
|------|----------------|------------|--------|
| TPR1 | State-sponsored actors, organized cybercriminals, and malicious insiders can steal, modify, or render ePHI unavailable, owing to weak access controls. | 4 | 5 |
| TPR2 | State-sponsored actors, organized cybercriminals, malicious insiders, or environmental events can render data unavailable, owing to weak availability processes. | 4 | 3 |
| TPR3 | Malicious insiders can cause data to be lost, owing to weak controls against data leakage. | 4 | 3 |
| TPR4 | Organized cybercriminals and malicious insiders can steal, modify, or render ePHI unavailable, by making malicious changes to the system or exploiting unmitigated vulnerabilities. | 4 | 3 |
| TPR5 | State-sponsored actors, organized cybercriminals, malicious insiders, or environmental events can render data unavailable, by exploiting weaknesses in cybersecurity governance. | 4 | 4 |

The risks of engaging with this example of a third-party provider must have the likelihood and impacts assessed as if a true risk analysis is to be completed. The factors influencing likelihood are

- Would this adversary know ePHI exists at this entity?

- How difficult is the vulnerability to exploit?

---

**Note**   As BA compliance with the HIPAA and the Security Rule specifically is required, this means that any entity engaging with covered entities or other BAs downstream must conduct the required risk analysis discussed throughout this book. However, some entities will not be compliant, and others may not share the details. Therefore, entities engaging with third parties must conduct this analysis. Even when a risk analysis is available, the cybersecurity and risk management teams should review it, to ensure relevance to the organization's risk tolerance.

---

These factors were considered when assigning likelihood values in Table 14-7. Because malicious insiders are likely to know the weaknesses that exist inside the entity, the conclusion is that the likelihood that these weaknesses can be exploited is high. The impact ratings are based on how much data can be affected.

The final step is to add these new risks into the heat map. Figure 14-7 shows the third-party risks (added in boldface).

| Risk Matrix | | | | | |
|---|---|---|---|---|---|
| | Very High 5 | Very Low | Low | Moderate R17, R20 | High R9,R10, R12,R13, R18,R21,**TPR1** | Very High R15, R19,R22 |
| | High 4 | Very Low | Low | Moderate R2, R8, R16, R23 | High R3, R5, R14, **TPR5** | Very High |
| **Impact** | Moderate 3 | Very Low | Low | Moderate R1,R6,R7,R11, R14,R24,R25 | Moderate R4,**TPR2,TPR3,TPR4** | High |
| | Low 2 | Very Low | Low R27 | Low R26 | Low | Moderate |
| | Very Low 1 | Very Low | Very Low | Very Low | Low | Low |
| | | Very Low 1 | Low 2 | Moderate 3 | High 4 | Very High 5 |
| | | Likelihood | | | | |

*Figure 14-7.* *The risks in boldface are newly identified, resulting from engaging with a third-party service provider with access to ePHI*

# A Word on Cloud Solutions

"Moving to the cloud" is a phrase used by businesses, especially those in healthcare. There are several myths about the cloud that warrant a discussion separate from those discussed earlier.

The negative aura surrounding the cloud is that it is some sort of digital Narnia, where data is mystically transmitted and may be lost forever. A cloud service means that the provider manages the technology and operations of the service offered. An example of this is healthcare providers outsourcing a billing application. The internal staff handles billing and collection operations, but external staff can access the application via a web interface. The service providers might own the application or the infrastructure the application sits on top of. In a cloud scenario, the service provider manages the operations and maintenance of the technologies used by the healthcare provider in the billing and collection processes.

A deep discussion on the nuances of cloud computing and the different models employed is not necessary for the purposes of this book. The key takeaway from this section is that assessing and understanding the risks to ePHI by engaging a provider in this type of model requires no additional steps than those already described. Know what information is required, obtain it either by independent reports or questionnaires, follow up until all necessary information is obtained, and assess all threats, vulnerabilities, likelihood, and impacts.

# Summary

Assessing third-party risk is essential to cybersecurity program management and compliance with HIPAA. The HITECH Act placed the onus on BAs, by making them responsible to protect ePHI to the same degree as covered entities. However, covered entities must take proper precautions when electing to engage with third parties. A breach at a third-party service provider with significant gaps in security controls also reflects upon the entity that chose the third party. When dealing with ePHI, it is a must that due diligence steps and risk assessments are completed for all third parties engaged. Other sensitive data types, such as personally identifiable information, intellectual property, and trade secrets, are also important, but for now, the focus is patient information.

# CHAPTER 15

# Social Media, BYOD, IOT, and Portability

Social media, Bring Your Own Device (BYOD), and the Internet of Things (IoT) are potential headaches and cybersecurity risks. Data moves so freely in the age of digitization that it places vast amounts of ePHI at risk in new and complicated ways. The diverse social media risks cover more than the typical concern over posting of sensitive information on these sites. End users often share sufficient intelligence about the companies they work at that attackers may not have to dig as much during the reconnaissance stage. Social media is a repository for attackers attempting to discover ways to exploit end users. Managing BYOD risks has come a long way in recent years, but risks still exist when allowing the workforce to use personal phones or tablets during the workday. Finally, the recent explosion surrounding IoT also creates risks that many practitioners are just beginning to understand. The volume of data collected is exploding, and entities are unsure of how to manage the protection, storage, and disposition of this data.

## Social Media

Social media plays a role in business. Entities use these channels for promotion and brand management. Employees use these same platforms for many of the same reasons. The best way to build a career and continually find new opportunities is through brand management,.building a brand and managing it through social media. Monitoring social media for signs of misuse is difficult. Quantifying risks arising from sharing intelligence is even harder. Despite the challenges, cybersecurity must understand the level of risk and implement protections. It is not possible to eliminate social media vulnerabilities through technical means.

© Eric C. Thompson 2017

E. C. Thompson, *Building a HIPAA-Compliant Cybersecurity Program*,
https://doi.org/10.1007/978-1-4842-3060-2_15

# Business Needs vs. Risks

Few entities in the current business landscape can afford to forego the use of social medial platforms. Nearly every corporate web site displays buttons enticing visitors to follow via Twitter, LinkedIn, Google+, YouTube, and others. In today's short attention span environment, the goal seems to be to inundate the public with short burst messages designed to keep the entity top-of-mind. Again, employees are always promoting their accomplishments. Bragging about one's success might produce more opportunities. Entities also benefit when able to show off high-caliber employees. This can be good for business, but these benefits do come with increased risk.

## Danger Lurks Around the Corner

Social media is a great launchpad for social engineering. The more details attackers can use, the more convincing they can be when attempting to get inside the network. The spear-phishing attack that led to Anthem's breach was attributed by Symantec to Black Vine.[1] Its report illustrated this point, noting that Black Vine used social media to gather the information required to launch the attack. Social media is a gold mine that does not require much digging to hit pay dirt. Job postings describe roles in great detail, and LinkedIn profiles clue attackers into the components of the IT landscape when users detail projects and job responsibilities. An attacker can quickly learn

- What applications, databases, operating systems, and network equipment are deployed

- What versions of the software are active

- The structure of the entity's leadership, IT department, and cybersecurity team and, possibly, the maturity of IT and cybersecurity programs

The goal of a threat actor is to marry this data and create a detailed picture of the target's IT systems.

---

[1]http://www.symantec.com/content/en/us/enterprise/media/security_response/ whitepapers/the-black-vinecyberespionage-group.pdf

# Addressing Social Media Risks

Analyzing the risks of social media requires addressing social media through policy enforcement and exception management and understanding the capabilities to prevent, detect, and respond to social media risks. The policy should dictate how social media is used on the entity's network and information assets. Some organizations block social media sites on the company network, and others take it a step further by never allowing users to visit social media sites with company assets, thus eliminating certain attack vectors. It is up to the cybersecurity or risk practitioner to evaluate the risks of social media in the following manner:

- Understand that sophisticated threat actors can and will exploit vulnerabilities related to social media.

- These vulnerabilities are end users posting information detailing the characteristics of the entity's business, IT processes, and information systems. The information posted is later used to exploit end users via social engineering or to craft other attacks based on the intelligence gathered.

- Likelihood and impact can match the values assigned to the risk, owing to immature training and awareness to simplify the process.

Potential intelligence is an assessment that provides value, if a third party with expertise in this arena can be found. Real data showing the entity's digital footprint makes it possible to quantitatively assess the risk posed by social media. If the cost of having an assessment such as this is too high, it is possible to conduct a high-level assessment to understand what social media risks may be present. In the end, it may not be possible to remediate assessment findings if risky social media findings are uncovered, but the information is useful for developing compensating controls. Figure 15-1 shows the steps for a social media audit plan.

> **Develop Audit scope**
> - LinkedIn
> - Twitter

> **Assessment steps**
> - Review corporate accounts
>   - Job Postings
>   - Marketing Posts
>   - Document Employee Connections
> - Review Employee Accounts
>   - Compile Intelligence

> **Assess Risk**
> - Likelihood and Impact of information being found and used
> - Adjust Risk and Report

***Figure 15-1.*** *Steps required to assess and evaluate risks to ePHI, based on an entity's social media presence*

Once the assessment is complete and updates are made to the risk analysis and risk register, identification of mitigation strategies and management reporting is required. These are not risks that can be eliminated, but close monitoring is a must.

# Internet of Things (IoT)

The term *Internet of Things* refers to the increased connectedness of devices with IP addresses that years ago were not common. These devices gather and use those IP addresses to transmit information. Businesses gather information used for innovation, enhanced customer service, and optimized processes. Because providing healthcare, adjudicating insurance claims, and providing services to covered entities are business-related, these business cases apply to all three types of entities. Providers gather data on patients, find new treatment methods, and increase efficiency by using data. This enhances a health system's ability to connect with the communities it serves. The challenges of how to deal with the amounts of data gathered and how to secure it remain.

# Bring Your Own Device (BYOD)

BYOD is a legacy cybersecurity issue in all sectors, healthcare being no different. BYOD risks should be managed through governance and mobile data management system controls, reducing the severity to low levels. End users' ability to access e-mail on their phones and tablets is a must now. Business leaders and customers expect 24/7 access with "reasonable" response times. This can only be achieved by allowing access on mobile phones and tablets. This does not mean that employees must access applications processing ePHI on mobile devices. Applications such as Good Enterprise and BlackBerry Work containerize e-mails, preventing the e-mail itself, or attachments, to be saved on the device. This way, if an employee is terminated, either voluntarily or involuntarily, that container can be erased, and company e-mail is no longer accessible by the former employee.

# Portable Devices

Years ago, about the time the Omnibus Rule took effect in 2013, lost or stolen thumb drives were to blame for breaches of ePHI. Resolution agreements subsequently focused on insufficient risk analysis and security controls, including the use of encryption. In 2017, thumb drives and other portable storage should not be relevant. Because so many solutions offer capabilities to prevent data transfer via USB (Universal Serial Bus), there is no excuse for blocking such uses of data. There might be a few examples of business units within healthcare providers, payers, or business associates that require the ability to store data on USB or other portable storage devices. If that is the case, risk analysis is required. Figure 15-2 outlines some of the details the analysis should capture.

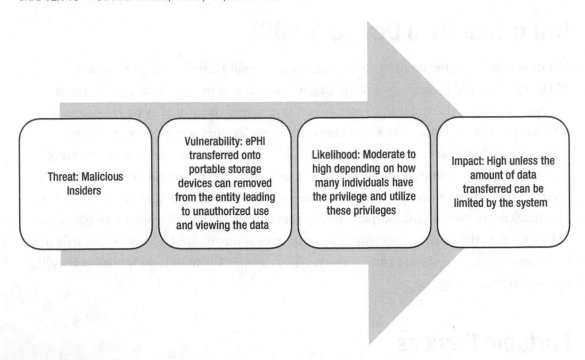

**Figure 15-2.**   *The risk analysis flow for portable devices. If the entity allows the use of these capabilities, it is important to assess the risk appropriately.*

This analysis concluded that malicious insiders pose the most significant threat to ePHI transferred to portable devices, such as thumb drives. These privileges must be governed by strong policy, procedures, and process controls. There also should be technical means to quickly disable this privilege, if unacceptable activity is discovered. That way, if end users decide to cut corners, or simply desire to steal vast amounts of ePHI, malicious activities are detected and the threats contained as quickly as possible.

# Summary

Social media, IoT, BYOD, and portable devices are all areas that the cybersecurity program and risk management must consider. The first two are growing and becoming more predominant issues in cybersecurity, while the last two remain considerations, although, with the solutions available today, their risk severity should be reduced to low or moderate.

Social media issues have moved beyond merely the risk of employees posting sensitive information publicly. Adversaries are resourceful and pull intelligence from many sources, increasing the odds for success when targeting entities with ePHI. Phishing e-mails spoof down to the tiniest details, with specifics gathered about the vulnerable end user exploited to increase the odds of success. Also increasing the odds against cybersecurity programs is the increased attack surface the explosion of IoT has brought to healthcare. The more data about patients that is created, captured, and retained, the larger the odds of a breach, and the greater the impact to the organization.

BYOD, involving end-user owned devices taking part in ePHI that is in use, motion, and at rest, also increases the odds of a breach. With the exception of letting workforce members use containerized e-mail applications, this privilege should not be allowed. End point security controls are needed to protect ePHI, and implementing such controls on nonentity-owned devices is too complicated. Finally, end point protection that prevents end users from transferring data to portable storage devices also requires strong consideration.

# CHAPTER 16

# Risk Treatment and Management

During the risk analysis and assessment process, risks specific to the entity's governance, processes, and capabilities were documented. Risks associated with engaging a third-party service provider and risks due to the use of social media were discovered and added during the testing phase. These risks range in severity from low to very high, based on the likelihood and impact to the confidentiality, integrity, and availability of ePHI if an adversary exploits one of them. Selecting security measures as a means of risk reduction or mitigation is an important step in the process, but it is not possible to eliminate the risk. That is where risk treatment and management come into play. When selecting security measures, entity management must choose the security measures, risk treatments, that reduce each risk to an acceptable level.

## Creating the Risk Treatment and Management Plan

Risks are treated by adopting security measures designed to reduce the risk to an acceptable level. These security measures or controls come in two forms: mitigating controls, which are implemented due to a gap, and compensating controls. Compensating controls are implemented when limiting factors do not allow for a leading practice control to function within the entity. This was touched upon in Chapter 8's discussion of cybersecurity program maturity and how maturity efforts can reduce risk. This process consists of three steps.

© Eric C. Thompson 2017
E. C. Thompson, *Building a HIPAA-Compliant Cybersecurity Program*,
https://doi.org/10.1007/978-1-4842-3060-2_16

1. Identify the cybersecurity controls that address each risk.

2. For cybersecurity controls already in place but lacking process maturity and/or capability to reduce risk sufficiently, a plan to correct these issues is required and must be approved by management.

3. Continuously monitor each control for progress against the corrective action plan and overall operational effectiveness.

Determining acceptable risk levels is important to risk management. It is not possible to mature all cybersecurity controls to the highest levels, so decisions are made on which cybersecurity controls require the most focus. Some entities will accept moderate risks and are only concerned with very high and high risks. Others look at each individual risk and determine how much reduction is desired. Neither approach is right or wrong, the difference being that the second scenario is more detailed and possibly optimizes resource allocation and risk management. Here, the goal is to reduce all risks to values of three or lower, in likelihood and impact. In Figure 16-1, the risks that need to be treated include the very high and high risks. Moderate risks: R17, R20, R2, R8, R16, R23 and R4 do not meet the criteria for acceptable risks and need treatment.

| Risk Matrix | | | | | |
|---|---|---|---|---|---|
| | **Very High**<br><br>5 | Very Low | Low | Moderate<br>R17, R20 | High<br>R9, R10, R12,<br>R13, R18, R21 | Very High<br>R15,R19, aR15, |
| | **High**<br><br>4 | Very Low | Low | Moderate<br>R2,  R8, R16, R23 | High<br>R3, R5, R14 | Very High |
| **Impact** | **Moderate**<br><br>3 | Very Low | Low | Moderate<br>R1,R6,R7,R11,R14,<br>R24, R25 | Moderate<br>R4 | High |
| | **Low**<br><br>2 | Very Low | Low<br>R27 | Low<br>R26 | Low | Moderate |
| | **Very Low**<br><br>1 | Very Low | Very Low | Very Low | Low | Low |
| | | **Very Low**<br>1 | **Low**<br>2 | **Moderate**<br>3 | **High**<br>4 | **Very High**<br>5 |
| | | Likelihood | | | | |

**Figure 16-1.** *The grid visually displays risks, so making it visually easier to view risks not within the acceptible risk range*

# Very High Risks

Very high risks, with scores of 5 for likelihood and impact, are the first group of risks to review. These risks require reductions in both likelihood and impact. As a reminder, the details of these risks are outlined in Table 16-1.

***Table 16-1.***  *Risks Identified As Very High, with Likelihood and Impact Values of 5*

| Risk | Description |
| --- | --- |
| R15 | Sophisticated attackers can gain access into the network, owing to inadequate training and awareness programs causing ePHI to be viewed, modified, or rendered unavailable. |
| R19 | Sophisticated attackers can move laterally and elevate privileges in the network, owing to inadequate monitoring controls and capabilities causing ePHI to be viewed, modified, or rendered unavailable. |
| R22 | Attacks by sophisticated attackers can go undetected, unquarantined, and fail to be eradicated, owing to missing log correlations processes and capabilities causing ePHI to be viewed, modified, or rendered unavailable. |

To reduce the likelihood factor, management must identify capabilities that limit the potential for success that a threat actor may have when exploiting the vulnerability. Figure 16-2 shows alternatives for management to consider.

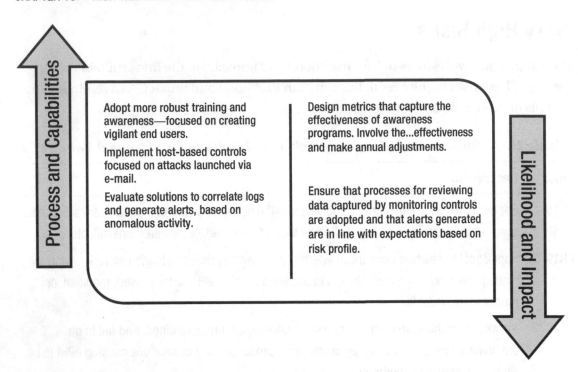

**Process and Capabilities**

Adopt more robust training and awareness—focused on creating vigilant end users.

Implement host-based controls focused on attacks launched via e-mail.

Evaluate solutions to correlate logs and generate alerts, based on anomalous activity.

Design metrics that capture the effectiveness of awareness programs. Involve the...effectiveness and make annual adjustments.

Ensure that processes for reviewing data captured by monitoring controls are adopted and that alerts generated are in line with expectations based on risk profile.

**Likelihood and Impact**

*Figure 16-2.* *The relationship between enhanced cybersecurity controls and risk reduction represents polar opposites*

The bullet points that follow indicate updates required to align NIST CSF controls with the three risks in Table 16-1. These improvements increase the maturity of the cybersecurity control process and, with it, reduce the likelihood a vulnerability tied to each being exploited. Policies that expect training and awareness to occur frequently and enforce sanctions against users consistently displaying risky behavior reduce the likelihood that threat actors can exploit end users to gain access to a network. Not only are end users less likely to click malicious links and documents in e-mails, or hand over credentials to attackers, but more vigilant end users will reduce the likelihood of a successful exploit. Following several improvements on how the entity monitors the environment and collects logs for analysis are highlighted:

- Document requirements for continuous monitoring, collection of logs, and correlation activities in policy documents. Specific technologies do not have to be outlined, but statements to this effect must be recorded.

- Procedure and control process documents outline how the environment is monitored and logs are collected, what is monitored and what logs are collected, and who owns the process and is accountable for ensuring effective operation.

- If technology investments and enhanced solutions have to be purchased, business cases outlining the cyber and compliance risk reduction requirements, reduction in business risks, and long-term benefits must be presented to the steering committee. If commitments for investments are denied, these decisions and their rationale must be recorded in the meeting minutes.

- These processes must be tested annually, either by internal resources or by engaging outside firms. The results and proposed corrective actions must be reviewed by management.

- As previously mentioned, metrics demonstrating effective operation and risk reduction must be identified, tracked, and reported to management, which reviews the results and makes necessary changes to the program, if the results are not satisfactory.

The third bulleted item discusses technology-based solutions. Monitoring, log collection, and correlation of events require investing in solutions such as SIEM technology. These services incur the costs of purchasing the product, fees based on events or log consumption, personnel or outside firms to monitor and investigate alerts, and many other additional ones. The amount of risk reduction is based on what the entity can afford to invest at any given time and the pace of implementation. For example,

- In phase one, a SIEM is purchased, and basic logs are ingested into the solution from firewalls, servers that process ePHI, and end point solutions protecting laptops.

- Phase one also includes assigning a member of the cybersecurity team to monitor the SIEM and review alerts.

- Phase two establishes a relationship with a third party that monitors and investigates alerts; logs are ingested from all servers; and new solutions, such as a IDS, or updates to end point protection, have logs forwarded to the SIEM.

- The final phase might include the purchase of machine-earning and/ or behavior analytics.

The first phase of the project may not result in a reduction of likelihood or impact to any risks. Once the second phase is completed, the impact can be reduced to somewhere between 3 and 4, depending on the entity's risk appetite. The final phase could reduce impact down to 2.

# High Likelihood and Very High Impact Risks

Table 16-2 shows the risks that are considered high, based on high likelihood of occurrence and very high impact to ePHI if vulnerabilities are exploited. These risks require reduction in both likelihood and impact.

*Table 16-2.* *High Risks to ePHI Requiring Reductions of Likelihood and Impact to Lower Each to an Acceptable Level. The First Seven Are High Likelihood and High Impact Risks. The Remaining Are Moderate Likelihood and High Impact Risks*

| Risk | Risk Description |
|------|------------------|
| R9 | Sophisticated attackers could view, modify, steal, or render ePHI unavailable, owing to a lack of access management controls. |
| R10 | Sophisticated attackers could view, modify, steal, or render ePHI unavailable, owing to database access management being ineffectively managed. |
| R12 | Sophisticated attackers could view, modify, steal, or render ePHI unavailable, owing to network access management being ineffectively managed. |
| R13 | Sophisticated attackers could view, modify, steal, or render ePHI unavailable, owing to the network infrastructure not being up to date. |
| R18 | Malicious insiders could view, modify, or steal ePHI, owing to removable media not being properly secured. |

(*continued*)

*Table 16-2.* (*continued*)

| Risk | Risk Description |
| --- | --- |
| R21 | Sophisticated attackers could view, modify, steal, or render ePHI unavailable because a logging process is not defined. |
| TPR1 | State-sponsored actors, organized cybercriminals, and malicious insiders can steal, modify, or render ePHI unavailable, owing to weak access controls. |
| R3 | Sophisticated attackers could view, modify, steal, or render ePHI unavailable, because cybersecurity needs and capabilities are not properly funded. |
| R5 | Sophisticated attackers could view, modify, steal, or render ePHI unavailable, owing to insecure configurations of network infrastructure and applications being inappropriately configured. |
| R14 | Malicious insiders could view, modify, steal, or render ePHI unavailable, owing to duties not being segregated appropriately within the environment. |
| TPR5 | State-sponsored actors, organized cybercriminals, malicious insiders, or environmental events can render data unavailable, by exploiting weaknesses in cybersecurity governance. |

Figure 16-3 shows the measures and steps required to reduce the following issues identified during the risk analysis.

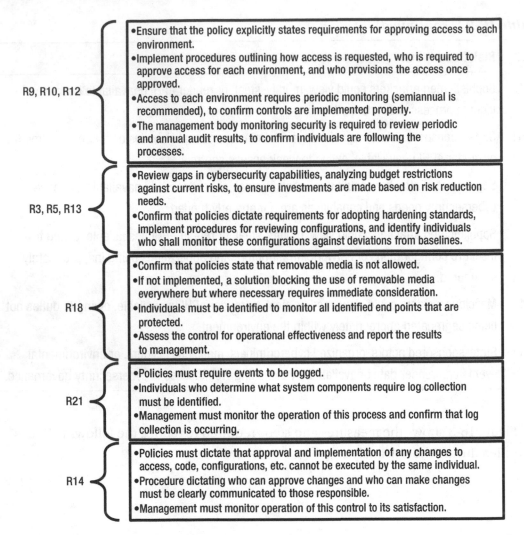

**R9, R10, R12**
- Ensure that the policy explicitly states requirements for approving access to each environment.
- Implement procedures outlining how access is requested, who is required to approve access for each environment, and who provisions the access once approved.
- Access to each environment requires periodic monitoring (semiannual is recommended), to confirm controls are implemented properly.
- The management body monitoring security is required to review periodic and annual audit results, to confirm individuals are following the processes.

**R3, R5, R13**
- Review gaps in cybersecurity capabilities, analyzing budget restrictions against current risks, to ensure investments are made based on risk reduction needs.
- Confirm that policies dictate requirements for adopting hardening standards, implement procedures for reviewing configurations, and identify individuals who shall monitor these configurations against deviations from baselines.

**R18**
- Confirm that policies state that removable media is not allowed.
- If not implemented, a solution blocking the use of removable media everywhere but where necessary requires immediate consideration.
- Individuals must be identified to monitor all identified end points that are protected.
- Assess the control for operational effectiveness and report the results to management.

**R21**
- Policies must require events to be logged.
- Individuals who determine what system components require log collection must be identified.
- Management must monitor the operation of this process and confirm that log collection is occurring.

**R14**
- Policies must dictate that approval and implementation of any changes to access, code, configurations, etc. cannot be executed by the same individual.
- Procedure dictating who can approve changes and who can make changes must be clearly communicated to those responsible.
- Management must monitor operation of this control to its satisfaction.

***Figure 16-3.*** *High-level outline of the risk treatment plan for high risks identified during the risk analysis process*

For the access controls, R9, R10, and R12, the objective of remediation is to reduce to a low level the likelihood of exploiting access vulnerabilities. Forcing strict policy and procedure documentation assigned to individuals accountable for successful operation will reduce the number of inappropriate access incidents.

Insufficient budget issues must be remediated through investment in capabilities required to bring infrastructure up to date and hardened to standards appropriate for protecting ePHI. As with access controls, these measures require policies that dictate hardening standards. These policies must also address who is responsible for ensuring that new hardware implementation adheres to these standards. The entity must also adopt a process for reviewing hardware configurations regularly, correcting any issues found, and for management to review the adopted standards, to ensure that they are appropriate for the entity.

Removable media poses a significant risk when users have access to ePHI and can transfer data to other devices. Technical solutions can block the ability of users to move data from an end point to portable media. Depending on the size of the entity, these solutions can be costly, but investing in this capability is a must. Too much is at stake to leave the door open for users to remove data from the environment in an unsecured manner. As with the other remediation activities discussed, strong policy and procedure documents are required to drive compliance from those expected to carry out this control process.

Management must monitor the operation of cybersecurity controls and review assessment results. These types of activities define highly mature cybersecurity programs. Metrics, which are derived from the testing and assessment of cybersecurity controls, are the means management must use to monitor the cybersecurity program. When metrics deviate, changes must be made to correct the situation.

## Moderate–High Likelihood and Moderate Impact

The risks in Table 16-3 require a reduction of one level, either in the likelihood or impact of the risk. The easiest path to reduction is focusing on likelihood. Again, this means making improvements to the cybersecurity controls. Here, the risk in question is R4, which is a risk to ePHI owing to missing integration between company policies and regulatory requirements. The other risks in this category exist because the entity engaged a third party with ePHI in its possession. The evaluation and mitigation of these risks should focus on measures the entity can employ to reduce the likelihood that this vulnerability can be exploited. The internal risk can be reduced through a review and updating of policy documents and accountability for enforcing those policies. The other risks cannot be directly mitigated by the entity; therefore, because these risks fall outside of the acceptable range, the entity must either choose not to not engage with the third party or management must accept the risks.

***Table 16-3.***  *High Likelihood and Moderate Impact Risks*

| Risk | Description |
| --- | --- |
| R4 | Malicious insiders can view, modify, steal, or render ePHI unavailable, owing to not integrating regulatory requirements into policy and procedure documents appropriately. |
| TPR2 | State-sponsored actors, organized cybercriminals, malicious insiders, or environmental events can render data unavailable, owing to weak availability processes. |
| TPR3 | Malicious insiders can cause data to be lost, owing to weak controls against data leakage. |
| TPR4 | Organized cybercriminals and malicious insiders can steal, modify, or render ePHI unavailable, by making malicious changes to the system or exploiting unmitigated vulnerabilities. |

Management response to these risks must be documented and reviewed periodically. Figure 16-4 shows the actions that can be taken to reduce this group of risks to an acceptable level.

---

### Risk 4

- Review all policies and map them to regulatory and third-party compliance requirements.
- Confirm that cybersecurity procedures and control wording reflect these policy requirements.
- Monitor the environment to ensure that cybersecurity controls implemented to meet compliance requirements are operating effectively.
- Metrics should be established to allow management to measure control effectiveness through annual reviews and adjustments.

### TPR2, 3 and 4

- Review the deficiency in availability with capabilities the vendor has to organizational needs and create an exception if the business cannot forgo the vendor relationship.
- Document the flow of data through the vendor system and identify the weaknesses in data leakage controls.  If governance or documentation weaknesses cause maturity issues with the control perhaps the residual risk can be accepted.
- Review the vulnerability management program and assess the weaknesses. If governance and oversight needs are required, the business agreement might allow for monitoring and reporting of vulnerability mitigation to the entity on a periodic basis.

***Figure 16-4.***  *Key actions that can be taken to reduce this group of risks to an acceptable level*

# Moderate–Moderate Likelihood and Very High Impact

These risks are very high impact risks, if exploited. Storing or allowing ePHI in test environments where security controls may lack robustness can cause a significant breach. The same is true of a lack of incident management and response documentation. This could cause a simple issue to turn into something more significant and more impactful. Table 16-4 documents the two risks in this category.

***Table 16-4.*** *Moderate Likelihood and Very High Impact Risks*

| Risk | Description |
| --- | --- |
| R17 | Sophisticated attackers could view, modify, steal, or render ePHI unavailable, because it exists in nonproduction environments, such as test and development. |
| R20 | Sophisticated attackers could view, modify, steal, or render ePHI unavailable, because cybersecurity incidents are not logged and investigated properly. |

These risks require reductions in likelihood to meet the risk acceptance criteria. Figure 16-5 illustrates several key document and activity implementations that will reduce the risk likelihood sufficiently.

---

**R17**

- Update cybersecurity policy to state that ePHI is not to be stored in nonproduction (dev and QA) environments.
- Assessments of nonproduction environments are required periodically, either annually or biannually, to confirm ePHI is not in use, motion, or rest in these authorized areas.
- Management reviews results and makes changes to the  environment, as necessary.

**R20**

- Policy documents require the production and maintenance of an incident response plan.
- The incident response plan and associated procedures determine characteristics for defining what is considered to be an incident.
- Management reviews the results of all incident responses to monitor adherence to the logging and response process.

---

*Figure 16-5.*  *Key actions that can be taken to reduce this group of risks to an acceptable level*

## Moderate–Moderate Likelihood and High Impact

Three of the four risks in Table 16-5, which are moderate likelihood and high impact, require improvement in governance processes. The last risk requires a technical component.

*Table 16-5.*  *Moderate Likelihood and High Impact Risks*

| Risk | Description |
|------|-------------|
| R2 | Sophisticated attackers could view, modify, steal, or render ePHI unavailable, owing to data not being managed appropriately, based on its classification. |
| R8 | Sophisticated attackers could view, modify, steal, or render ePHI unavailable, because standard time lines for remediation are not established. |
| R16 | Sophisticated attackers could view, modify, steal, or render ePHI unavailable, because data at rest is not encrypted. |
| R28 | Sophisticated attackers could view, modify, steal, or render ePHI unavailable, because third-party service providers are not vetted through proper due diligence. |

To get these risks reduced within acceptable parameters, reducing their likelihood through increased control maturity is the focus. Figure 16-6 shows the key activities and documentation improvements required to meet the objectives.

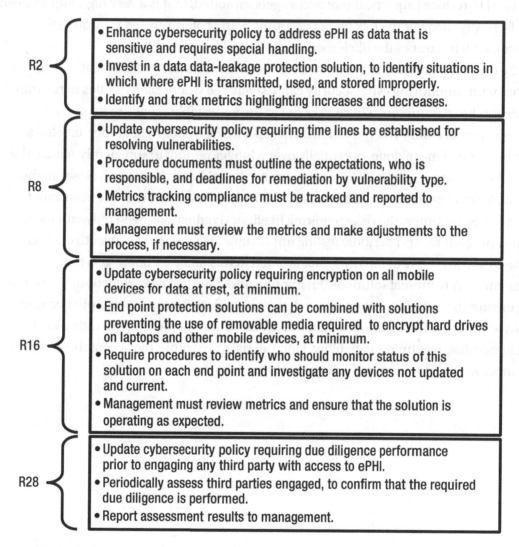

**Figure 16-6.** *Key actions that can be taken to reduce this group of risks to an acceptable level*

# Summary

Here, risk reductions occur primarily by reducing the likelihood of a successful exploit. It is hard to reduce impacts. If root access gets exploited, that is a very high impact event. The best way to lower the risk of root accounts being compromised is through tight control, which reduces the likelihood.

By using the grid layout in Figure 16-1, risk managers and members of management tasked with monitoring cybersecurity can visually see where each risk lies in relation to acceptable parameters. Those risks not in the acceptable range are treated to achieve the necessary risk reductions. The risks in the upper right corner, labeled as very high, need more done, potentially over a longer period, to sufficiently reduce the risks. As the entity reviews risks moving left on the grid and downward, closer to the center, actions necessary to reduce risk can focus on fewer and more concentrated activities. Sometimes, the risks requiring likelihood reductions need only enhanced policy, procedure, and periodic testing improvements to reach the objectives. This is the case with many of the risks documented in this analysis. Some also require investment in technical solutions. Encryption and data-leakage protection, for example, can ensure that ePHI is protected, used, transmitted, and stored in compliance with entity standards. This cannot be achieved by any other means than investing in and implementing a technical capability. Once all risks are within the acceptable range, the organization can focus on reducing other risks.

# CHAPTER 17

# Customizing the Risk Analysis

Risk analysis is customizable, if the required elements exist. It is thorough and covers the entire enterprise. Here, it is possible to show an example of a risk analysis customized using Monte Carlo simulations when assigning values to the likelihood and impact ratings for given risks. Risk analysis is part art, part science. The art to risk analysis is to achieve results that reflect the true state of the environment. Qualitative risk assessments can suffer if careful thought is not given to assigning likelihood and impact values, yet it is not possible to be 100% quantitative. Evidence must be interpreted by the person doing the analysis. Monte Carlo simulations allow the risk practitioner to use his or her judgment to determine a range of possible values, agree on a likely value, and use a simulation to assign likelihood and impact values.

## Risk Analysis Parameters

The first place to begin this process is to establish the parameters for the likelihood and impact values to be used in the risk analysis. This occurs once the inventory of ePHI is complete, threats are identified, vulnerabilities are documented, and risk statements are written.

© Eric C. Thompson 2017
E. C. Thompson, *Building a HIPAA-Compliant Cybersecurity Program*,
https://doi.org/10.1007/978-1-4842-3060-2_17

# Likelihood

As stated earlier, likelihood is a function of the maturity that the cybersecurity controls assigned to reduce a specific risk have achieved. Here, the PRISMA[1] model is used to assess the maturity for each control. As a refresher, PRISMA measures control maturity based on the following components:

- Policy

  - Policies must use "we" and "shall."

  - There is a continuous cycle of assessing risk, implementing controls, and monitoring for program effectiveness.

  - Policies cover the entire organization.

  - Policies define roles and responsibilities.

  - Sanctions for noncompliance are integrated into the policies.

- Procedure

  - This is the who, what, where, when, and how of implementing security controls.

- Implementation

  - Procedures are communicated to individuals who are required to follow them.

  - IT security procedures are implemented everywhere the procedure applies.

- Test

  - Periodic testing is conducted to evaluate the effective operation of policy, procedure, and control implementation.

- Integration

  - Management reviews assessments and metrics on a continuous basis and makes necessary adjustments to ensure proper operation.

---

[1]NIST, "Program Review for Information Security Assistance," http://csrc.nist.gov/groups/SMA/prisma/security_maturity_levels.html, December 7, 2016; updated July 31, 2017.

## Assessing the Level of Maturity

To gauge the level of maturity for a control, each component is scored in its respective categories on a scale of zero to a maximum of five points for each control. Table 17-1 shows the breakdown of the likelihood scale, based on the maturity score assigned to the control operation.

***Table 17-1.*** *Maturity Levels, Based on the Scores Applied in Each of the Five Components of the PRISMA Model*

| Maturity Level | Score Range |
| --- | --- |
| Very High | 5 |
| High | 4–4.5 |
| Moderate | 2.5–4 |
| Low | 1–2.5 |
| Very Low | 0–1 |

## Assigning Impact Values

Impact values are assigned based on the potential number of records that could be lost during a breach. Creating parameters that place values for impact, using potential records lost, is loosely tied into risk tolerance but focuses on how tightly the entity intends to control the environment. The Ponemon[2] Institute listed the average cost of a breach at $4 million and the average cost per record, for sensitive records, at $158. Healthcare records had a cost of $355 per record. For this analysis, the $158 per record metric is used.

Using an average total cost of $4 million and a per-record cost of $158, a breach just north of 25,000 records would reach the $4 million mark. Here, the upper limit, worst possible scenario, and highest impact was set at 30,000 records lost. Table 17-2 outlines the thresholds set for number of records lost in each category.

---

[2]Bernie Monegain, "Cost of data breaches climbs to $4 million as healthcare incidents are most expensive, Ponemon finds," Healthcare IT News, www.healthcareitnews.com/news/cost-data-breaches-climbs-4-million-healthcare-events-most-expensive-ponemon-finds, June 20, 2016.

**Table 17-2.** *Breakdown of Impact Ranges, by Number of Records, That May Be Breached*

| Impact Level | Impact Rating | Threshold |
|---|---|---|
| Very High | 4.5–5 | 24,000 to 30,000 |
| High | 3.5–4.5 | 18,000 to 24,000 |
| Moderate | 2.5–3.5 | 12,000 to 18,000 |
| Low | 1.5–2.5 | 6,000 to 12,000 |
| Very Low | 0–1 | 0 to 6,000 |

# Very Low

The impacts for very low risks are 0.55 for a breach of 300 records to an upper limit of 1.5 if 6,000 records are affected. Table 17-3 displays impact based on records affected.

**Table 17-3.** *Impact Ratings for Very Low Risks, Based on the Number of Records Affected by a Breach*

| Impact Level | Potential Breach Total (Up To) |
|---|---|
| 0.55 | 300 |
| 0.60 | 600 |
| 0.65 | 900 |
| 0.70 | 1,200 |
| 0.75 | 1,500 |
| 0.80 | 1,800 |
| 0.85 | 2,100 |
| 0.90 | 2,400 |
| 0.95 | 2,700 |

*(continued)*

***Table 17-3.*** (*continued*)

| Impact Level | Potential Breach Total (Up To) |
|---|---|
| 1 | 3,000 |
| 1.05 | 3,300 |
| 1.10 | 3,600 |
| 1.15 | 3,900 |
| 1.20 | 4,200 |
| 1.25 | 4,500 |
| 1.3 | 4,800 |
| 1.35 | 5,100 |
| 1.4 | 5,400 |
| 1.45 | 5,700 |
| 1.5 | 6,000 |

The precise impacts based on 300 record increments are broken down further in this chapter in the low, moderate, high, and very high categories.

# Low

The impact of a low risk ranges from 1.55 for a breach affecting 6,300 records to 2.5 for 12,000 records affected. Table 17-4 shows the impact ranges for low risks, based on the number of records affected.

**Table 17-4.** *Impact Ranges of Low Risks, Based on the Number of Records Affected by a Breach*

| Impact Level | Potential Breach Total (Up To) |
|---|---|
| 1.55 | 6,300 |
| 1.6 | 6,600 |
| 1.65 | 6,900 |
| 1.7 | 7,200 |
| 1.75 | 7,500 |
| 1.8 | 8,000 |
| 1.85 | 8,300 |
| 1.9 | 8,400 |
| 1.95 | 8,700 |
| 2 | 9,000 |
| 2.05 | 9,300 |
| 2.1 | 9,600 |
| 2.15 | 9,900 |
| 2.2 | 10,200 |
| 2.25 | 10,500 |
| 2.3 | 10,800 |
| 2.35 | 11,100 |
| 2.4 | 11,400 |
| 2.45 | 11,700 |
| 2.5 | 12,000 |

# Moderate

Moderate risks range from 2.55 for breaches affecting 12,300 records to 3.5 for 18,000 records affected. Table 17-5 shows the impact ranges for moderate risks, based on number of records affected.

***Table 17-5.***  *Impact Ranges of Moderate Risks, Based on the Number of Records Affected by a Breach*

| Impact Level | Potential Breach Total (Up To) |
|---|---|
| 2.55 | 12,300 |
| 2.6 | 12,600 |
| 2.65 | 12,900 |
| 2.7 | 13,200 |
| 2.75 | 13,500 |
| 2.8 | 13,800 |
| 2.85 | 14,100 |
| 2.9 | 14,400 |
| 2.95 | 14,700 |
| 3.0 | 15,000 |
| 3.05 | 15,300 |
| 3.1 | 15,500 |
| 3.15 | 15,800 |
| 3.2 | 16,100 |
| 3.25 | 16,400 |
| 3.3 | 16,700 |
| 3.35 | 17,000 |
| 3.4 | 17,300 |
| 3.45 | 17,600 |
| 3.5 | 18,000 |

# High

The impact ratings for high risks range from 3.55 for breaches of 18,300 to 4.5 for breaches of 24,000 records. Table 17-6 shows the impact levels, based on the number or records affected by a breach.

***Table 17-6.*** *Impact Ranges for High Risks, Based on the Number of Records Affected by a Breach*

| Impact Level | Potential Breach Total (Up To) |
|---|---|
| 3.55 | 18,300 |
| 3.6 | 18,600 |
| 3.65 | 19,100 |
| 3.7 | 19,400 |
| 3.75 | 19,700 |
| 3.8 | 20,000 |
| 3.85 | 20,300 |
| 3.9 | 20,600 |
| 3.95 | 20,900 |
| 4 | 21,200 |
| 4.05 | 21,500 |
| 4.1 | 21,500 |
| 4.15 | 21,800 |
| 4.2 | 22,100 |
| 4.25 | 22,400 |
| 4.3 | 22,700 |
| 4.35 | 23,000 |
| 4.4 | 23,300 |
| 4.45 | 23,600 |
| 4.5 | 24,000 |

## Very High

The impact levels for very high risks range from 4.55 for a breach affecting 24,600 records to 5 for breaches affecting 30,000 records. Table 17-7 shows the impact ranges, based on number of records affected by a breach.

*Table 17-7.* *Impact Ranges for Very High Risks, Based on the Number of Records Affected by a Breach*

| Impact Level | Potential Breach Total (Up To) |
| --- | --- |
| 4.55 | 24,600 |
| 4.6 | 25,200 |
| 4.65 | 25,800 |
| 4.7 | 26,400 |
| 4.75 | 27,000 |
| 4.8 | 27,600 |
| 4.85 | 28,200 |
| 4.9 | 28,800 |
| 4.95 | 29,400 |
| 5 | 30,000 |

# Risk Analysis Walkthrough: Two Examples

With the risk analysis parameters established, two risks documented in Chapter 7 will now be assessed using Monte Carlo simulations. These simulations are used to assign values for likelihood and impact, based on best estimates outcomes. Monte Carlo simulations are not new to cybersecurity. A SANS Institute white paper written by Dan Lyons outlines the process for using Monte Carlo simulations to evaluate security investments[3] and is available in the SANS Reading Room. This white paper uses

---

[3]Dan Lyon, "Modeling Security Investments With Monte Carlo Simulations," www.sans.org/reading-room/whitepapers/modeling/modeling-security-investments-monte-carlo-simulations-35457, September 16, 2014.

Oracle's Crystal Ball software, a plug-in for Excel,[4] to run the simulations. For a cyber-risk practitioner, the Monte Carlo technique and Crystal Ball are methods available to enhance the risk analysis process. During the risk analysis process, the practitioner establishes the low, high, and most likely thresholds for likelihood and impact as inputs. Another parameter is deciding how many simulations the program will run during the scenario. The process here set Crystal Ball to run 9,000 simulations on the inputs and display the values at the 90th percentile. Likelihood and impact build this analysis based on values that occurred 90% more often than the other values during the risk simulations.

# Access Management Risk

Risks associated with access are listed in Table 17-8. These are application, database, and network access risks, which have high likelihood and very high impact values that drive these high risks.

***Table 17-8.*** *Risks Appearing on the Risk Analysis Associated with Access Management*

| Risk No | Risk | Likelihood | Impact |
|---------|------|------------|--------|
| R9 | Application access management is ineffectively managed. | 4 | 5 |
| R10 | Database access management is ineffectively managed. | 4 | 5 |
| R12 | Network access management is ineffectively managed. | 4 | 5 |

## Evaluating Likelihood

The likelihood was initially measured at 4. During the analysis of risk treatments, it was documented that the approach to reducing the risks should focus on updating policies to implement strong governance, establishing that procedures exist for adding, removing, and reviewing user access, and defining ownership for those procedures. Accountability for ensuring processes exist and are operating effectively is a must. Again, to increase cybersecurity control maturity to its maximum, testing operational effectiveness must

---

[4]Oracle, "Oracle Crystal Ball," www.oracle.com/us/products/applications/crystalball/ overview/index.html, 2008.

occur, and management must monitor performance metrics and make necessary adjustments.

Access controls are immature here, as evidenced by only one out of five points credited to the process. The analysis concluded that only partial credit could be given for policy, procedure, and implementation. Monte Carlo simulations are useful in assigning the likelihood value, based on a range of possible outcomes. The ranges for this simulation are illustrated in Table 17-9.

***Table 17-9.*** *Value Ranges for Each of the Maturity Elements for Access Controls*

| Maturity Element | Range of Values | Most Likely Value |
|---|---|---|
| Policy | 0–0.25 | 0 |
| Procedure | 0.25–0.75 | 0.50 |
| Implementation | 0.25–0.75 | 0.50 |

## Evaluating Impact

The impact for weak access control is 5, which means any successful exploit could cause 30,000 or more records to be viewed, stolen, modified, or rendered unavailable. To add more precision to the risk analysis, it is important to go a step further. Understanding what each type of account, or role, in an application does adds more quantitative elements to the risk analysis. If a user account in an application storing, processing, and transmitting ePHI were compromised, what is the likely number of records between 0 and 30,000 that could be compromised? Questions the risk practitioner might ask include the following:

- Is access to the application role-based?

- Can it be determined how many records the average user can access, and, if so, what is the range?

- Are there auditing or monitoring tools, and do these mechanisms generate automated alerts, or is manual intervention required?

If this example is a healthcare provider, it would be prudent to understand if the availability of patient information is limited by clinical environment, department, or other access-limitation controls. If access is limited, what is the average number of records for each role? Or, if access is not limited, it must be assumed that all records are at risk by each compromised account. And if a user account is rapidly accessing patient records, it is important to understand if any thresholds are available to alert the cybersecurity team to these activities.

The same thought process can be used at healthcare payers and business associates. Understand how access to the application in question is provisioned and attempt to understand the threshold of records at risk. The risk analysis enhances cybersecurity control and distribution of resources only if the inputs are of sufficient quality. Assuming every access compromise is the worst possible outcome does not help if only certain accounts have close monitoring.

Here, an account that is compromised is not limited by any mitigating controls. Access management is immature, so it is probable that a compromised application account can lead to a breach of 30,000 or more records. To simulate the impact, a low-range and a most likely value have to be determined. The lowest limit for this scenario is 0, the upper limit is 30,000, and the median is 15,000.

At the database and network level, if administrator accounts are compromised, it is likely that the 30,000-record threshold will be reached. Simulating these scenarios for impact is not necessary for this analysis.

## Monte Carlo Simulations of Likelihood and Impact

Figure 17-1 shows the screen in Crystal Ball on which the values for policy ranges are entered. For each component, policy, procedure, and implementation, the low limit, high limit, and most likely value are entered. For the scenarios outlined, the values used in the simulation are laid out in Table 17-10.

***Table 17-10.*** *Value ranges for Likelihood and Impact of Access Control Risks*

| Risk No | Low Likelihood | High Likelihood | Likely Value | Low Impact | High Impact | Likely Impact |
|---------|---------------|-----------------|--------------|------------|-------------|---------------|
| R9 | 4.5 | 5 | 4.75 | 4 | 5 | 4.5 |

# Insecure Development and Quality Assurance Environments

During the risk analysis process, Risk 17 (R17) was documented as a risk to ePHI, owing to it resting in Development and Quality Assurance (QA), which are known to be less secure than production environments. The concern is that members of the workforce developing changes and others who test those changes prior to implementation to production should not have access to ePHI in these environments.

## Evaluating Likelihood

This risk was rated at a level 3, moderate, for likelihood, again because of control maturity. The existence of a policy and procedure are enough to rate this as a high risk, given that two of the five criteria are met. Once partial credit is added for some environments not having ePHI in use or at rest in DEV or QA and the testing performed that found ePHI in DEV and QA, the control process aligned to this vulnerable situation is reduced to a moderate level. The subjective parts of this assessment relate to the implementation credit and testing credit. If half the DEV and QA environments were found to have ePHI and half did not, does that mean half the implementation value should be assigned to measure the control maturity? This may not be static for a given time. The range of likelihood values for this vulnerability can look like those in Table 17-11.

***Table 17-11.***  *Range of Values for This Vulnerability's Likelihood*

| Low | High | Most Likely |
| --- | --- | --- |
| 2.5 | 3.25 | 3 |

## Evaluating Impact

The impact of this risk was originally valued at a level 5, based on the lack of protection of records in the DEV and QA environments. The technical testing uncovered ePHI in the environments, but not all of them. If it can be assumed that this entity is a business associate with no more than 30,000 records at risk, and each system has 18,000 and 12,000 records, respectively, we can use the following values, listed in Table 17-12, for the impact valuation.

**Table 17-12.** *The Impact Ranges for the Risk Related to Insecure Development and Quality Assurance Environments*

| Low | High | Most Likely |
|-----|------|-------------|
| 2.5 | 3.5  | 3           |

# Monte Carlo Simulation Assumptions

Crystal Ball offers many options for defining assumptions. Here, triangular distribution is used when data is limited, because the program recommends this when data is minimal. Figure 17-1 illustrates the ranges for likelihood and impact for the two risks in question.

| Ranges | Risk 9 | | | Risk 17 | |
|--------|------------|--------|---|------------|--------|
|        | Likelihood | Impact |   | Likelihood | Impact |
| High   | 5          | 5      |   | 3.25       | 3.5    |
| Likely | 4.75       | 4.5    |   | 3          | 3      |
| Low    | 4.5        | 4      |   | 2.5        | 2.5    |

**Figure 17-1.** *The high, low, and most likely values for the two risks under evaluation*

Once these values are input into Crystal Ball, as seen in Figure 17-2, 9,000 trials are run. The values that occur in the 90th percentile are chosen for the likelihood and impact values used in the analysis.

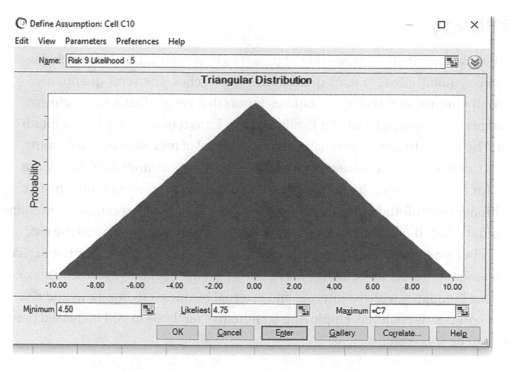

**Figure 17-2.** *The minimum, likeliest, and maximum values assigned in Crystal Ball prior to running all 9,000 trials*

# Comparing the Results

For the access management risk, the original likelihood and impact values were 5 for each. The other risk, insecure development and QA environments, originally valued likelihood and impact at 3. The access management numbers based on the Monte Carlo simulations performed were lower. The likelihood was 4.89, and the impact was 4.78. The risk related to insecure environments was higher than the risk analysis originally completed. The likelihood was 3.11, and impact was 3.27. If the entity choses to graph these risks with more granularity, the level of precision the risk analysis provides increases.

# Summary

NIST 800-30 outlines risk assessment approaches in section 2.3.2. These include qualitative, quantitative, or semi-quantitative approaches. The semi-quantitative approach outlined in this chapter requires inputs that are qualitative. Agreeing on the ranges of values applicable for likelihood and impact of each risk is a qualitative factor. The goal is to use the simulations to add a level of precision to those inputs used to calculate the level of severity for each risk. There are other models that are useful for these purposes. It is important that the approach selected is one the risk practitioner is comfortable with and understands. If the approach cannot be explained and understood, the credibility for the conclusions drawn decreases, and the risk analysis becomes worthless. Often, it makes sense to begin the risk analysis and risk management program by focusing on assessing through qualitative means. Then, once increased familiarity with the internal and external business environment and risk analysis process is achieved, employing quantitative methods to add increased precision is likely to be successful.

# CHAPTER 18

# Think Offensively

Executing and continuously updating the risk analysis is a challenging task. Things change daily in the cybersecurity world, including an entity's risk profile. Healthcare providers, payers, and business associates collectively struggle with assessing and keeping up to date a comprehensive and thorough risk analysis. Analyzing and assessing risk are not only required by the HIPAA Security Rule but are necessary to build an effective cybersecurity program. There are many challenges. Situational awareness and knowledge of all places in which ePHI is in use, in motion, and at rest is a big concern. Understanding the application of risk analysis guidance in a way that meets regulatory requirements is another. The last is how to conduct the risk analysis in a way that brings value to the entity. Organizations that accept these challenges and face them one step at a time can build cybersecurity programs that are compliant with HIPAA, invest resources where risk exists, and focus on continuous improvement.

## The Risk Analysis Journey

Guidance exists publicly for entities to execute upon the risk analysis requirements. HHS directs healthcare professionals to NIST 800-30, but it emphasizes that no specific framework is required. No matter the framework chosen, required elements must exist. In this book, the risk analysis focused on these elements.

- Who are the threat actors and threat scenarios that could affect the confidentiality, integrity, and availability of ePHI?

- What vulnerabilities exist that these threats can exploit?

- How likely is it these vulnerabilities will be exploited?

- If exploited, what is the impact to ePHI?

© Eric C. Thompson 2017
E. C. Thompson, *Building a HIPAA-Compliant Cybersecurity Program*,
https://doi.org/10.1007/978-1-4842-3060-2_18

## Threat Actors and Scenarios

Sophisticated attackers—state-sponsored actors and organized cybercriminals—were combined into a single threat group. This decision was made in part because it was difficult to differentiate between each group. This streamlined the process and the output of the risk analysis. This was a scoping and planning decision that other entities may not agree with, and that is acceptable as well. Other documented threats included malicious insiders, users who circumvent controls or find weaknesses to exploit for personal gain, and natural and environmental scenarios.

## Vulnerabilities

Vulnerabilities are weaknesses in the environment that threats and threat scenarios can exploit to view, steal, modify, or render ePHI unavailable. Several sources exist to aid entities trying to identify and document weaknesses in the environment. Appendix F in NIST SP 800-30 outlines ways to identify and document vulnerabilities and predisposing conditions. Reviewing previously completed assessments, which show gaps in the cybersecurity program and document key details about the entity's program, are also useful. Organizational experiences by those conducting the analysis or interviewing members of the workforce provide insights into missing governance, process, and security configurations. Identifying detailed vulnerabilities increases the usefulness and value of the risk analysis.

## Impact

Impact measures the effect of successful exploits on ePHI. It is up to each entity to document the levels of severity for a breach. Very high impacts can begin as low as 500 records exposed or start in the millions. These levels are dependent on organizational factors each entity must establish.

## Get Offensive

It is hard not to fall into the compliance trap when thinking about the risk analysis. To date, the prominence of it in the news is unquestionable. With the challenges faced by cybersecurity leaders, it's understandable why some consider it a complicated compliance requirement. Those who have not studied the issue or understood the risk analysis sufficiently, are left feeling that the requirement is daunting and hoping it never becomes an issue. In reality, the risk analysis process brings control and power to cybersecurity program management. Instead of blindly purchasing solutions claiming to remove cybersecurity risk from the environment, investement choices are made based on risk acceptance criteria and the risk treatment plan. The consistent narrative of how attackers are well-funded and loaded with smart people always places healthcare entities at a disadvantage. But not every breach suffered in the last five or six years required a genius to pull it off. Many occurred because simple and avoidable mistakes were made. Risk is a function of the environment in which ePHI lives; therefore, understanding each risk intimately yields knowledge and direction to do something about the issues at hand.

## The HIPAA Compliant Program

The risk analysis was the first step in a journey that led to complying with the HIPAA Security Rule. Not only did it allow a key safeguard to be met, but it leads entities to adopt cybersecurity controls meant to reduce risks to and protect ePHI. After cybersecurity controls are identified and assessed, a key final piece to the process is mapping the cybersecurity controls to the HIPAA Security Rule. In Appendix B of this book, that mapping exists and outlines the NIST CSF subcategories that achieve compliance with the assigned safeguard.

## Take Ten Minutes Each Day and Get the Process Started

In an average of ten minutes a day, it is possible to create or enhance the current risk analysis in six months. It takes planning and discipline to dedicate time every day and protect that time from other priorities, but it can be done. The six steps of the risk analysis covered in this book included

1. Identify locations of ePHI, which are at risk.

2. Consider all reasonably anticipated threats to the confidentiality, integrity, and availability of ePHI.

3. Document all known vulnerabilities in the environment.

4. Measure the likelihood that a weakness could be exploited.

5. Evaluate the impact of a breach to the environment exposed by the risk.

6. Identify and measure cybersecurity controls meant to reduce the risks to ePHI.

The first step in planning this project is to assign each of these steps to months one through six. Then, for minutes each day, two hundred minutes each month, or three hours and twenty minutes over the duration of this project, set the objectives to be completed and what must be done every day to achieve those objectives. The two most important factors of success for this initiative are commitment to finishing and setting proper expectations.

# Month One: Identifying All Instances of ePHI

Prior to beginning the risk analysis, and before attempting to inventory the ePHI, it is important to understand several factors.

- Does executive management understand the importance of this endeavor, and will you have its backing when obstacles occur?

- How well do you know the organization? Is this a new role or are you a long-time employee?

- Are individuals inside the entity that are willing to assist available? That is, will they sit down and have an honest discussion?

Having seniority at an organization with connections and relationships in many departments makes this process easier. The first few days, or week, can be spent documenting all the applications, databases, data warehouses, and other systems that are known to store, process, or transmit ePHI. Healthcare providers, payers, and business associates have core systems that are used to conduct business, and those systems are the key starting point. Once this process is completed, the rest of the month should be spent setting up quick meetings with key individuals in each disparate business unit, gathering information on other systems that interact with ePHI but are not part of the core systems.

# Month Two: Vulnerabilities

Again, this should not be a difficult or laborious process. The list of vulnerabilities can be gathered through reading guidance provided by NIST, reviewing previous assessments, and knowledge of the environment. This can be accomplished in a few days. The rest of month should be spent talking with members of the workforce. Each day, interviews of five minutes can be conducted, asking one question: What do you feel are the biggest security weaknesses in the organization? Interviewing 15 people from 15 different areas of the business can yield details that enhance the comprehensive list of vulnerabilities.

# Month Three: Threat Actors and Vulnerability Mapping

The list of threats and threat actors can be documented rather quickly and the rest of the month spent mapping the threats to vulnerabilities each may exploit. The process should be set up the same way it was outlined early in this book. Starting with a list of threats on one side of a page, white board, or in the electronic workbooks used for the analysis, the vulnerabilities can be reviewed and mapped to appropriate threats each day for ten minutes. Attack scenarios can be documented. These detail how an attack might be carried out and include several vulnerabilities linked together. Realistically, this process can be done in about one week. That leaves close to ten workdays, depending on the month, to write risk statements. Because the premise of choosing the highest caliber threat to focus risk treatment actions against is used, the process of writing all the risk statements can be accomplished during the month.

# Month Four: Measure the Likelihoods

The routine is the same for this month. Each day, for ten minutes, evaluate each of the risks and assign the likelihood value. The best bet is to try and understand ahead of time how many must be completed each day to finish, and just keep plugging away at them. If they have not already, by this time, most begin to find additional pockets of time to work on the analysis. Once progress is visible, the desire to finish and see the results is unavoidable.

## Month Five: Measure the Impacts

By now, the cadence is established, and momentum has swung in favor of finishing the process. Use the guidance and tools in this book to evaluate the impact for each risk. This should not be done arbitrarily; however, if there are risks posing challenges to assessment because the data is not available to make precise estimates, use a best-guess approach, erring on the conservative side. This means that it is better to round the impact up, causing the overall risk to be measured more severely, than to round down and assume the risk is moderate vs. high or very high. If remediation actions are inappropriate, owing to overinvestment in risk reduction, that is better than appearing to ignore a risk that might be perceived to be much higher.

## Month Six: Identify Cybersecurity Controls

On the home stretch of this journey, the final step is to identify the cybersecurity controls that will reduce the risks to ePHI. It is hoped that a framework is in place, but if one does not exist, no worries, one can be adopted immediately. Whatever the case, review the risks and associate a specific cybersecurity control or controls to each. These cybersecurity controls must be assessed, so that risk reduction can be measured. This can be completed after the analysis is complete.

# Get Better

So much effort goes to waste if this process stops after the risk analysis and control mapping process ends. Elite organizations try to get better every day. This does not mean that there are never failures, and, for cybersecurity teams, it does not mean that a breach will never occur. The goal is to be ready to act when things go wrong. The best way to do this is to know the environment inside and out. The risk analysis guides or forces cybersecurity teams to do this, depending on one's outlook. Teams whose purpose is to protect the health information in its possession to the best of its abilities should see risk analysis as a way to develop a game plan. Study the information systems and the end users every day. Understanding more each day how business is done, how data flows within the entity, and how risks are shifting provides an opportunity for the team to mentally prepare for incidents. This preparation could make the difference in the impact of a breach.

# Summary

There are many factors that cybersecurity leaders cannot control. They cannot control which threat actors target their entity, which members of the workforce will fall victim to phishing attacks, or which end users recklessly use company assets. These are the events that cybersecurity leaders cannot control, and at times, cybersecurity leaders cannot control the outcomes of events. What can be controlled is identifying the risks to patient information and the response to those risks. If end users are high-risk vulnerabilities, taking awareness efforts to the next level is the right response. Focusing investment and resources to mitigate those risks is an appropriate response. Doing nothing, or acting helpless against the actions of reckless end users is not the correct response. There is power in action and in taking ownership of the actions within one's control. The risk analysis is the blueprint for creating the response when attackers strike. It is a battle plan displaying where and how entities should fight. The risk analysis allows cybersecurity leaders to choose how to respond to threats, and the goal should be to get better every day.

# APPENDIX A

# NIST CSF Internal Controls

As discussed in Chapter 3, the NIST cybersecurity framework gives direct guidance on how to build cybersecurity programs. The categories and subcategories specify the activities required to establish the program. Controls that outline the "how" of implementing the requirements of each subcategory must be defined, which requires someone to own the control and a time factor in which control activities can be established. Table A-1 shows the controls aligned to the subcategories within the protect, detect, and respond functions.

***Table A-1.*** *NIST CSF Internal Controls*

| Category | Subcategory | Internal Control |
|---|---|---|
| Access Control | PR.AC-1: Identities and credentials are managed for authorized devices and users. | Access must be approved by the application, OS, or database owner prior provisioning. |
| | PR.AC-2: Physical access to assets is managed and protected. | Facilities are protected by badge access and limited to those who require access for their job function; visitors must sign in and be escorted. |
| | PR.AC-3: Remote access is managed. | Remote access requires two factor authentications and is limited to those who require it for job function. |
| | PR.AC-4: Access permissions are managed, incorporating the principles of least privilege and separation of duties. | Access reviews are performed semiannually by each application or infrastructure owner, to confirm that access is still required. Any exceptions found must be removed within ten business days. |

(*continued*)

© Eric C. Thompson 2017
E. C. Thompson, *Building a HIPAA-Compliant Cybersecurity Program*,
https://doi.org/10.1007/978-1-4842-3060-2

***Table A-1.*** (*continued*)

| Category | Subcategory | Internal Control |
|---|---|---|
| | PR.AC-5: Network integrity is protected, incorporating network segregation where appropriate. | Network segments processing ePHI are segregated from other networks using firewalls and other solutions. The CISO conducts assessments annually to ensure that the segments are established and operating appropriately. |
| Awareness and Training | PR.AT-1: All users are informed and trained. | |
| | PR.AT-2: Privileged users understand roles and responsibilities. | Written job descriptions identify responsibilities and performance indicators related to securing sensitive information. |
| | PR.AT-3: Third-party stakeholders (e.g., suppliers' customers, partners) understand roles and responsibilities. | All nonemployees are required to complete security awareness training and acknowledge their understanding of all organizational policies related to expected use and security of data. |
| | PR.AT-4: Senior executives understand roles and responsibilities. | Written job descriptions include expectations of all executives to facilitate and enforce information security. |
| | PR.AT-5: Physical and information security personnel understand roles and responsibilities. | Human resource managers create and distribute written job descriptions that include expected performance requirements of all information security personnel. |

(*continued*)

*Table A-1.*  (*continued*)

| Category | Subcategory | Internal Control |
|---|---|---|
| Data Security | PR.DS-1: Data at rest is protected. | The chief information security officer confirms that all instances of ePHI at rest are encrypted. For instances in which exceptions are necessary, those exceptions are logged, monitored, and have sufficient mitigating controls identified and placed into operation. |
| | PR.DS-2: Data in transit is protected. | The manager of network services is responsible for ensuring that all external data transmissions are encrypted. |
| | PR.DS-3: Assets are formally managed throughout removal, transfers, and disposition. | The manager of network services and desktop support maintains an up-to-date inventory of hardware and software assets and reconciles it monthly. |
| | PR.DS-4: Adequate capacity to ensure availability is maintained. | The manager of computer operations monitors capacity and investigates alerts generated by the system. |
| | PR.DS-5: Protections against data leaks are implemented. | The cybersecurity team monitors DLP alerts and investigates potential loss of ePHI leaving the network boundary. |
| | PR.DS-6: Integrity-checking mechanisms are used to verify software, firmware, and information integrity. | Integrity check alerts are investigated by the application owner or designated individual and resolved prior to completion of data processing. |

(*continued*)

***Table A-1.*** (*continued*)

| Category | Subcategory | Internal Control |
|---|---|---|
| Information Protection | PR.IP-1: A baseline configuration of information technology/industrial control systems is created and maintained. | Baseline configurations for network devices and IT assets are documented by the security team, as are automated alerts and corrections of unauthorized configuration changes. |
| | PR.IP-2: A systems development life cycle to manage systems is implemented. | System owners are responsible for ensuring that all changes to applications are developed in accordance with a systems development life cycle (SDLC), which includes testing and approval of changes prior to migration into production. Additionally, each change must adhere to segregation of duties. |
| | PR.IP-3: Configuration change control processes are in place. | Changes to configurations require authorization from the CISO or IT asset owner and have a documented business case for the change. |
| | PR.IP-4: Backups of information are conducted, maintained, and tested periodically. | Daily incremental and weekly full backups are performed. The network operations team tests backups quarterly, to confirm successful restoration. |
| | PR.IP-5: Policy and regulations regarding the physical operating environment for organizational assets are met. | All entrances to entity facilities require badge access. Guests and visitors are required to sign in, provide valid ID, and be escorted on premise. |
| | PR.IP-6: Data is destroyed according to policy. | The manager of network services ensures that hard drives and other retired storage assets are destroyed, to prevent data recovery from these assets by unauthorized individuals. |

(*continued*)

***Table A-1.*** (*continued*)

| Category | Subcategory | Internal Control |
|---|---|---|
| | PR.IP-7: Protection processes are continuously improved. | The CISO shall engage a third-party assessor to evaluate the cybersecurity program annually. |
| | PR.IP-8: Effectiveness of protection technologies is shared with appropriate parties. | Results of annual security tests are shared with appropriate stakeholders. External stakeholders must be approved by the general counsel and CIO prior to report distribution. |
| | PR.IP-9: Response plans (Incident Response and Business Continuity) and recovery plans (Incident Recovery and Disaster Recovery) are in place and managed. | The manager of network services and CISO document business continuity and disaster recovery plans that are reviewed and updated annually. |
| | PR.IP-10: Response and recovery plans are tested. | The manager of network services and CISO test recovery plans and review results annually, to ensure that the plan meets organization requirements. |
| | PR.IP-11: Cybersecurity is included in human resources practices (e.g., deprovisioning, personnel screening). | The manager of network services provisions Active Directory and e-mail accounts only when HR provides notification of the new hire. When employees and nonemployees leave the organization, HR provides notification to disable network and e-mail accounts. |
| | PR.IP-12: A vulnerability management plan is developed and implemented. | The network security manager scans network devices weekly, compiling and tracking remediation progress against documented time lines. |

(*continued*)

***Table A-1.*** (*continued*)

| Category | Subcategory | Internal Control |
|---|---|---|
| Maintenance | PR.MA-1: Maintenance and repair of organizational assets is performed and logged in a timely manner, with approved and controlled tools. | The network security manager approves, logs and monitors maintenance activities and requirements for assets processing ePHI. |
| | PR.MA-2: Remote maintenance of organizational assets is approved, logged, and performed in a manner that prevents unauthorized access. | Remote maintenance must be approved by the asset owner prior to commencement. Details of the maintenance must be logged, and temporary access is granted only to assets, as necessary. |
| Protective Technology | PR.PT-1: Audit/log records are determined, documented, implemented, and reviewed in accordance with policy. | The cybersecurity policy requires logging to occur, and procedures exist to outline the assets and events that are required to be captured in logs. |
| | PR.PT-2: Removable media is protected, and its use restricted, according to policy. | The use of removable media is blocked on all laptops and monitored by the desktop analyst. Removable media is restricted on servers and network devices to necessary instances only. These instances must be logged and approved by the CISO and/or CIO. |
| | PR.PT-3: Access to systems and assets is controlled, incorporating the principle of least functionality. | Elevated access to IT assets is reviewed semiannually by the CIO. Any necessary changes to access are recorded and implemented within five business days. |
| | PR.PT-4: Communications and control networks are protected. | The network security team implements, manages. and monitors perimeter security solutions. Events are investigated and, if necessary, reported to the CISO and CIO. |

(*continued*)

*Table A-1.* (*continued*)

| Category | Subcategory | Internal Control |
|---|---|---|
| Anomalies and Events | DE.AE-1: A baseline of network operations and expected data flows for users and systems is established and managed. | The network management team monitors network traffic, utilizing solutions that alert the team to potentially abnormal traffic patterns. |
| | DE.AE-2: Detected events are analyzed to understand attack targets and methods. | The network security team investigates alerts, escalating events, as appropriate, to the CISO, who may invoke the incident response plan. |
| | DE.AE-3: Event data are aggregated and correlated from multiple sources and sensors. | Logs are collected in a SIEM solution, which correlates and analyzes the logs to detect suspected intrusions. |
| | DE.AE-4: Impact of events is determined. | Events and incidents are investigated and triaged, based on the sensitivity of data and assets involved. |
| | DE.AE-5: Incident alert thresholds are established. | The incident response plan is maintained by the CISO and contains thresholds used by team members to conclude whether an event must be declared an incident. |
| Security Continuous Monitoring | DE.CM-1: The network is monitored to detect potential cybersecurity events. | The network is monitored by members of the security operations team for events that require further investigation. |
| | DE.CM-2: The physical environment is monitored to detect potential cybersecurity events. | Security cameras are installed in the data center and are continuously monitored by members of the network operations team. |
| | DE.CM-3: Personnel activity is monitored to detect potential cybersecurity events. | End point and network protection tools are implemented and managed by the desktop support team that allow for monitoring end-user behavior for dangerous activity. |

(*continued*)

***Table A-1.*** (*continued*)

| Category | Subcategory | Internal Control |
|---|---|---|
| | DE.CM-4: Malicious code is detected. | End point protection solutions detect occurrences of malicious code execution and alert members of the cybersecurity team. The network devices are monitored by the network management team to confirm that all end points are up to date. |
| | DE.CM-5: Unauthorized mobile code is detected. | End point protection solutions detect occurrences of malicious code execution and alert members of the cybersecurity team. The network devices are monitored by the network management team to confirm that all end points are up to date. |
| | DE.CM-6: External service provider activity is monitored to detect potential cybersecurity events. | All external connections by vendors supporting IT applications or infrastructure must be secured and actively monitored to ensure that only permissible actions occur during the connection. |
| | DE.CM-7: Monitoring for unauthorized personnel, connections, devices, and software is performed. | The network management team monitors the network and responds to alerts of unknown assets connecting or to unauthorized use of network resources. |
| | DE.CM-8: Vulnerability scans are performed. | Network security analysts confirm that scheduled vulnerability scans are completed weekly. |

(*continued*)

**Table A-1.** (*continued*)

| Category | Subcategory | Internal Control |
|---|---|---|
| Detection Processes | DE.DP-1: Roles and responsibilities for detection are well-defined to ensure accountability. | The CISO assigns ownership of detection processes and receives weekly reports of events detected and mitigating actions taken. |
| | DE.DP-2: Detection activities comply with all applicable requirements. | The detection function is audited annually by either internal audit or an external firm at the direction of the CISO. |
| | DE.DP-3: Detection processes are tested. | Annual penetration tests are conducted to test the entity's ability to detect attacks. The CISO is responsible for selecting and monitoring remediation actions. |
| | DE.DP-4: Event detection information is communicated to appropriate parties. | The incident response plan includes steps for escalating incidents to the executive response team, which determines the appropriate stakeholders and when to communicate details of the incident. |
| | DE.DP-5: Detection processes are continuously improved. | Results of testing or incidents are reviewed for lessons learned, which are incorporated into the cybersecurity process. |

(*continued*)

*Table A-1.* (*continued*)

| Category | Subcategory | Internal Control |
|---|---|---|
| Communications | RS.CO-1: Personnel know their roles and order of operations when a response is needed. | An incident response plan is maintained by the CISO, which outlines the roles and responsibilities of team members when events occur. |
| | RS.CO-2: Events are reported consistent with established criteria. | Reviews of the incident response process are conducted annually to confirm that events were reported as expected, based on cybersecurity policy and procedure. |
| | RS.CO-3: Information is shared consistent with response plans. | The incident response plan includes steps for escalating incidents to the executive response team, which determines the appropriate stakeholders and when to communicate details of the incident. |
| | RS.CO-4: Coordination with stakeholders occurs consistent with response plans. | The incident response plan includes steps for escalating incidents to the executive response team, which determines the appropriate stakeholders and when to communicate details of the incident. |
| | RS.CO-5: Voluntary information sharing occurs with external stakeholders, to achieve broader cybersecurity situational awareness. | The incident response plan includes steps for escalating incidents to the executive response team, which determines the appropriate stakeholders and when to communicate details of the incident. |

(*continued*)

**Table A-1.** (*continued*)

| Category | Subcategory | Internal Control |
|---|---|---|
| Analysis | RS.AN-1: Notifications from detection systems are investigated. | Network security personnel investigate alerts, to determine if an event or incident must be investigated. If escalation is not required, the alert is closed. |
| | RS.AN-2: The impact of the incident is understood. | Events and incidents are investigated and triaged, based on the sensitivity of data and assets involved. |
| | RS.AN-3: Forensics are performed. | The CISO retains and engages an external forensics firm for incidents requiring forensic investigation. |
| | RS.AN-4: Incidents are categorized consistent with response plans. | Post incident reviews are conducted to confirm an incident or event was classified appropriately. |
| Mitigation | RS.MI-1: Incidents are contained. | The CISO is maintains and incident response plan that includes steps necessary to contain incidents. |
| | RS.MI-2: Incidents are mitigated. | The CISO is maintains and incident response plan that includes steps necessary to mitigate incidents. |
| | RS.MI-3: Newly identified vulnerabilities are mitigated or documented as accepted risks. | The CISO receives and reviews monthly vulnerability reports to ensure all vulnerabilities are mitigated within expected timeframes. |
| Improvement | RS.IM-1: Response plans incorporate lessons learned. | The CISO leads the incident response team through a lesson learned meeting after an incident response. |
| | RS.IM-2: Response strategies are updated. | The CISO updates the incident response plan once all lessons learned are collected. |

(*continued*)

***Table A-1.*** (*continued*)

| Category | Subcategory | Internal Control |
|---|---|---|
| Recovery Planning | RC.RP-1: Recovery plan is executed during or after an event. | The CISO ensures that the recovery plan is utilized during events that require a formal response. |
| Improvement | RC.IM-1: Recovery plans incorporate lessons learned. | The CISO leads the incident response team through a lesson-learned meeting after an incident response. |
| | RC.IM-2: Recovery strategies are updated. | The information security steering committee reviews the recovery strategies annually and recommends necessary changes. |
| Communication | RC.CO-1: Public relations are managed. | The VP of marketing and communications is responsible for managing official messages during incidents. |
| | RC.CO-2: Reputation after an event is repaired. | The VP of marketing and other members of the executive team determine necessary steps for repairing reputational damage and communicate with external stakeholders. |
| | RC.CO-3: Recovery activities are communicated to internal stakeholders and executive and management teams. | The CISO and/or CIO report to executives and the board throughout the response and recovery process. |

# APPENDIX B

# NIST CSF to HIPAA Crosswalk

This appendix illustrates the relationships between subcategories of the NIST Cybersecurity Framework (CSF) and the safeguards of the HIPAA Security Rule. These tables are meant to highlight the importance of associating the cybersecurity controls to the HIPAA elements and not the other way around. Entities should focus on securing ePHI, with compliance a result of the process. Focusing on compliance does not allow for security. The relationships are broken down by function and category. For example, the first table contains the asset management category of the identify function, so that users can see, for each subcategory, which safeguards relate.

## Identification: Asset Management

Table B-1 shows the asset management subcategory mapped to HIPAA Security Rule safeguards.

***Table B-1.*** *Asset Management Subcategory Cybersecurity Controls Mapped to the HIPAA Security Rule Safeguards*

| Subcategory | HIPAA Regulation |
| --- | --- |
| ID.AM-1 | HIPAA Security Rule 45 C.F.R. §§ 164.308(a)(1)(ii)(A), 164.310(a)(2)(ii), 164.310(d) |
| ID.AM-2 | HIPAA Security Rule 45 C.F.R. §§ 164.308(a)(1)(ii)(A), 164.308(a)(7)(ii)(E) |
| ID.AM-3 | HIPAA Security Rule 45 C.F.R. §§ 164.308(a)(1)(ii)(A), 164.308(a)(3)(ii)(A), 164.308(a)(8), 164.310(d) |
| ID.AM-4 | HIPAA Security Rule 45 C.F.R. §§ 164.308(a)(4)(ii)(A), 164.308(b), 164.314(a)(1), 164.314(a)(2)(i)(B), 164.314(a)(2)(ii), 164.316(b)(2) |
| ID.AM-5 | HIPAA Security Rule 45 C.F.R. § 164.308(a)(7)(ii) (E) |

© Eric C. Thompson 2017
E. C. Thompson, *Building a HIPAA-Compliant Cybersecurity Program*,
https://doi.org/10.1007/978-1-4842-3060-2

# Identification: Business Environment

Table B-2 shows the business environment subcategory mapped to HIPAA Security Rule safeguards.

***Table B-2.*** *Business Environment Subcategory Cybersecurity Controls Mapped to the HIPAA Security Rule Safeguards*

| Subcategory | HIPAA Regulation |
| --- | --- |
| ID.BE-1 | HIPAA Security Rule 45 C.F.R. §§ 164.308(a)(1)(ii)(A), 164.308(a)(4)(ii), 164.308(a)(7)(ii)(C), 164.308(a)(7)(ii)(E), 164.308(a)(8), 164.310(a)(2)(i), 164.314, 164.316 |
| ID.BE-2 | HIPAA Security Rule 45 C.F.R. §§ 164.308(a)(1)(ii)(A), 164.308(a)(4)(ii), 164.308(a)(7)(ii)(C), 164.308(a)(7)(ii)(E), 164.308(a)(8), 164.310(a)(2)(i), 164.314, 164.316 |
| ID.BE-3 | HIPAA Security Rule 45 C.F.R. §§ 164.308(a)(7)(ii)(B), 164.308(a)(7)(ii)(C), 164.308(a)(7)(ii)(D), 164.308(a)(7)(ii)(E), 164.310(a)(2)(i), 164.316 |
| ID.BE-4 | HIPAA Security Rule 45 C.F.R. §§ 164.308(a)(7)(i), 164.308. (a)(7)(ii)(E), 164.310(a)(2)(i), 164.312(a)(2)(ii), 164.314(a)(1), 164.314(b)(2)(i) |
| ID.BE-5 | HIPAA Security Rule 45 C.F.R. §§ 164.308(a)(1)(ii)(B), 164.308(a)(6)(ii), 164.308(a)(7), 164.308(a)(8), 164.310(a)(2)(i), 164.312(a)(2)(ii), 164.314(b)(2)(i) |

# Identification: Governance

Table B-3 shows the governance subcategory mapped to HIPAA Security Rule safeguards.

***Table B-3.*** *Governance Subcategory Cybersecurity Controls Mapped to the HIPAA Security Rule Safeguards*

| Subcategory | HIPAA Regulation |
| --- | --- |
| ID.GV-1 | HIPAA Security Rule 45 C.F.R. §§ 164.308(a)(1)(i), 164.316 |
| ID.GV-2 | HIPAA Security Rule 45 C.F.R. §§ 164.308(a)(1)(i), 164.308(a)(2), 164.308(a)(3), 164.308(a)(4), 164.308(b), 164.314 |
| ID.GV-3 | HIPAA Security Rule 45 C.F.R. §§ 164.308(a)(1), 164.308(b) |
| ID.GV-4 | HIPAA Security Rule 45 C.F.R. §§ 164.308(a)(1), 164.308(b) |

# Identification: Risk Assessment

Table B-4 shows the risk assessment subcategory mapped to HIPAA Security Rule safeguards.

***Table B-4.*** *Risk Assessment Subcategory Cybersecurity Controls Mapped to the HIPAA Security Rule Safeguards*

| Subcategory | HIPAA Regulation |
| --- | --- |
| ID.RA-1 | HIPAA Security Rule 45 C.F.R. §§ 164.308(a)(1)(ii)(A), 164.308(a)(7)(ii)(E), 164.308(a)(8), 164.310(a)(1), 164.312(a)(1), 164.316(b)(2)(iii) |
| ID.RA-2 | |
| ID.RA-3 | No direct mapping to HIPAA for ID.RA-2 |
| ID.RA-4 | |
| ID.RA-5 | |
| ID.RA-6 | |

# Identification: Risk Management

Table B-5 shows the risk management subcategory mapped to HIPAA Security Rule safeguards.

***Table B-5.*** *Risk Management Subcategory Cybersecurity Controls Mapped to the HIPAA Security Rule Safeguards*

| Subcategory | HIPAA Regulation |
| --- | --- |
| ID.RM-1 | HIPAA Security Rule 45 C.F.R. § 164.308(a)(1)(ii)(B) |
| ID.RM-2 | HIPAA Security Rule 45 C.F.R. § 164.308(a)(1)(ii)(B) |
| ID.RM-3 | HIPAA Security Rule 45 C.F.R. §§ 164.308(a)(1)(ii)(B), 164.308(a)(6)(ii), 164.308(a)(7)(i), 164.308(a)(7)(ii)(C),164.308(a)(7)(ii)(E), 164.310(a)(2)(i) |

# Protect: Access Control

Table B-6 shows the access control subcategory mapped to HIPAA Security Rule safeguards.

***Table B-6.*** *Access Control Subcategory Cybersecurity Controls Mapped to the HIPAA Security Rule Safeguards*

| Subcategory | HIPAA Regulation |
| --- | --- |
| PR.AC-1 | HIPAA Security Rule 45 C.F.R. §§ 164.308(a)(3)(ii)(B), 164.308(a)(3)(ii)(C), 164.308(a)(4)(i), 164.308(a)(4)(ii)(B), 164.308(a)(4)(ii)(C), 164.312(a)(2)(i), 164.312(a)(2)(ii), 164.312(a)(2)(iii), 164.312(d) |
| PR.AC-2 | HIPAA Security Rule 45 C.F.R. §§ 164.308(a)(1)(ii)(B), 164.308(a)(7)(i), 164.308(a)(7)(ii)(A), 164.310(a)(1), 164.310(a)(2)(i), 164.310(a)(2)(ii), 164.310(a)(2)(iii), 164.310(b), 164.310(c), 164.310(d)(1), 164.310(d)(2)(iii) |
| PR.AC-3 | HIPAA Security Rule 45 C.F.R. §§ 164.308(a)(4)(i), 164.308(b)(1), 164.308(b)(3), 164.310(b), 164.312(e)(1), 164.312(e)(2)(ii) |
| PR.AC-4 | HIPAA Security Rule 45 C.F.R. §§ 164.308(a)(3), 164.308(a)(4), 164.310(a)(2)(iii), 164.310(b), 164.312(a)(1), 164.312(a)(2)(i), 164.312(a)(2)(ii) |
| PR.AC-5 | HIPAA Security Rule 45 C.F.R. §§ 164.308(a)(4)(ii)(B), 164.310(a)(1), 164.310(b), 164.312(a)(1), 164.312(b), 164.312(c), 164.312(e) |

# Protect: Awareness and Training

Table B-7 shows the awareness and training subcategory mapped to HIPAA Security Rule safeguards.

***Table B-7.*** *Awareness and Training Subcategory Cybersecurity Controls Mapped to the HIPAA Security Rule Safeguards*

| Subcategory | HIPAA Regulation |
| --- | --- |
| PR.AT-1 | HIPAA Security Rule 45 C.F.R. § 164.308(a)(5) |
| PR.AT-2 | HIPAA Security Rule 45 C.F.R. §§ 164.308(a)(2), 164.308(a)(3)(i), 164.308(a)(5)(i), 164.308(a)(5)(ii)(A), 164.308(a)(5)(ii)(B), 164.308(a)(5)(ii)(C), 164.308(a)(5)(ii)(D) |
| PR.AT-3 | HIPAA Security Rule 45 C.F.R. §§ 164.308(b), 164.314(a)(1), 164.314(a)(2)(i), 164.314(a)(2)(ii) |
| PR.AT-4 | HIPAA Security Rule 45 C.F.R. §§ 164.308(a)(2), 164.308(a)(3)(i), 164.308(a)(5)(i), 164.308(a)(5)(ii)(A), 164.308(a)(5)(ii)(B), 164.308(a)(5)(ii)(C), 164.308(a)(5)(ii)(D) |
| PR.AT-5 | HIPAA Security Rule 45 C.F.R. §§ 164.308(a)(2), 164.308(a)(3)(i), 164.308(a)(5)(i), 164.308(a)(5)(ii)(A), 164.308(a)(5)(ii)(B), 164.308(a)(5)(ii)(C), 164.308(a)(5)(ii)(D), 164.530(b)(1) |

# Protect: Data Security

Table B-8 shows the data security subcategory mapped to HIPAA Security Rule safeguards.

***Table B-8.*** *Data Security Subcategory Cybersecurity Controls Mapped to the HIPAA Security Rule Safeguards*

| Subcategory | HIPAA Regulation |
| --- | --- |
| PR.DS-1 | HIPAA Security Rule 45 C.F.R. §§ 164.308(a)(1)(ii)(D), 164.308(b)(1), 164.310(d), 164.312(a)(1), 164.312(a)(2)(iii), 164.312(a)(2)(iv), 164.312(b), 164.312(c), 164.314(b)(2)(i), 164.312(d) |
| PR.DS-2 | HIPAA Security Rule 45 C.F.R. §§ 164.308(b)(1), 164.308(b)(2), 164.312(e)(1), 164.312(e)(2)(i), 164.312(e)(2)(ii), 164.314(b)(2)(i) |
| PR.DS-3 | HIPAA Security Rule 45 C.F.R. §§ 164.308(a)(1)(ii)(A), 164.310(a)(2)(ii), 164.310(a)(2)(iii), 164.310(a)(2)(iv), 164.310(d)(1), 164.310(d)(2) |
| PR.DS-4 | HIPAA Security Rule 45 C.F.R. §§ 164.308(a)(1)(ii)(A), 164.308(a)(1)(ii)(B), 164.308(a)(7), 164.310(a)(2)(i), 164.310(d)(2)(iv), 164.312(a)(2)(ii) |
| PR.DS-5 | HIPAA Security Rule 45 C.F.R. §§ 164.308(a)(1)(ii)(D), 164.308(a)(3), 164.308(a)(4), 164.310(b), 164.310(c), 164.312(a), 164.312(e) |
| PR.DS-6 | HIPAA Security Rule 45 C.F.R. §§ 164.308(a)(1)(ii)(D), 164.312(b), 164.312(c)(1), 164.312(c)(2), 164.312(e)(2)(i) |
| PR.DS-7 | HIPAA Security Rule 45 C.F.R. § 164.308(a)(4)4 |

# Protect: Information Protection

Table B-9 shows the information protection subcategory mapped to HIPAA Security Rule safeguards.

***Table B-9.*** *Information Protection Subcategory Cybersecurity Controls Mapped to the HIPAA Security Rule Safeguards*

| Subcategory | HIPAA Regulation |
| --- | --- |
| PR.IP-1 | HIPAA Security Rule 45 C.F.R. §§ 164.308(a)(8), 164.308(a)(7)(i), 164.308(a)(7)(ii) |
| PR.IP-2 | HIPAA Security Rule 45 C.F.R. § 164.308(a)(1)(i) |
| PR.IP-3 | HIPAA Security Rule 45 C.F.R. § 164.308(a) (8) |
| PR.IP-4 | HIPAA Security Rule 45 C.F.R. §§ 164.308(a)(7)(ii)(A), 164.308(a)(7)(ii)(B), 164.308(a)(7)(ii)(D), 164.310(a)(2)(i), 164.310(d)(2)(iv) |
| PR.IP-5 | HIPAA Security Rule 45 C.F.R. §§ 164.308(a)(7)(i), 164.308(a)(7)(ii)(C), 164.310, 164.316(b)(2)(iii) |
| PR.IP-6 | HIPAA Security Rule 45 C.F.R. §§ 164.310(d)(2)(i), 164.310(d)(2)(ii) |
| PR.IP-7 | HIPAA Security Rule 45 C.F.R. §§ 164.306(e), 164.308(a)(7)(ii)(D), 164.308(a)(8), 164.316(b)(2)(iii) |
| PR.IP-8 | HIPAA Security Rule 45 C.F.R. § 164.308(a)(6)(ii) |
| PR.IP-9 | HIPAA Security Rule 45 C.F.R. §§ 164.308(a)(6), 164.308(a)(7), 164.310(a)(2)(i), 164.312(a)(2)(ii) |
| PR.IP-10 | HIPAA Security Rule 45 C.F.R. § 164.308(a)(7)(ii)(D) |
| PR.IP-11 | HIPAA Security Rule 45 C.F.R. §§ 164.308(a)(1)(ii)(C), 164.308(a)(3) |
| PR.IP-12 | HIPAA Security Rule 45 C.F.R. §§ 164.308(a)(1)(i), 164.308(a)(1)(ii)(A), 164.308(a)(1)(ii)(B) |

# Protect: Maintenance

Table B-10 shows the maintenance subcategory mapped to HIPAA Security Rule safeguards.

***Table B-10.*** *Maintenance Subcategory Cybersecurity Controls Mapped to the HIPAA Security Rule Safeguards*

| Subcategory | HIPAA Regulation |
| --- | --- |
| PR.MA-1 | HIPAA Security Rule 45 C.F.R. §§ 164.308(a)(3)(ii)(A), 164.310(a)(2)(iv) |
| PR.MA-2 | HIPAA Security Rule 45 C.F.R. §§ 164.308(a)(3)(ii)(A), 164.310(d)(1), 164.310(d)(2)(ii), 164.310(d)(2)(iii), 164.312(a), 164.312(a)(2)(ii), 164.312(a)(2)(iv), 164.312(b), 164.312(d), 164.312(e), 164.308(a)(1)(ii)(D) |

# Protect: Protective Technology

Table B-11 shows the protective technology subcategory mapped to HIPAA Security Rule safeguards.

***Table B-11.*** *Protective Technology Subcategory Cybersecurity Controls Mapped to the HIPAA Security Rule Safeguards*

| Subcategory | HIPAA Regulation |
| --- | --- |
| PR.PT-1 | HIPAA Security Rule 45 C.F.R. §§ 164.308(a)(1)(ii)(D), 164.308(a)(5)(ii)(C), 164.310(a)(2)(iv), 164.310(d)(2)(iii), 164.312(b) |
| PR.PT-2 | HIPAA Security Rule 45 C.F.R. §§ 164.308(a)(3)(i), 164.308(a)(3)(ii)(A), 164.310(d)(1), 164.310(d)(2), 164.312(a)(1), 164.312(a)(2)(iv), 164.312(b) |
| PR.PT-3 | HIPAA Security Rule 45 C.F.R. §§ 164.308(a)(3), 164.308(a)(4), 164.310(a)(2)(iii), 164.310(b), 164.310(c), 164.312(a)(1), 164.312(a)(2)(i), 164.312(a)(2)(ii), 164.312(a)(2)(iv) |
| PR.PT-4 | HIPAA Security Rule 45 C.F.R. §§ 164.308(a)(1)(ii)(D), 164.312(a)(1), 164.312(b), 164.312(e) |

# Detect: Anomalies and Events

Table B-12 shows the anomalies and events subcategory mapped to HIPAA Security Rule safeguards.

***Table B-12.*** *Anomalies and Events Subcategory Cybersecurity Controls Mapped to the HIPAA Security Rule Safeguards*

| Subcategory | HIPAA Regulation |
| --- | --- |
| DE.AE-1 | HIPAA Security Rule 45 C.F.R. §§ 164.308(a)(1)(ii)(D), 164.312(b) |
| DE.AE-2 | HIPAA Security Rule 45 C.F.R. § 164.308(6)(i) |
| DE.AE-3 | HIPAA Security Rule 45 C.F.R. §§ 164.308(a)(1)(ii)(D), 164.308(a)(5)(ii)(B), 164.308(a)(5)(ii)(C), 164.308(a)(6)(ii), 164.308(a)(8), 164.310(d)(2)(iii), 164.312(b), 164.314(a)(2)(i)(C), 164.314(a)(2)(iii) |
| DE.AE-4 | HIPAA Security Rule 45 C.F.R. § 164.308(a)(6) |
| DE.AE-5 | HIPAA Security Rule 45 C.F.R. § 164.308(a)(6)(i) |

# Detect: Continuous Monitoring

Table B-13 shows the continuous monitoring subcategory mapped to HIPAA Security Rule safeguards.

***Table B-13.*** *Continous Monitoring Subcategory Cybersecurity Controls Mapped to the HIPAA Security Rule Safeguards*

| Subcategory | HIPAA Regulation |
| --- | --- |
| DE.CM-1 | HIPAA Security Rule 45 C.F.R. §§ 164.308(a)(1)(ii)(D), 164.308(a)(5)(ii)(B), 164.308(a)(5)(ii)(C), 164.308(a)(8), 164.312(b), 164.312(e)(2)(i) |
| DE.CM-2 | HIPAA Security Rule 45 C.F.R. §§ 164.310(a)(2)(ii), 164.310(a)(2)(iii) |
| DE.CM-3 | HIPAA Security Rule 45 C.F.R. §§ 164.308(a)(1)(ii)(D), 164.308(a)(3)(ii)(A), 164.308(a)(5)(ii)(C), 164.312(a)(2)(i), 164.312(b), 164.312(d), 164.312(e) |
| DE.CM-4 | HIPAA Security Rule 45 C.F.R. §§ 164.308(a)(1)(ii)(D), 164.308(a)(5)(ii)(B) |

(*continued*)

***Table B-13.*** (*continued*)

| Subcategory | HIPAA Regulation |
| --- | --- |
| DE.CM-5 | HIPAA Security Rule 45 C.F.R. §§ 164.308(a)(1)(ii)(D), 164.308(a)(5)(ii)(B) |
| DE.CM-6 | HIPAA Security Rule 45 C.F.R. § 164.308(a)(1)(ii)(D) |
| DE.CM-7 | HIPAA Security Rule 45 C.F.R. §§ 164.308(a)(1)(ii)(D), 164.308(a)(5)(ii)(B), 164.308(a)(5)(ii)(C), 164.310(a)(1), 164.310(a)(2)(ii), 164.310(a)(2)(iii), 164.310(b), 164.310(c), 164.310(d)(1), 164.310(d)(2)(iii), 164.312(b), 164.314(b)(2)(i) |
| DE.CM-8 | HIPAA Security Rule 45 C.F.R. §§ 164.308(a)(1)(i), 164.308(a)(8) |

# Detection: Detection Processes

Table B-14 shows the detection processes subcategory mapped to HIPAA Security Rule safeguards.

***Table B-14.*** *Detection Processes Subcategory Cybersecurity Controls Mapped to the HIPAA Security Rule Safeguards*

| Subcategory | HIPAA Regulation |
| --- | --- |
| DE.DP-1 | HIPAA Security Rule 45 C.F.R. §§ 164.308(a)(2), 164.308(a)(3)(ii)(A), 164.308(a)(3)(ii)(B), 164.308(a)(4), 164.310(a)(2)(iii), 164.312(a)(1), 164.312(a)(2)(ii) |
| DE.DP-2 | HIPAA Security Rule 45 C.F.R. §§ 164.308(a)(1)(i), 164.308(a)(8) |
| DE.DP-3 | HIPAA Security Rule 45 C.F.R. § 164.306(e) |
| DE.DP-4 | HIPAA Security Rule 45 C.F.R. §§ 164.308(a)(6)(ii), 164.314(a)(2)(i)(C), 164.314(a)(2)(iii) |
| DE.DP-5 | HIPAA Security Rule 45 C.F.R. §§ 164.306(e), 164.308(a)(8) |

# Response: Response Planning

Table B-15 shows the response planning subcategory mapped to HIPAA Security Rule safeguards.

***Table B-15.*** *Response Planning Subcategory Cybersecurity Controls Mapped to the HIPAA Security Rule Safeguards*

| Subcategory | HIPAA Regulation |
|---|---|
| RS.RP-1 | HIPAA Security Rule 45 C.F.R. §§ 164.308(a)(6)(ii), 164.308(a)(7)(i), 164.308(a)(7)(ii)(A), 164.308(a)(7)(ii)(B), 164.308(a)(7)(ii)(C), 164.310(a)(2)(i), 164.312(a)(2) (ii) |

# Response: Communications

Table B-16 shows the Communications subcategory mapped to HIPAA Security Rule safeguards.

***Table B-16.*** *Communications Subcategory Cybersecurity Controls Mapped to the HIPAA Security Rule Safeguards*

| Subcategory | HIPAA Regulation |
|---|---|
| RS.CO-1 | HIPAA Security Rule 45 C.F.R. §§ 164.308(a)(2), 164.308(a)(7)(ii)(A), 164.308(a)(7)(ii)(B), 164.308(a)(7)(ii)(C), 164.310(a)(2)(i), 164.308(a)(6)(i), 164.312(a)(2)(ii) |
| RS.CO-2 | HIPAA Security Rule 45 C.F.R. §§ 164.308(a)(5)(ii)(B), 164.308(a)(5)(ii)(C), 164.308(a)(6)(ii), 164.314(a)(2)(i)(C), 164.314(a)(2)(iii) |
| RS.CO-3 | HIPAA Security Rule 45 C.F.R. §§ 164.308(a)(5)(ii)(B), 164.308(a)(5)(ii)(C), 164.308(a)(6)(ii), 164.314(a)(2)(i)(C) |
| RS.CO-4 | HIPAA Security Rule 45 C.F.R. §§ 164.308(a)(6), 164.308(a)(7), 164.310(a)(2)(i), 164.312(a)(2)(ii) |
| RS.CO-5 | HIPAA Security Rule 45 C.F.R. § 164.308(a)(6) |

# Response: Analysis

Table B-17 shows the analysis subcategory mapped to HIPAA Security Rule safeguards.

***Table B-17.*** *Analysis Subcategory Cybersecurity Controls Mapped to the HIPAA Security Rule Safeguards*

| Subcategory | HIPAA Regulation |
| --- | --- |
| RS.AN-1 | HIPAA Security Rule 45 C.F.R. §§ 164.308(a)(1)(i), 164.308(a)(1)(ii)(D), 164.308(a)(5)(ii)(B), 164.308(a)(5)(ii)(C), 164.308(a)(6)(ii), 164.312(b) |
| RS.AN-2 | HIPAA Security Rule 45 C.F.R. §§ 164.308(a)(6)(ii), 164.308(a)(7)(ii)(B), 164.308(a)(7)(ii)(C), 164.308(a)(7)(ii)(E) |
| RS.AN-3 | HIPAA Security Rule 45 C.F.R. § 164.308(a) (6) |
| RS.AN-4 | HIPAA Security Rule 45 C.F.R. § 164.308(a)(6)(ii) |

# Response: Mitigation

Table B-18 shows the mitigation subcategory mapped to HIPAA Security Rule safeguards.

***Table B-18.*** *Mitigation Subcategory Cybersecurity Controls Mapped to the HIPAA Security Rule Safeguards*

| Subcategory | HIPAA Regulation |
| --- | --- |
| RS.MI-1 | HIPAA Security Rule 45 C.F.R. § 164.308(a)(6)(ii) |
| RS.MI-2 | HIPAA Security Rule 45 C.F.R. § 164.308(a)(6)(ii) |
| RS.MI-3 | HIPAA Security Rule 45 C.F.R. §§ 164.308(a)(1)(ii)(A), 164.308(a)(1)(ii)(B), 164.308(a)(6)(ii) |

# Response: Improvement

Table B-19 shows the improvement subcategory mapped to HIPAA Security Rule safeguards.

***Table B-19.*** *Improvement Subcategory Cybersecurity Controls Mapped to the HIPAA Security Rule Safeguards*

| Subcategory | HIPAA Regulation |
| --- | --- |
| RS.IM-1 | HIPAA Security Rule 45 C.F.R. §§ 164.308(a)(7)(ii)(D), 164.308(a)(8), 164.316(b)(2)(iii) |
| RS.IM-2 | HIPAA Security Rule 45 C.F.R. §§ 164.308(a)(7)(ii)(D), 164.308(a)(8) |

# Recovery: Recovery Planning

Table B-20 shows the recovery planning subcategory mapped to HIPAA Security Rule safeguards.

***Table B-20.*** *Recovery Planning Subcategory Cybersecurity Controls Mapped to the HIPAA Security Rule Safeguards*

| Subcategory | HIPAA Regulation |
| --- | --- |
| RC.RP-1 | HIPAA Security Rule 45 C.F.R. §§ 164.308(a)(7), 164.310(a)(2)(i) |

# Recovery: Improvements

Table B-21 shows the improvements subcategory mapped to HIPAA Security Rule safeguards.

***Table B-21.*** *Improvements Subcategory Cybersecurity Controls Mapped to the HIPAA Security Rule Safeguards*

| Subcategory | HIPAA Regulation |
|---|---|
| RC.IM-1 | HIPAA Security Rule 45 C.F.R. §§ 164.308(a)(7)(ii)(D), 164.308(a)(8), 164.316(b)(2)(iii) |
| RC.IM-2 | HIPAA Security Rule 45 C.F.R. §§ 164.308(a)(7)(ii)(D), 164.308(a)(8) |

# Recovery: Communications

Table B-22 shows the communications subcategory mapped to HIPAA Security Rule safeguards.

***Table B-22.*** *Communications Subcategory Cybersecurity Controls Mapped to the HIPAA Security Rule Safeguards*

| Subcategory | HIPAA Regulation |
|---|---|
| RC.CO-1 | HIPAA Security Rule 45 C.F.R. § 164.308(a)(6)(i) |
| RC.CO-2 | HIPAA Security Rule 45 C.F.R. § 164.308(a)(6)(i) |
| RC.CO-3 | HIPAA Security Rule 45 C.F.R. §§ 164.308(a)(6)(ii), 164.308(a)(7)(ii)(B), 164.308(a)(7)(ii)(C), 164.310(a)(2)(i), 164.314(a)(2)(i)(C) |

# Risk Analysis Templates

Two templates are available for readers of this book. You can download them by going to www.apress.com/9781484230596. The first is a workbook useful for executing the risk analysis. The second is specifically for assessing third parties engaged to provide a service. It is like the first but adds the nuances of assessing risks when outsourcing services or allowing other entities access to ePHI.

## Risk Analysis Template

The risk analysis template consists of five tabs. These are aligned to the steps covered under NIST 800-30 for conducting a risk analysis. These steps include documenting instances of ePHI, threats, vulnerabilities, risks and risk measurement, and a heat map displaying grids and associated risk levels. The risk and risk measurement tab combines several steps, including assigning likelihood and impact values to each risk.

## Instances of ePHI

This tab is where all instances of ePHI and the characteristics are documented. The application or system processing the data, supporting infrastructure, and other factors, both qualitative and quantitative, are documented in this section. Figure C-1 is an example of these in an Excel document.

© Eric C. Thompson 2017
E. C. Thompson, *Building a HIPAA-Compliant Cybersecurity Program*,
https://doi.org/10.1007/978-1-4842-3060-2

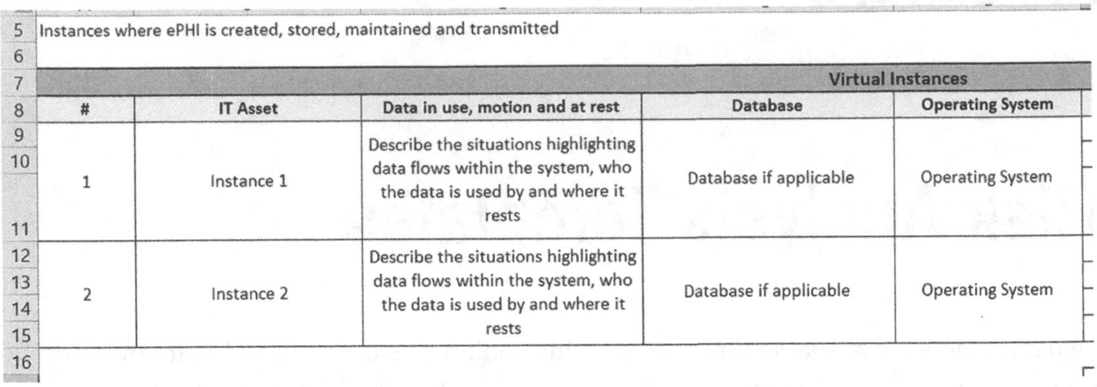

| 5 | Instances where ePHI is created, stored, maintained and transmitted | | | | |
|---|---|---|---|---|---|
| 6 | | | | | |
| 7 | | | | Virtual Instances | |
| 8 | # | IT Asset | Data in use, motion and at rest | Database | Operating System |
| 9 | | | | | |
| 10 | 1 | Instance 1 | Describe the situations highlighting data flows within the system, who the data is used by and where it rests | Database if applicable | Operating System |
| 11 | | | | | |
| 12 | | | Describe the situations highlighting data flows within the system, who the data is used by and where it rests | | |
| 13 | 2 | Instance 2 | | Database if applicable | Operating System |
| 14 | | | | | |
| 15 | | | | | |
| 16 | | | | | |

***Figure C-1.*** *Example of the information captured in instances of the ePHI tab of the risk analysis workbook*

# Threats

Threat actors, sophisticated attackers, cybercriminals, and malicious insiders and associated characteristics are documented in this tab, as shown in Figure C-2.

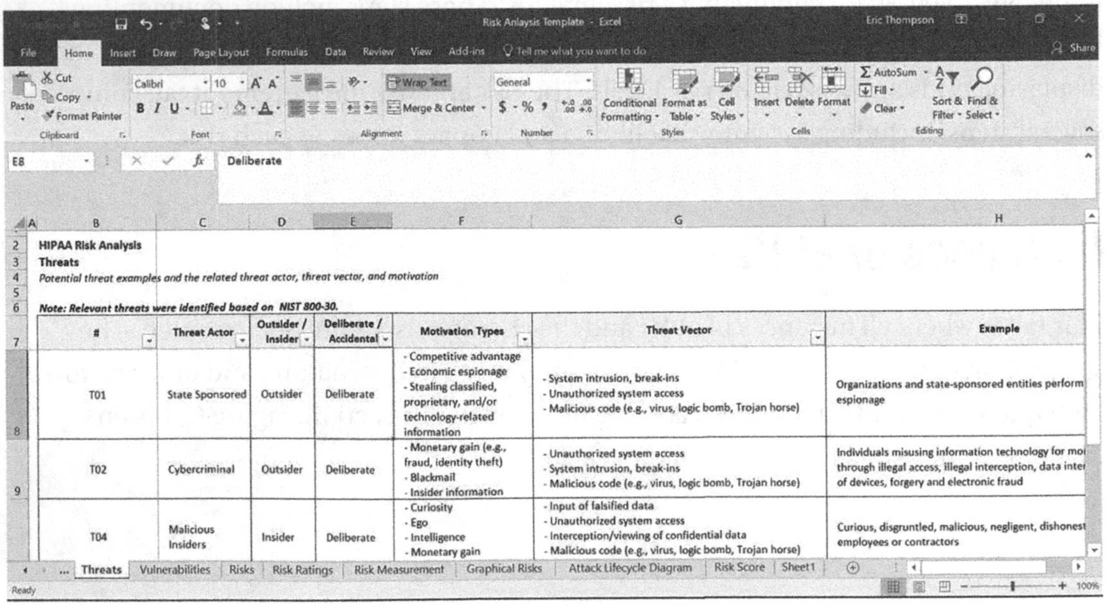

***Figure C-2.*** *Threats, with characteristics of each, documented in the Excel workbook*

# Vulnerabilities

This tab shows vulnerabilities and controls identified for risk reduction by category and subcategory, as shown in Figure C-3.

| | Vulnerability | NIST Category | NIST Sub-category |
|---|---|---|---|
| | **HIPAA Risk Analysis** | | |
| | **Vulnerabilities** | | |
| | *Potential vulnerabilities and the related domain, process and sub-process* | | |
| Ref | Vulnerability | NIST Category | NIST Sub-category |
| V01 | Infrastructure and applications(including web applications and interfaces) are inappropriately configured | PR.IP | PR.IP-1 |
| V02 | Design specifications are not effectively developed, reviewed, and approved | PR.IP | PR.IP-3 |
| V03 | Solutions are not appropriately developed according to standards and requirements | PR.IP | PR.IP-2 |
| V04 | Implementation and deployment planning is not performed | PR.IP | PR.IP-2 |
| V05 | Users and support staff are not adequately educated on new systems/ functionalities | PR.IP | PR.IP-2 |
| V06 | Requirements for changes and new system developments are not adequately identified | PR.IP | PR.IP-2 |
| V07 | Change requirements are not appropriately reviewed and prioritized | PR.IP | PR.IP-2 |
| V08 | Key stakeholders do not approve change | PR.IP | PR.IP-3 |
| V09 | Changes and configurations are not developed to satisfy business requirements | PR.IP | PR.IP-2 |
| V10 | QA testing is not performed | PR.IP | PR.IP-3 |
| V11 | Requirements are not validated and approved by key stakeholders | PR.IP | PR.IP-3 |
| V12 | The test environment does not support testing standards and requirements | PR.IP | PR.IP-2 |
| V13 | Testing plans are not effectively created | PR.IP | PR.IP-3 |
| V14 | IT ownership and accountability is not clearly defined and documented | ID.AM | ID.AM-5 |
| V15 | The organizational IT structure is not designed to adequately support business objectives | ID.BE | ID.BE-3 |

... | Threats | **Vulnerabilities** | Risks | Risk Ratings | Risk Measurement | Graphical Risks | Attack Lifecycle

Ready

***Figure C-3.*** *Vulnerabilities and security controls identified for risk reduction, documented in the vulnerabilities tab*

# Risk Ratings and Graph

In the Risk Ratings and Graph tab, the risk, impact, likelihood, and a graphical representation of the risks are shown. Figure C-4 highlights the display of this information.

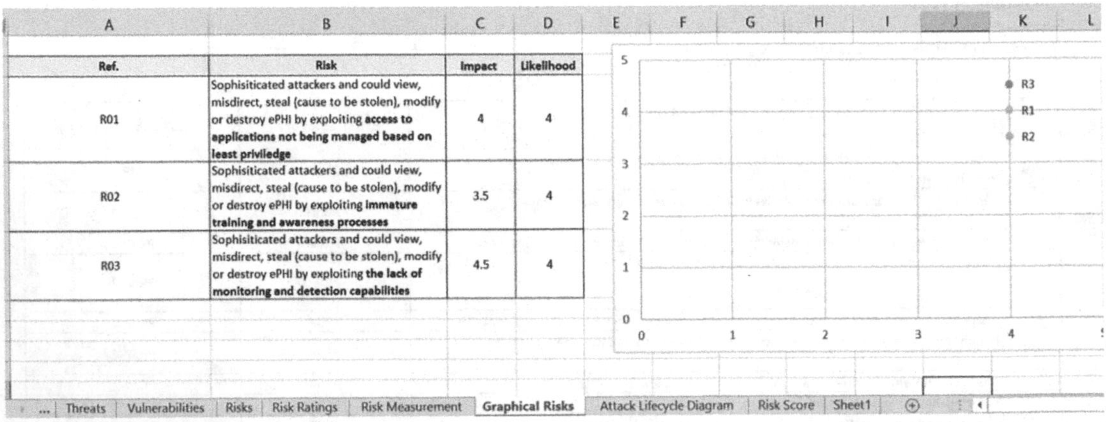

| Ref. | Risk | Impact | Likelihood |
|------|------|--------|------------|
| R01 | Sophisiticated attackers and could view, misdirect, steal (cause to be stolen), modify or destroy ePHI by exploiting access to applications not being managed based on least priviledge | 4 | 4 |
| R02 | Sophisiticated attackers and could view, misdirect, steal (cause to be stolen), modify or destroy ePHI by exploiting immature training and awareness processes | 3.5 | 4 |
| R03 | Sophisiticated attackers and could view, misdirect, steal (cause to be stolen), modify or destroy ePHI by exploiting the lack of monitoring and detection capabilities | 4.5 | 4 |

Threats | Vulnerabilities | Risks | Risk Ratings | Risk Measurement | **Graphical Risks** | Attack Lifecycle Diagram | Risk Score | Sheet1

***Figure C-4.*** *Risks, the assignment of impact and likelihood, and a graphical representation of risks are displayed in this tab*

## Risk Heat Map

This heat map is the same template used during the risk analysis process, highlighting the grids and associated risk severity, as shown in Figure C-5.

**HIPAA Risk Analysis**
**Risk Identification**
*The impact and likelihood indicators that will be used to rank identified risks*

**Risk Matrix**
Level of risk determined by a combination of likelihood and impact

| Impact | | | | | |
|---|---|---|---|---|---|
| Critical 5 | Very Low | Low | Moderate | High | Very High |
| Significant 4 | Very Low | Low | Moderate | High | Very High |
| High 3 | Very Low | Low | Moderate | Moderate | High |
| Moderate 2 | Very Low | Low | Low | Low | Moderate |
| Low 1 | Very Low | Very Low | Very Low | Low | Low |
| | Highly Unlikely 1 | Unlikely 2 | Somewhat Likely 3 | Highly Likely 4 | Almost Certain 5 |
| | **Likelihood** | | | | |

***Figure C-5.*** *Grids displaying the associated risks*

## Third-Party Risk Template

The Third-Party Risk Template is a simple Excel document used to track risks. The workbook consists of the cover sheet, which is used to describe the service performed, the inherent risks of engaging the third party, and procedures performed to assess risk. There are also tabs to list threats, vulnerabilities, control assessment, and risk analysis. Ultimately, there needs to be a list of risks compiled, so that the entity can determine if the risks are acceptable, or if other alternatives must be considered.

# Cover Sheet

Figure C-6 is the cover sheet, which is where the description of the third party, inherent risks, and steps undertaken to assess risk are documented.

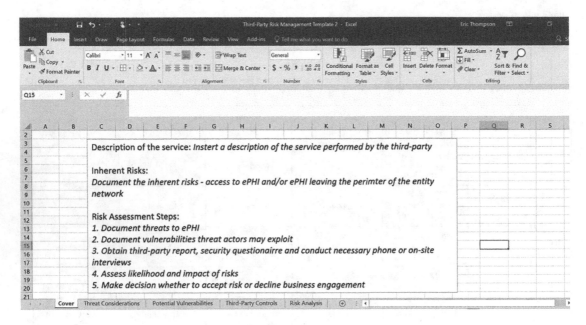

***Figure C-6.*** *Cover sheet where characteristics of the third-party relationship are documented*

# Threats

In this analysis, threats are documented the same as internal risk analysis steps require. Figure C-7 shows an example.

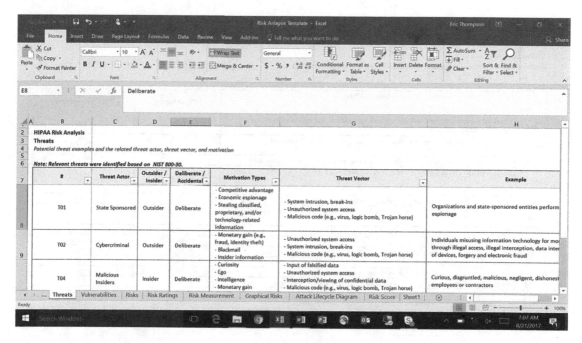

***Figure C-7.*** *Threats to ePHI at third parties are documented in this tab.*

# Potential Vulnerabilities

Potential vulnerabilities must be assessed as well. Figure C-8 shows the list of vulnerabilities that may exist and require assessment to confirm if each presents a risk to ePHI.

| Ref | Vulnerability | NIST Category | NIST Sub-category |
|-----|---------------|---------------|-------------------|
| | **HIPAA Risk Analysis** | | |
| | **Vulnerabilities** | | |
| | *Potential vulnerabilities and the related domain, process and sub-process* | | |
| V01 | Infrastructure and applications(including web applications and interfaces) are inappropriately configured | PR.IP | PR.IP-1 |
| V02 | Design specifications are not effectively developed, reviewed, and approved | PR.IP | PR.IP-3 |
| V03 | Solutions are not appropriately developed according to standards and requirements | PR.IP | PR.IP-2 |
| V04 | Implementation and deployment planning is not performed | PR.IP | PR.IP-2 |
| V05 | Users and support staff are not adequately educated on new systems/ functionalities | PR.IP | PR.IP-2 |
| V06 | Requirements for changes and new system developments are not adequately identified | PR.IP | PR.IP-2 |
| V07 | Change requirements are not appropriately reviewed and prioritized | PR.IP | PR.IP-2 |
| V08 | Key stakeholders do not approve change | PR.IP | PR.IP-3 |
| V09 | Changes and configurations are not developed to satisfy business requirements | PR.IP | PR.IP-2 |
| V10 | QA testing is not performed | PR.IP | PR.IP-3 |
| V11 | Requirements are not validated and approved by key stakeholders | PR.IP | PR.IP-3 |
| V12 | The test environment does not support testing standards and requirements | PR.IP | PR.IP-2 |
| V13 | Testing plans are not effectively created | PR.IP | PR.IP-3 |
| V14 | IT ownership and accountability is not clearly defined and documented | ID.AM | ID.AM-5 |
| V15 | The organizational IT structure is not designed to adequately support business objectives | ID.BE | ID.BE-3 |

... | Threats | **Vulnerabilities** | Risks | Risk Ratings | Risk Measurement | Graphical Risks | Attack Lifecycle

Ready

***Figure C-8.*** *Potential vulnerabilities that may pose a risk to ePHI at the third party*

# Third-Party Controls

Figure C-9 displays the tab where security controls at the third party are evaluated to assess the existence of vulnerabilities for the analysis.

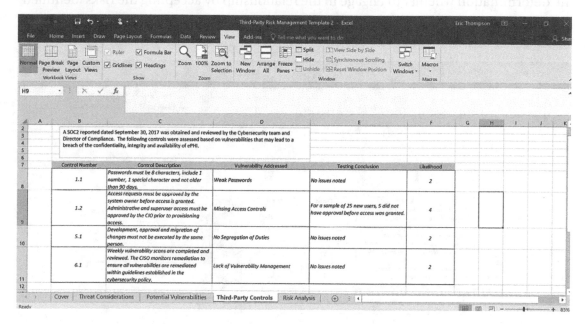

***Figure C-9.*** *Vulnerabilities aligned with security controls at the third party*

# Third-Party Risk Analysis

In this tab, the analysis is completed. The vulnerabilities are assigned to threat actors with risk values assigned. This information is presented to management, which makes the determination whether to engage in the relationship by accepting the risks identified in Figure C-10.

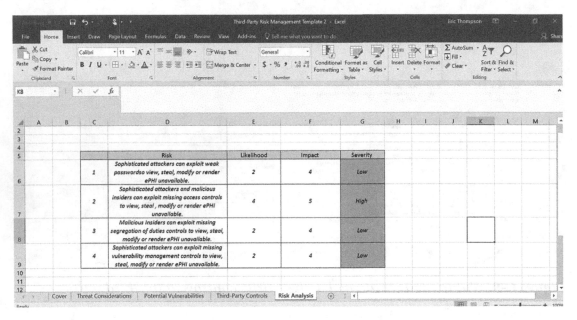

***Figure C-10.*** *Documented risks of engaging with a third-party service provider*

# Index

E. C. Thompson, *Building a HIPAA-Compliant Cybersecurity Program*,
https://doi.org/10.1007/978-1-4842-3060-2

# Get the eBook for only $5!

Why limit yourself?

With most of our titles available in both PDF and ePUB format, you can access your content wherever and however you wish—on your PC, phone, tablet, or reader.

Since you've purchased this print book, we are happy to offer you the eBook for just $5.

To learn more, go to http://www.apress.com/companion or contact support@apress.com.

# Apress®

Printed in the United States
By Bookmasters